T0281844

BRUCE WILLIS

BRUCE WILLIS

Celebrating the Cinematic Legacy of an Unbreakable Hollywood Icon

SEAN O'CONNELL

APPLAUSE
THEATRE & CINEMA BOOKS

Essex, Connecticut

APPLAUSE
THEATRE & CINEMA BOOKS

An imprint of Globe Pequot, the trade division of
The Rowman & Littlefield Publishing Group, Inc.
4501 Forbes Blvd., Ste. 200
Lanham, MD 20706
www.rowman.com

Distributed by NATIONAL BOOK NETWORK

Library of Congress Cataloging-in-Publication Data
Names: O'Connell, Sean, 1974- author.
Title: Bruce Willis : celebrating the cinematic legacy of an unbreakable Hollywood icon /
     Sean O'Connell.
Description: Essex, Connecticut : Applause, [2024]. | Includes bibliographical references and
     index.
Identifiers: LCCN 2023050962 (print) | LCCN 2023050963 (ebook) | ISBN
     9781493076338 (cloth) | ISBN 9781493076345 (epub)
Subjects: LCSH: Willis, Bruce, 1955- | Actors—United States—Biography.
Classification: LCC PN2287.W474 O26 2024 (print) | LCC PN2287.W474 (ebook) |
     DDC 791.4302/8092 [B]—dc23/eng/20240207
LC record available at https://lccn.loc.gov/2023050962
LC ebook record available at https://lccn.loc.gov/2023050963

♾™ The paper used in this publication meets the minimum requirements of American
National Standard for Information Sciences—Permanence of Paper for Printed Library
Materials, ANSI/NISO Z39.48-1992.

CONTENTS

AUTHOR'S NOTE

An entertainment journalist once asked Bruce Willis if he'd ever consider writing his own memoir. "Too many people would get hurt," the star replied. "Because I'd have to tell the truth. But it'd be a great book, let me tell you."[1]

I don't doubt that for a second. Hopefully this book keeps you entertained until the official story gets told.

Treat this book as a companion piece. It pairs best with a towering stack of Willis movies, programmed into your own personal film festival. Take the time to watch the films that are discussed, even the ones you feel like you've seen a dozen times. Revisit his classics. Catch up on undiscovered gems. Try to view each film through the specific lens of Willis's performance choices, and appreciate his valuable contributions.

Willis launched his career with the uproarious romantic-comedy television series *Moonlighting*, where his seemingly off-the-cuff bravado gelled effortlessly with Cybill Shepherd's grace and composure. Willis went on to appear in more than one hundred feature films, forging a singular career populated with astronomical hits, unforeseen misses, risky creative detours, and relatively safe sequels. His body of work reflects the doors that were opened by his early success, but also spotlights trends in the industry that theoretically shaped his project choices.

By breaking his career into distinct sections of Comedy, Action, Science Fiction, Auteur Director Collaborations, and (of course) the *Die Hard* franchise, I'm establishing a versatility that too many overlook in Willis. In an industry that's quick to apply labels and pigeonhole talent to specified career paths, Willis bucked those limitations to prove how capable he was at excelling in multiple genres. Just watch the four films he released in 1991—which required him to play an abusive, alcoholic husband (*Mortal Thoughts*), a singing cat burglar on a globetrotting jaunt (*Hudson Hawk*), a Jewish gangster (*Billy Bathgate*), and a burned-out private detective who teams with a washed-up NFL quarterback (*The Last Boy Scout*)—to comprehend Willis's ambidexterity as an actor.

I hope you learn more about Willis through his movies, and my analysis. I hope you receive a greater appreciation for his confident self-awareness, his eagerness to go to bat for storytellers who needed the benefit of his star power, and the quiet skill set he offered—which often allowed his costars to shine. This is a win-win assignment. Not only do you have an excuse to absorb a healthy dose of Willis-driven cinema. You also possess an informative guide to Willis's uncommon oeuvre. Dive into both with an open heart, and enjoy the ride.

Yippee Ki-Yay!

INTRODUCTION

THE RETIREMENT OF BRUNO

—1—

On a nondescript Wednesday morning in the waning days of March, one of the biggest movie stars on the planet called it quits.

The absence of fanfare was remarkable. No press conference was organized. The Hollywood trades received no advanced notice. Instead, a simple statement posted to Demi Moore's Instagram page on March 30, 2022, revealed that Bruce Willis—her former husband, the father of their three daughters, and the one-time holder of the title "highest-paid actor in Hollywood"—would retire from show business, effective immediately.

"To Bruce's amazing supporters, as a family we wanted to share that our beloved Bruce has been experiencing some health issues and has recently been diagnosed with aphasia, which is impacting his cognitive abilities," the note read, in part. "As a result of this and with much consideration, Bruce is stepping away from the career that has meant so much to him."[1]

And so much to the world. In the days and weeks following the announcement, social media erupted with an outpouring of condolences and support for the movie star who'd played a pivotal role in audiences' lives. While film journalists argued over the man's influence and placement in the Hollywood pantheon of big-screen legends, Willis's *The Sixth Sense* costar Haley Joel Osment allowed himself to be more personal. He posted a photo of Bruce alongside a tender message that said, "It's been difficult to find the right words for someone I've always looked up to—first on the big screen, and then by some wild stroke of luck, in person. . . . I am so grateful for what

I got to witness firsthand, and for the enormous body of work he built for us to enjoy for years and years to come."[2]

Fellow Hollywood staple John Travolta spoke on his collaborations with Willis when he shared on Instagram the day of the announcement, "Bruce and I became good friends when we shared 2 of our biggest hits together, *Pulp Fiction* and *Look Who's Talking*. Years later, he said to me, 'John, I just want you to know that when something good happens to you, I feel like it's happening to me.' That's how generous a soul he is. I love you, Bruce."[3]

That passion was shared by Willis's *Looper* costar, Emily Blunt. "He just was that wry, clever, quiet cool thing he had. It's just amazing," she said. "I loved being around him, and I love him, as a person."[4]

Leave it to action icon, longtime Willis colleague, and king of the one-liners Arnold Schwarzenegger to perfectly capture the sentiment of movie fans when he concluded, "He will always be remembered as a great, great star. And a kind man. I understand that under his circumstances, health-wise, that he had to retire. But in general, we never really retire. Action heroes, they reload."[5]

—2—

Willis is a Hollywood legend by every definition of the word, and the last of a dying breed. His professional career spanned five decades, an impressive feat in an industry that consistently discards talent while hunting for the next shiny plaything.

Willis told people he wanted to be an actor since he was nineteen, and his early career choices suggested that Willis was just as interested in entertaining himself as he was in entertaining the audience. There's a reason the Seagram's wine coolers ad campaign that Willis headlined in the late 1980s utilized the slogan, "This is where the fun starts." Willis had that "It" factor. Audiences identified him as someone they wanted to hang out with, and infiltrating his inner circle in those early days seemed possible. His friendship seemed attainable.

Fellow actor John Goodman hung out with Willis in those early days. He jokes that they were unknowns. "I didn't know him. He didn't know me." But

Goodman knew, even just by watching Willis tend to customers from behind the New York City bars, that a career in entertainment was in the cards.

"He's still one of the best bartenders I've ever seen in my life. Bruce had a running tatter going constantly. It was like a pro wrestling rap, or Three Stooges bits, or Little Rascals stuff . . . calling out basketball scores while he was bartending. He was great," Goodman recalled. "I never saw him act until much later, but I knew he'd be good. Just the way that he was behind a bar. Like I said, it was the best free show in town."[6]

It didn't stay free for very long. Willis's 120 feature films have grossed a grand total of $8.35 billion in worldwide tickets sold as of 2022.[7] Factor in DVD sales, digital streams, merchandise deals, and licensing agreements associated with Willis's movies over the years, the totality of his financial contributions to the film industry are astronomical. He even earned the remarkable distinction of being the highest paid actor for a single movie in Hollywood history in 1999. Thanks to shrewd negotiations that promised him 17.5 percent of *The Sixth Sense*'s global box-office gross, as well as rights to its home video sales, Willis pocketed somewhere in the vicinity of $115 million for headlining M. Night Shyamalan's unnerving drama.

But Willis wasn't *just* a bankable movie star. Critics lauded a wide range of the actor's performances over the years, whether he was playing a blue-collar cop fighting terrorists to save his wife (Bonnie Bedelia) in John McTiernan's *Die Hard*, a time-traveling prisoner in Terry Gilliam's *12 Monkeys*, or a washed-up boxer who just wants to retrieve his father's gold watch in Quentin Tarantino's transformational *Pulp Fiction*. To be fair, critics also took more than enough jabs at other credits on Willis's résumé. The versatile performer was anything but Teflon. Yet the criticisms never prevented him from finding work.

Willis once remarked, when talking about his reviews both positive and negative, "I don't believe that anything that gets said about films when they come out really has any meaning or longevity. It's only 10 or 15 years down the road, you look back and you say, 'This film really holds up.'"[8]

The actor has a healthy number of those on his résumé. Together, they map out a long-lasting career for a versatile movie star who started in one genre but succeeded in many. By breaking Willis's storied career into categories, one also can make interesting parallels between his choices and the shifts the industry endured as it marched forward. His career arc paints a portrait of Hollywood during a unique time, when movie stars could open pictures to robust opening weekends, and cinema's biggest talents held audience members captivated in theaters, long before their stories ended up on our home-video systems, our laptops, or our handheld devices.

"Bruce is one of the all-time great movie stars of our generation. He's a fantastic actor who has left some incredible performances that I think are going to only grow in estimation over the years to come," said *Knives Out* and *Glass Onion* director Rian Johnson, who cast Willis in the intelligent time-traveling thriller *Looper*. While Johnson would go on to direct a *Star Wars* sequel and one of the finest episodes of the spectacular drug thriller *Breaking Bad*, he was still relatively unproven in 2012 while working on *Looper* and needed the participation of a star like Willis to help get his original screenplay greenlit. Willis did this a handful of times for talented up-and-coming filmmakers with whom he wanted to collaborate, be it Tarantino for *Pulp Fiction* or Shyamalan on *Sixth Sense*.

"When he committed to a role and threw himself into it," Johnson concluded, "there was nobody better."[9]

—3—

Any celebration of Willis's life work has to begin with his first massive professional break in the razor-sharp television program *Moonlighting*. No doubt you'll begin singing Al Jarreau's theme song for the program the moment it's mentioned. ("Some walk by night, some fly by day . . .") Willis portrayed David Addison, a fast-talking and irreverent private investigator at the Blue Moon Detective Agency, which served as one of many tax write-offs for one-time fashion model Maddie Hayes (Cybill Shepherd). The show's creator and executive producer, Glenn Gordon Caron, modeled his ABC program after both the film noir crime stories and the rapid-fire romantic comedies of the 1940s. Imagine Cary Grant and Rosalind Russell's *His Girl Friday* having a baby with Humphrey Bogart and Lauren Bacall's *The Big Sleep*, but delivered in one-hour chunks structured for network television.

"(It was) a romantic comedy, I suppose, set against the facade of a detective agency," Willis recalls about the show that made him a star. "But it was about the jokes, more than anything else. It was about the comedy. Based upon, more than anything else, the screwball comedies of Howard Hawks and Preston Sturges."[10]

Caron envisioned *Moonlighting* as a vehicle for leading lady Shepherd, whose appearances in the acclaimed films *The Last Picture Show* (1971) and Martin Scorsese's *Taxi Driver* (1976) brought immediate credibility to the series. But Willis's attention-grabbing performance as the snarky, flirtatious, and egotistic Addison very quickly became the reason audiences considered the show appointment television. The actor admits to borrowing heavily from the Three Stooges and Bob Hope when fleshing out his character. He looked to rapid-fire wisenheimers of the past for inspiration, and the media responded kindly to his choices.

"As Addison, Willis is as much conman as detective," television critic Richard Hack wrote in a *Hollywood Reporter* review of the show's pilot. "He's a cross between Bill Murray and Dan Aykroyd with a touch of Roseanne Roseannadanna thrown in. And is the reason *Moonlighting* works and works well."[11]

Echoing the importance of Willis's contributions to *Moonlighting*, *New York Times* critic John J. O'Connor wrote, "Confronted with Miss Shepherd's Maddie, a flamboyantly insinuating creature, Mr. Willis becomes almost debonair as, the battle of the sexes raging, he appears to be constantly bemused, complete with twinkling eyes. Miss Shepherd gets most of the flashy turns, but without Mr. Willis, there would be no show."[12]

Ironically, Willis remembers facing "a great deal of resistance" from ABC's decision makers when it came to casting him as David Addison, surmising, "I just don't think that they thought that I was TV leading man material."[13] But Caron refused to back down, insisting to the network that Willis was the right man for the role. It was a career-making decision.

The actor received three Primetime Emmy Award nominations over the course of his career, which led to two wins—one for playing Addison on *Moonlighting* in 1987, and another for his guest role as one of Jennifer Aniston's love interests on NBC's smash sitcom *Friends* in 2000. The Hollywood

Foreign Press Association also nominated Willis four times in the Golden Globe category for Best Actor in a Television Series: Comedy or Musical for *Moonlighting*, eventually bestowing him the award in 1987.

An amusing bit of trivia: Willis's award-winning *Friends* cameo was the result of a bet he made, then lost, to the late Matthew Perry, his costar in the feature film *The Whole Nine Yards*. The action star doubted that the duo's gangster comedy could open to number one at the box office (a reflection of his opinion of the material, no doubt). *The Whole Nine Yards* not only opened to number one over President's Day weekend in February 2000, but it also held that top spot for two additional weekends. Months later, Willis made good on his wager, then donated his *Friends* paycheck to five of his preferred charities: the American Foundation for AIDS Research; AIDS Project Los Angeles; the Elizabeth Glaser Pediatric AIDS Foundation; the Rape Treatment Center, and UCLA Unicamp for underprivileged children.

"He oozed A-list," Perry wrote about Willis in his 2022 memoir *Friends, Lovers, and the Big Terrible Thing*. "He didn't just take over a room, he *was* the room. . . . Sometimes, at the end of the night, when the sun was just about to come up and everyone else had gone, and the party was over, Bruce and I would just sit and talk. That's when I saw the real Bruce Willis—a good-hearted man, a caring man, selfless. A wonderful parent. And a wonderful actor. And most important, a good guy."[14]

Willis's celebrity naturally extended far beyond his acting credits, and past the boundaries of Hollywood. Though tight-lipped about his party affiliations, Willis's public political moves have generated headlines. He has thrown his weight behind various political candidates, speaking at the 2000 Republican National Convention in support of George W. Bush, or publicly refusing to endorse Bob Dole in his 1996 presidential bid after the senator criticized Moore and her provocative crime-comedy *Striptease*. Dole waged war on the entertainment industry at the time, criticizing rap artists for "[debasing] our nation and [threatening] our children for the sake of corporate profits," but labeling James Cameron's 1994 blockbuster *True Lies* as "friendly to the family" (likely because it starred noted Republican Arnold Schwarzenegger). Willis later dismissed Dole as "a nitwit."[15]

During the height of his *Moonlighting* run, the versatile Willis made hay as a recording artist, releasing a well-received rhythm and blues album titled "The Return of Bruno" on Motown Records in 1987. The album charted as high as fourth in the UK and reached fourteenth on the US Billboard 200, while two singles from the record—cover versions of the Staples Singers' "Respect Yourself" and the Drifters' "Under the Boardwalk"—remained in heavy rotation on MTV, firmly establishing Willis as a household name.

The "Respect Yourself" video especially painted Willis as a Springsteen-esque working-class hero from the streets of his home state, New Jersey—an image he would cultivate over the course of his career. Director James Yukich (the genius behind Genesis's *Land of Confusion* video) begins his clip with Willis wiping down a neon-drenched neighborhood bar and stacking pint glasses before the performer starts strutting around the establishment, singing into a broom handle and playing pool while a dish towel dangles from the back pocket of his broken-in blue jeans. In the late 1980s, this was the epitome of cool.

Willis often made calculated decisions like this to keep his image grounded and on a level playing field with his target demographic: the blue-collar laborers. One need only to watch the actor's forty-four credited appearances on *The Late Show with David Letterman* when making the press rounds to promote his latest projects to get an understanding of the image Willis liked to project. His humorous visits and casual banter, matching wits with the acerbic talk show host, pushed the narrative that Willis was a regular Joe, eager to make jokes at his own expense. He'd ride a motorcycle into Letterman's television studio in Manhattan's Theater District. He'd rappel down from the rafters instead of walking out like a routine guest, one time even riding on the hood of a speeding truck that catapulted him into a fake wall, so he could emerge all bloodied and bruised. These elaborate, self-deprecating skits became watercooler conversation the next day, and allowed the superstar actor to increase his household recognizability. Letterman became so close to Willis over the years, he even asked the A-lister to host *The Late Show* when Letterman had to call out sick with an eye infection. Willis agreed, and ended up interviewing news anchor Dan Rather, reality-TV starlet Carmen Electra, and Grammy winner John Mayer.

Reluctantly, Willis and Moore also fed the world's hunger for Hollywood gossip with their highly publicized courtship and subsequent marriage in 1987. The two were enormously popular movie stars at the time. Willis alternated *Die Hard* sequels with critical darlings such as *12 Monkeys* and *Pulp Fiction* during their whirlwind marriage, while Moore parlayed her "Brat Pack" status into starring roles in box-office juggernauts *Ghost* (the highest-grossing domestic release of 1990), *A Few Good Men* (1992), and *Indecent Proposal* (1993). And even though the couple attempted to flee Hollywood's intense spotlight by retreating to rural Hailey, Idaho, around 1988, incessant curiosity about their personal lives fueled tabloid magazines and infotainment programs throughout the late 1980s and 1990s.

By his own account, Willis never understood—or accepted—the right the media believed they had to his personal life. "I don't feel the need to give out the details of my life. Some people tell you everything they ever did, but nobody really cares," he said in 1988. "I never really thought that because I became a successful actor, that what I had to say became that much more important. Nobody was asking me my opinion while I was acting in New York. I guess people want to know that stuff now, but I don't feel it's my responsibility to open up my private life. My work ends when I go home at the end of the day. Then it becomes my life. You can talk about what's up there on the screen, or what's down there on the television, but I always wanted it to be about the work."[16]

Willis's movie star status, and his reputation for being the gregarious life of the party, only increased when he, Moore, Schwarzenegger, and Sylvester Stallone invested heavily in the Planet Hollywood theme-restaurant chain. The foursome agreed to be unofficial faces of the food-service business, frequently turning the opening-night celebrations held for new locations into all-star affairs that were heavily publicized by the media. Excited patrons (usually tourists) were teased with the promise that Schwarzenegger might show up at a location for a surprise visit, possibly posing with George Clooney next to their *Batman and Robin* costumes. Or maybe Stallone would commemorate a *Rocky* anniversary by donating boxing gloves, star-spangled shorts, or some other valuable prop from the boxing franchise and posing for pictures. Over the years, Willis took on more of an emcee role at these restaurant openings, hopping on a Planet Hollywood stage to sing and play harmonica with the house band, or saunter behind the bar to serve cocktails to the patrons—a way to remain connected to his pre-celebrity days tending bar in New York City establishments like Cafe Central, Kamikaze, and Chelsea Central. When Willis was present, a party seemed poised to pop.

Celebrity isn't all red carpets, lavish awards ceremonies, and raucous Planet Hollywood openings, though. The toll of living their lives in the public eye eventually wore on Willis and Moore. The couple amicably split in June 1998, then officially filed for divorce in 2000.

"It's difficult to live your life and marriage under a magnifying glass, which is what happens to movie star couples," Willis explained to *Rolling Stone*. "[But] I still love Demi. We're very close. We have three children whom we will continue to raise together, and we're probably as close now as we ever were. We realize we have a lifelong commitment to our kids."[17]

Moore, when writing about Willis in her 2019 memoir *Inside Out*, elaborated, "We had a whirlwind, truncated infatuation that morphed into a full-on family."[18]

That family got referenced in the Instagram post confirming Willis's retirement from acting. Moore referred to the aphasia diagnosis as "a really challenging time for our family," but relayed that they were "moving through this as a strong family unit."

The post concluded with a hopeful promise, "As Bruce always says, 'Live it up!' And together we plan to do just that."

—5—

Filmmaker Mike Burns first noticed possible issues with Willis's reading and speech comprehension on the set of the 2021 action thriller *Out of Death*. Though Burns had composed original music for an earlier Willis vehicle, *Midnight in the Switchgrass*, this was his first directorial assignment, and he could tell something wasn't right with his leading man.

"After the first day of working with Bruce, I could see it firsthand," Burns said, "and I realized that there was a bigger issue at stake here and why I had been asked to shorten his lines."[19]

Once *Out of Death* wrapped, Burns immediately was offered another directing gig on a Willis project titled *Wrong Place*. Burns reached out to the actor's reps to see how Willis was feeling ahead of the shoot, and was informed that he was "a whole different person . . . way better than last year."

Willis wasn't, and his cognitive decline is evident in his *Wrong Place* scenes. His speech is slurred to a mumble. Body doubles stand in for him in any framing situation where you don't have to see Willis's face. Burns finished production on *Wrong Place*, but swore he'd never do another film under these conditions. Only a few months later, Moore posted the Instagram message informing everyone of Willis's diagnosis.

The American Speech-Language-Hearing Association (ASHA) defines aphasia as a language disorder associated with brain damage to the left half of the brain. Per medical experts, the brain's left hemisphere is responsible for language and speech, and aphasia "may make it hard for you to understand, speak, read, or write," though ASHA claims it "does not make you less smart or cause problems with the way you think." Side effects found in people diagnosed with aphasia can include muscle weakness in your mouth (referred to as dysarthria), as well as an individual's inability to make the muscles in their mouth move the right way to say words. Finally, patients with aphasia often have swallowing problems, called dysphagia.

The most common cause of aphasia is a stroke, which is how fellow film star and *Basic Instinct* sensation Sharon Stone ended up diagnosed with the ailment following a cerebral hemorrhage that lasted for nine days in 2001. "I was hemorrhaging so much that my brain had been pushed into the front of my face," the actress told *Harper's Bazaar* in a 2015 profile centered around her Hollywood comeback. "It took two years for my body just to absorb all the internal bleeding I had. It almost feels like my entire DNA changed. My brain isn't sitting where it used to, my body type changed, and even my food allergies are different."[20]

Stone's condition began with an aneurysm. The same thing happened to *Terminator: Genisys* star Emilia Clarke shortly after filming wrapped on the first season of her enormously successful HBO series *Game of Thrones*. It was during an exercise session in North London shortly after *Thrones* had wrapped its first season that Clarke entered into a plank position at the request of her physical trainer and immediately "felt as though an elastic band was squeezing my brain."[21] According to an emotional recollection she penned for the *New Yorker* in 2019, Clarke attempted to push through the workout but eventually had to wave off her trainer and retreat to the gym's locker room, where she, in her own words, "proceeded to be violently, voluminously ill."

"At some level, I knew what was happening: my brain was damaged," Clarke surmised.

Surgeons officially diagnosed Clarke with a subarachnoid hemorrhage (SAH), a life-threatening stroke that is caused by bleeding into the space surrounding the brain. One third of SAH patients die immediately following the aneurysm that triggers the bleeding. Clarke avoided a fatality by enduring multiple surgeries at the National Hospital for Neurology and Neurosurgery in central London. It was during her recovery period when Clarke was diagnosed with aphasia. Nurses asked her simple questions such as, "What is your name?" Clarke was unable to answer.

"In my worst moments, I wanted to pull the plug," Clarke confessed. "I asked the medical staff to let me die. My job—my entire dream of what my life would be—centered on language, on communication. Without that, I was lost."

Like Stone, Clarke would recover from aphasia, though she never forgot the impact her brief stint with the ailment had on her psyche. Both actors returned to their careers, where they thrived on both television and in the movies. Clarke also went on to partner with financial backers to launch SameYou, a charitable organization that strives to assist brain injury survivors gain access to high-quality neurohabilitation and end brain injury recovery inequality. Aphasia was but a stop on their professional journey, not the final destination.

—**6**—

Stone and Clarke recovered from their diagnoses. Willis will not. On February 16, 2023, the actor's family issued a statement confirming that his condition had progressed, and now included a diagnosis of frontotemporal dementia or FTD.

"FTD is a cruel disease that many of us have never heard of and can strike anyone," the statement read. "For people under 60, FTD is the most common form of dementia, and because getting the diagnosis can take years, FTD is likely much more prevalent than we know. Today there are no treatments for the disease, a reality that we hope can change in the years ahead.

"Bruce has always found joy in life—and has helped everyone he knows to do the same," the statement continued. "It has meant the world to see that sense of care echoed back to him and to all of us. We have been so moved by the love you have all shared for our dear husband, father, and friend during this difficult time. Your continued compassion, understanding, and respect will enable us to help Bruce live as full a life as possible."[22]

Future books will be written about Willis's health struggles and the overwhelming emotional support he received from second wife Emma Heming Willis, his ex-wife Moore, and their blended family. They did an admirable job protecting Willis from the white-hot glare of media attention, while also utilizing social media to keep invested fans up to date on his rapidly changing condition.

This book, instead, is dedicated to the incredible body of work Willis will leave behind. The New Jersey native catapulted toward Hollywood like the *Armageddon* asteroid, and his impact has been felt throughout the industry from the moment he wrapped a firehose around his waist and leapt from the top of Nakatomi Plaza. During a 1988 conversation following the release of *Die Hard*, Willis was asked if he feared getting typecast as an action hero following the movie's enormous success.

"I like to keep challenging myself. I like to keep forcing myself to do new things," the actor said. "One of the scariest things about that is that you have the opportunity to fail when you try new things. But it's the only thing I can do to continue to grow as an actor."[23]

Willis always has promised audiences something unexpected, particularly when the industry tried to categorize him alongside his Planet Hollywood counterparts while discussing his Hollywood legacy. After all, the blue-collar Willis reshaped the image of the 1980s action star, convincing audiences (and studio heads) that heroes didn't need to be chiseled from marble to prevail.

Stallone never bought into the fact that these men were in line for the same parts, or even trying to mimic each other in their action features. "All the parts that we've played have been defined, and very definitive. Like, I couldn't have played the Terminator. I know that," Stallone said. "And Bruce, what he did with *Die Hard*, is again a definitive character. You align it to Rambo, but that's not true. It's a totally different kind of character. I think we've all carved out our niches, and they really don't overlap that much."[24]

But while Stallone and Schwarzenegger opted for safer material as they extended their careers, Willis attempted more gambles. For every *Die Hard* sequel or predictable action vehicle, Willis made sure to also branch out into unexpected genres, expand his audience, amplify the voice of an untested director, and challenge his perceived limits. These are some of the reasons his inevitable retirement has sent shockwaves through the industry that possibly has taken Willis for granted for too many years.

Willis never hesitated to put himself into the hands of proven directors for material that was outside of his comfort zone. Rob Reiner cast him opposite Michelle Pfeiffer for a painfully honest look at a failing marriage titled *The Story of Us*. The actor would lampoon his oversized Hollywood reputation by playing himself for a screamingly funny cameo in Steven Soderbergh's *Ocean's Twelve*. Willis bet on the cutting-edge talents of Robert Rodriguez when the *Desperado* director brought Frank Miller's *Sin City* graphic novel to life in eye-catching black and white.

Gradually, Willis found himself at the center of the 1990s film-school boom thanks to his role in Quentin Tarantino's *Pulp Fiction*, a masterpiece that inspired the next generation of storytellers—and produced far too many Tarantino clones. In the mid-1990s, when the industry executives chased a trend of flashy sci-fi blockbusters, Willis championed both rule-bending visionaries (Luc Besson for *The Fifth Element*, Terry Gilliam for *12 Monkeys*) and commercial workhorses (Michael Bay for *Armageddon*).

Willis's counterparts, outside of possibly Harrison Ford, can't brag about that range. His fearless approach to projects helped make him bankable, highly sought after, and respected. And his detours led to experimental science fiction stories, conversation-starting adult dramas, and awards-worthy collaborations with celebrated auteurs that make up some of the most beloved films of the last thirty years.

SECTION ONE
THE COMEDIES OF
BRUCE WILLIS

". . . Or would you rather be a fish?"

Official movie poster for Blake Edwards's *Blind Date*, starring Bruce Willis. *Author's Collection*

As *Clerks* director Kevin Smith pointed out, the natural comparisons for Bruce Willis in his earliest days weren't Chuck Norris, Jean-Claude Van Damme, Arnold Schwarzenegger, or Sylvester Stallone. It was Bill Murray, a lanky comedian with a fading tuft of perpetually tousled hair who masked his sharp comedic timing behind a goofy class-clown likeability. For a brief period, Willis mirrored Murray's career path, earning a following on television before moving into feature-film roles that were tailored to each actor's strengths. *Caddyshack* and *Stripes* for Murray. *Blind Date* and *Sunset* for Willis.

Their two breakout hits, however, steered them toward different destinies. Ivan Reitman's 1984 smash *Ghostbusters* (with a little help from *Stripes*) established Murray as a rabble-rousing agent of chaos, the disruptor who earned cool points by metaphorically flipping the middle finger at authority. Willis, on the other hand, broke through the barriers of movie stardom in *Die Hard*, turning the motor-mouthed hero of *Moonlighting* into a viable action candidate. Where Murray parlayed *Ghostbusters* into *Little Shop of Horrors*, *Scrooged*, *Quick Change*, and *What about Bob?*, Willis worked on *Die Hard* sequels, serious character dramas (*In Country*, *Mortal Thoughts*), and mainly flexed his comedic muscles lending his voice to a toddler in two *Look Who's Talking* movies.

A thousand tiny decisions shape a performer's career. It's possible Willis purposefully avoided straight comedies in the late 1980s to prove to the industry he wasn't just David Addison, *Moonlighting*'s sarcastic detective. "I get to do all kinds of things," Willis once told professional interviewer Charlie Rose when reflecting on his career. "Comedy is the hardest one to do. To try and make people laugh, and to be successful at it."[1]

But I look at the Murray comparison and wonder what might have happened if Willis had enjoyed a massive comedic hit during those formative years. Would he have flipped his script and constructed a formidable résumé of comedies, only detouring into action when the project intrigued him? Because as the following five movies prove, Willis could be extremely funny whenever he wanted to be, and was proficient in multiple styles of comedy.

CHAPTER ONE
BLIND DATE

Director: Blake Edwards
Cast: Bruce Willis, Kim Basinger, John Larroquette,
Phil Hartman, William Daniels, Joyce Van Patten
Release Date: March 27, 1987

> *There's a school of comedy that I've studied for a long time. Directors like Frank Capra, Preston Sturges, Ernst Lubitsch.*
> *These guys kind of created that screwball comedy genre. And Blake Edwards is one of the last masters of that comedy style.*[1]
>
> —BRUCE WILLIS ON *BLIND DATE*

—1—

An oft-told Hollywood myth goes something like this: sixteen-year-old Julia Jean "Judy" Turner ditched her boring slate of high school classes in January of 1937, and headed to the famous Schwab's Drug Store, located on Los Angeles's Sunset Strip. The pharmacy had earned a reputation for being the film industry's unofficial hub, where movers and shakers met on the regular to strike deals. Turner wasn't seeking stardom that afternoon. All she wanted was a Coke from the shop's soda fountain. She ended up with so much more.

As the story goes, Turner caught the eye of Mervyn LeRoy, a famous movie director and screenwriter who would go on to produce *The Wizard of Oz* in 1939. So struck was LeRoy by the teenager's wholesome beauty, he allegedly introduced himself and offered Turner a screen test, which went so well it resulted in a studio contract. Judy Turner switched her name to Lana, and one of Hollywood's silver-screen icons was born.

That's not exactly how the "legend" of Lana Turner happened, mind you. Young Julia Jean did play hooky from Hollywood High School, though she spent that January afternoon at the Top Hat Cafe, an establishment located roughly two miles east of Schwab's. That's where Billy Wilkerson, owner and operator of the *Hollywood Reporter*, eyeballed the beauty and put her in touch with Zeppo Marx (of the famed Marx Brothers), who worked as a successful talent agent at the time. And it was Marx who introduced Turner to LeRoy, connecting the dots that eventually launched her career.

But Turner's story isn't commemorated for its details. Her chance encounter gets shared and re-shared by Hollywood dreamers because of what it represents, in general: Possible passage into the insular film community, and tangible proof that all it takes to break into show business is being recognized by the right person.

Drugstore soda shops no longer were in fashion by the time Bruce Willis sought his entrance into the entertainment industry. An aspiring actor had as much chance of winning the lottery in the mid-1980s as they did being discovered by a Hollywood powerbroker in a Los Angeles pharmacy. Around that time, however, a different proving ground was steadily developing young talent and exposing them to movie studio decision makers: television.

—2—

Hollywood never used to view movies and TV as equals. To use a baseball analogy, television usually operated as the farm team system, where a minor league player could develop his or her skills in hopes of graduating to a movie marquee. Few would dispute that cable television networks and digital streaming services such as Netflix, HBO Max, and Amazon Prime Video have closed the quality gap that once separated motion pictures from dramatic and comedic television. But actors historically found it easier to start in television with the hope of transitioning to films, rarely looking back after making the successful leap.

A handful of legends parlayed television stints into sustainable film gigs. *The Honeymooners* icon Jackie Gleason landed a role in Robert Rossen's pool-shark drama *The Hustler* opposite Paul Newman, earning an Oscar nomination for his performance. Sally Field entertained audiences as *Gidget* and *The Flying Nun*, among other characters, before she landed a part opposite Burt Reynolds in 1977's *Smokey and the Bandit* (also starring Gleason, ironically).

These examples, though, acted as the exceptions to the rule that for a long period of time, TV actors stayed busy on the medium lovingly nicknamed "the idiot box," movie stars occupied a more prestigious rung on the Hollywood hierarchy, and movement between the two rarely occurred.

In the 1980s and early 1990s, however, an abnormal number of eventual A-listers could be found in showcase roles on weekly sitcoms and dramas. They would become some of the industry's top earners, their ranks consisting of Robin Williams (*Mork and Mindy*), George Clooney (*The Facts of Life*), Johnny Depp (*21 Jump Street*), Denzel Washington (*St. Elsewhere*), Will Smith (*The Fresh Prince of Bel Air*), Leonardo DiCaprio (*Parenthood, Growing Pains*), and Tom Hanks (*Bosom Buddies*). Outside of Depp and Washington, the rest cut their teeth on comedy, which some mistakenly believe is easier to master than drama. Perhaps coincidentally, Lorne Michaels's late-night sketch comedy staple *Saturday Night Live* also started graduating cast members from its ranks around this same time, turning "not-ready-for-prime-time" players like Chevy Chase, Bill Murray, Dan Aykroyd, and Eddie Murphy into bankable movie stars.

And following a similar trajectory to the above names was a blue-collar bartender from Carney's Point, New Jersey, with a hunger for performing, a few college credits from Montclair State University under his belt, and a dream.

—**3**—

Moonlighting isn't Bruce Willis's first official screen credit. That distinction goes to a lone episode of NBC's sleek hit *Miami Vice*, where Willis turned up as a short-tempered, sadistic arms dealer named Tony Amato, who was being investigated by Don Johnson and Philip Michael Thomas. And prior to *Miami Vice*, Willis had two uncredited appearances in 1980's *The First Deadly Sin* (where he played Man Entering Diner), and the Paul Newman legal drama *The Verdict*. Willis, cast as an extra, can be spotted over Newman's shoulder in a few courtroom scenes. He'd later tell casting agents he was playing a court reporter in the film. Whatever it takes to get your foot in the door, and elevate your status.

But *Moonlighting* is the program most audience members would say introduced them to this supernova of charm and attitude. Five years prior to Willis joining Shepherd at the Blue Moon Detective Agency, however, another up-and-coming star was using an ABC sitcom as his springboard to the movies. Tom Hanks spent two seasons in women's clothing opposite Peter Scolari for the boundary pushing sitcom *Bosom Buddies*. Their characters, Kip and Henry, pretended to be Buffy and Hildegard to obtain affordable housing in a hotel designated for women. Hanks, like Willis, stood out from his ensemble and received the bulk of the show's praise. And when *Bosom Buddies* went off the air in 1982, Hanks immediately transitioned into the rowdy comedies *Splash* and *Bachelor Party* in 1984.

It's unclear if Willis observed Hanks's career path and opted to closely follow it. But once *Moonlighting* put him on the map, he too shifted into his first leading-man role, and chose a slapstick comedy that basically asked him to replicate a chunk of what he already was doing on his full-time, weekly television gig.

Die Hard forever will be Willis's most celebrated movie. *Pulp Fiction* and *The Sixth Sense* arguably are his most respected. But only Blake Edwards's comedy of errors, the 1987 farce *Blind Date*, gets proper credit for being Willis's first feature-film leading role, earning it a special place on the star's timeline.

The plot's hardly complicated. Worker bee Walter (Willis) needs a female escort for an important work event. Walter's brother, Ted (Phil Hartman), introduces him to Nadia (Kim Basinger, red hot thanks to 1986's provocative *9 1/2 Weeks*), and passes along one directive for the evening: Don't let her drink. Alcohol drives her wild. Naturally, Walter ignores the advice, lets Nadia sip some champagne, and spends the rest of the evening trying to corral the party animal he accidentally unleashed.

Moonlighting made terrific use of Willis's unique skill set. Eighty percent of each episode capitalized on the actor's ability to quickly turn a phrase, fire back a sharp quip, or dance verbal circles around an unsuspecting adversary. Average *Moonlighting* episode scripts were twice as long as similar TV dramas, simply because of the amount of dialogue the writers gave Willis and Shepherd. For the other 20 percent of the episodes, though, the street-wise Addison often held his own against ruffians he and Maddie were paid to investigate, and Willis had to make these scuffles look believable. The actor's evolving physicality would help carry his third feature, *Die Hard*. Edwards, though, seemed more interested in the madcap, rat-a-tat-tat line deliveries that Willis brought to his television series, and sought to translate it to the bigger screen.

"There's a school of comedy that I've studied for a long time," Willis said when reflecting on his work in *Blind Date*. "Directors like Frank Capra, Preston Sturges, Ernst Lubitsch. These guys kind of created that screwball comedy genre, and Blake Edwards is one of the last masters of that comedy style."[1]

Screwball comedies were derived from the romantic-comedy formula, and often relied on a dominant female character whose actions challenged the masculinity of her male costar. They usually contained ridiculously exaggerated and farcical scenarios that had the central couple at each other's throats before allowing their natural chemistry to seep in, leading to love. *Moonlighting* followed this time-honored template, as did Willis's feature film debut.

Not that Willis was merely "doing David Addison" in *Blind Date*. He's not, and that's appreciated. For starters, Walter's nowhere near as cool as Willis's television detective. And instead of delivering the punchlines, Willis's Walter mainly is asked by the screenplay to play the straight man reacting to every zany twist thrown at him by a drunken Basinger or a furiously jealous John Larroquette. Walter's a wallflower. He's unassuming, very accommodating, and mostly does for his costars what Shepherd had been doing for Willis on a weekly basis on *Moonlighting*: Lobs soft pitches straight over the plate so his scene mates can swing for the fences.

This doesn't mean Willis disappears during his debut feature. Late in the story, when Nadia's antics have all but destroyed every facet of Walter's humdrum existence, Willis finally gets to cut loose and flash his center-of-attention charisma that we know lurks beneath his scruffy surface. He tries to embarrass Nadia at a party attended by her close friends by juggling pâté. He shoots a black olive basketball-style into a well-endowed woman's healthy cleavage ("Boston fans?" Walter asks the horrified patrons when they don't applaud his accomplishment). He knocks a waiter into a swimming pool. During this stretch, Willis finally begins to match Larroquette's lunacy and cranks up the manic energy we know he's capable of displaying. Once Willis's internal party animal is allowed to emerge, the movie gets a needed jolt from its presence.

—5—

Most critics came out of *Blind Date* mixed. Some of the sight gags, particularly one involving a Great Dane named Rambo, received thumbs up, though the material was recognized as weak, no matter how hard Willis, Basinger, and Larroquette tried to make it memorable. "Most of the time I wasn't laughing," *Chicago Sun Times* critic Roger Ebert wrote. "But when I was laughing, I was genuinely laughing—there are some absolutely inspired moments. This is the kind of movie that serves as a reminder that comedy is agonizingly difficult when it works, and even more trouble when it doesn't."[2]

But entertaining the audience wasn't the sole accomplishment of *Blind Date*. At least not from the perspective of this proven TV star looking to take the next big step, like several of his colleagues around this same time.

"It did something that I was unaware needed to be done," Willis said of *Blind Date*. "And that was to somehow send a signal to the people who make films that someone that can come out of TV can also work in films and be successful."[3]

You can even spot the exact moment in *Blind Date* when that signal is sent. With three minutes left in the film's brisk 92-minute run time, Willis emerges from a pool cabana, having successfully disrupted Nadia and David's wedding ceremony. He stands on the ledge of an oversized swimming pool, beckons to his love interest from across the water, and flashes that signature movie-star grin, the one that would help propel his career. *Blind Date* was neither a financial hit, nor a critical darling. But it proved Willis's talents could work outside of the weekly television format. And by the time *Moonlighting* went off the air in 1989, Willis had become a certified movie star who only had to return to television when he wanted to.

CHAPTER TWO

HUDSON HAWK

Director: Michael Lehmann
Cast: Bruce Willis, Danny Aiello, Andie MacDowell, Richard E. Grant,
Sandra Bernhard
Release Date: May 24, 1991

> *I don't think the response that the film got in the media had anything to do*
> *with the film. I think it was my turn to catch a beating in the press.*
> *And when it's your turn, it's just your turn.*
> —BRUCE WILLIS ON *HUDSON HAWK*

—1—

Hudson Hawk promised everything Bruce Willis thought his fans wanted out
of a movie. The globetrotting, madcap caper blended three ingredients that
were very appealing to the *Die Hard* star at the time of production: cheeky
musical numbers that allowed the semi-professional singer to cover jazz-pop
show tunes by Bing Crosby and Frank Sinatra; snarky yet clever comedic
dialogue delivered at expedited rhythms, reminiscent of his *Moonlighting* heyday; and inventive action set pieces that made good use of Willis's energetic
yet smooth physicality. The finished product ping-pongs crazily like a helium
balloon in a breeze, striving for the wit of a Hope and Crosby road picture
but usually stalling out in buffoonish Three Stooges territory. Still, it's easy to
understand why, in the summer of 1991, Willis believed this movie would
connect.

"Before you start shooting any film," the actor once opined, "they're all
hits."[1]

This one was not. *Inside the Actor's Studio* fixture James Lipton tip-
toed into a discussion of *Hudson Hawk* during a 2001 taping with Willis

by mentioning, in the host's signature complimentary style, that the movie "failed to find its audience." This phrasing made Willis chuckle.

"Very generous, very kind way of saying that," Willis fired back, dryly. "'Failed to find its audience.' There *was* an audience for it. It just had kind of an underground culture audience for it."[2]

That's also generous. In reality, *Hudson Hawk* bombed when it opened. Critics ripped the film to shreds. Audiences didn't jive with the movie's goofy tone. Despite Willis's presence in a movie marketed around his appeal as an action-savvy jokester, *Hudson Hawk* earned only $7 million over the Memorial Day weekend (always a prime frame for new releases) and failed to lure crowds away from Ron Howard's suspenseful firefighter thriller *Backdraft* (which more than doubled the *Hawk* with its $15.7 million opening-weekend haul).

No Hollywood star, no matter how famous, is immune to a flop. And occasionally, those misses reach mythic proportions. Dustin Hoffman and Warren Beatty's reputations were plagued for years by *Ishtar*. Kevin Costner's bankability as a leading man temporarily sank following *Waterworld*. Eddie Murphy was responsible for more than a few duds, notably *Norbit* and *The Adventures of Pluto Nash*. For John Travolta, it's *Battlefield Earth*. It's not just that these movies lost money or generated fierce critical scorn. It's that they were identified as passion projects for their central creators, and the stench of their failure became the stuff of legend.

Hudson Hawk belongs on that list of maligned misfires. The affable movie has become a punchline over the years, a cautionary tale of what could happen when an eager studio gives a meteoric star what amounts to a blank check, then steps back and hopes for the best. But there were reasons, at the time, for executives to have a modicum of faith in the project. Willis, of course, was a proven commodity in 1991, having propelled not one but two franchises—*Die Hard* and *Look Who's Talking*—into profitability. Director Michael Lehmann also was coasting on a wave of goodwill for the high school–set black comedy *Heathers* when he signed on to this unorthodox hybrid of broad physical comedy and historical espionage.

It could be argued however that, thanks to a pair of consecutive flatliners, the bloom did start to come off Willis's rose around December 1990. That month, Brian De Palma's star-studded adaptation of novelist Tom Wolfe's *The Bonfire of the Vanities*, which cast Willis as an alcoholic tabloid reporter, opened to thunderous boos. Critics unanimously labeled the effort an inept, shallow, and miscast calamity. "You may have read that preview audiences have hooted (at) the film's revisionist ending, which concludes with a sermon," film critic Gene Siskel wrote in the *Chicago Tribune*. "I didn't hoot because I was too sad. I gave up on the movie well before the ending, because it was utterly devoid of drama. And I don't care how De Palma moves his camera or how many overhead shots he uses. He is photographing emptiness here."[3]

Four months later, barely enough time for *Bonfire*'s corpse to grow cold, Willis appeared alongside real-life spouse Demi Moore in the intentionally sleazy *Mortal Thoughts*, where he played against type as a womanizing, abusive drunk of a husband. The lure of seeing the celebrity couple on screen attracted a few curious onlookers, though overall reaction to the thriller was lukewarm. Which partially explains why Willis still contends that *Hudson Hawk*, no matter its quality, was destined to crash and burn.

"[Critics] had been trying to tear down [and] come after me since the first *Die Hard*," the actor said, looking back on *Hudson Hawk*'s legacy. "The films were successful anyway. But they had started to review this film long before anybody saw any of it."[4]

There's probably some truth to that assessment. It also, however, lets *Hudson Hawk* off the hook. A handful of critics may have approached Willis's fanciful vanity project with sharpened daggers, ready to puncture his inflated, celebrity ego. But the actor definitely provided his detractors with more than enough ammunition once he served up this ambitious yet, at times, cartoonishly immature concoction of singing cat burglars, assassins named after candy bars, a papal network of spies assigned to protect the Vatican, and a centuries-old invention by Leonardo da Vinci that converts lead into gold.

Discussing the film on their syndicated program *Siskel & Ebert*, Siskel dismissed the picture as "overstuffed" and lamented that "every character, and I mean every character including the villains, tries too hard to be funny."[5]

Both sides, in fact, are right. *Hudson Hawk* is an enjoyable mess that takes enormous swings. And critics probably judged it too harshly, given its comedic intent. "This is really my attempt . . . to just do a film that makes people laugh, that cracks people up and entertains them," Willis said while promoting the movie. "There's no message here. No moral code or anything like that. Just trying to make you laugh. . . . It's pretty silly. There's a lot of very stupid, broad, sophomoric humor in there. I'm a big fan of sophomoric humor."[6]

But because of where *Hudson Hawk* lands on Willis's timeline, and the creative decisions that he made in the wake of its failure, it's interesting to contemplate how different the actor's trajectory might have been had this very personal project found its following.

—2—

Hudson Hawk was Bruce Willis's "baby," an original concept on which he'd tinkered for years before earning enough juice to get it greenlit. Because of his unprecedented level of involvement in the development of the picture, it's fair to conclude that *Hudson Hawk* gives us our most unfiltered glimpse into what amuses Willis as a storyteller. The *Die Hard* star was so responsible for the shaping of the *Hudson Hawk* clay that he received a "story by" credit, the first and (to date) only of his career.

Willis came up with the Hudson Hawk character while tending bar in Manhattan in the early 1980s. The very loose idea started out as a song that Willis and fellow New York City musician Robert Kraft would scat at each other while the duo walked from bar to bar. One guy might launch the tune by improvising a lyric about prominent jazz saxophonist Coleman Hawkins, nicknamed "The Hawk." The other would fire back a verse about the frigid winds that blew through Chicago, which also are known as "The Hawk."

"Nickel in his pocket. Time on both his hands. Little Tommy 'Five-Tone,' Forty-Ninth and Tenth," Willis would sing.

"Let it rain, let it snow. Let the north wind blow," Kraft would counter. "It's the . . . Hudson Hawk again."

Before long, the two had imagined an entire narrative about a New York–based character whose name derives from the river that runs down the west side of Manhattan. Willis saw potential in the gag.

"He said at one point . . . 'Someday, I'm going to make a movie called the Hudson Hawk,'" Kraft recalls. "And I thought, 'Yeah, sure. You're working in a bar. I'm trying to get a record deal, and you're already making this movie.'"[7]

Years would pass before Willis found himself blessed with enough cachet to push *Hudson Hawk* through the studio system. And over that period of time, he and Kraft constantly changed the story's direction. They first assumed *Hudson Hawk* would play as a serious action movie, the kind of picture for which Willis was starting to become known. But the *Die Hard* lead never fully embraced the movie when it played this material straight, and repeatedly looked for opportunities to inject levity. An early version of the story involved Hawk stealing a heart off of a transplant list. Another would have set the story in the American frontier, and involved the theft of a buffalo.

"One of the first things we said was that it was like James Bond before he became James Bond. 'What was James Bond like when he was twenty years old?'" Willis remembered.

Eventually, the friends designated Italy as a prime location for the plotline—possibly because Willis and Kraft wanted to hang out in Venice, Florence, and Rome—and a new draft of the *Hudson Hawk* screenplay was submitted to TriStar Pictures, the studio behind *Blind Date* that had signed Willis to a first-look deal.

"And then boom," Kraft said, "one day we were shooting in New York, and taking the Concord to Rome."

—3—

Hudson Hawk represents the closest Willis came to blatantly rehashing his *Moonlighting* shtick for a film, particularly during his charming flirtations with Andie MacDowell or his sarcastic jabs aimed at his colorful array of criminal competition. Either David Addison learned how to soft-shoe through a scene while singing a tune from Hawk, or Hudson Hawk picked up tips from Addison on how to pass judgment with exaggerated facial expressions.

Both supremely confident antiheroes believe themselves to be the coolest guy in any room and understand how to let the audience in on their jokes. These parts were comfort zones for Willis, and we can only wonder how long he might have stayed in them—delivering multiple *Hudson Hawk* sequels instead of *Die Hard* follow ups—if the audience had shared his passion.

"It's easy to envision an alternate timeline in which Willis avoided macho action-hero roles and instead became something akin to a blue-collar Cary Grant: a cagey, self-aware, silver-tongued charmer who rarely punched anybody because he was so good at talking himself out of tight spots," culture critic and author Matt Zoller Seitz observed for Vulture in 2022.[8]

Willis didn't completely abandon unconventional projects following *Hudson Hawk*. He collaborated with esteemed director Robert Altman (*The Player*) and Robert Zemeckis (*Death Becomes Her*) on films that were interesting to him, but balanced those endeavors with the audience-friendly action installments *The Last Boy Scout* and *Striking Distance* before his career completely detoured thanks to Quentin Tarantino's *Pulp Fiction* in 1994. Still, he never gambled on anything quite as silly and satirical as *Hudson Hawk* for the remainder of his career. As Zoller Seitz observed about Willis's post-*Hawk* choices, "His transformation was among the most drastic in pop-culture history. By 1998, Michael Bay's science fiction actioner *Armageddon* was casting Willis as a cynical, surly, know-it-all oil driller loosely modeled on real-life oil-well firefighter Red Adair, previously fictionalized in the John Wayne epic *Hellfighters*. David Addison was being scrubbed away a bit more each year. In his place was a vision of American manhood that would have been at home in the 1950s."

—4—

Willis, Kraft, Lehmann and the core contributors to *Hudson Hawk* still to this day spend their time defending the film. "When the movie came out, a lot of people said, 'This doesn't make any sense.' Well duh, that's the point," Lehmann remarks on an audio commentary track recorded for the DVD. "We were playing around with the conventions of action-adventure movies, very deliberately and, I think, all in good fun. People either got it, or they didn't."[9]

Film critic Fred Topel echoed this conclusion about the movie's intentionally absurd tone.

"I have a theory that movies should make less sense. It's a fictional world, so why should they all follow the same rules as real life?" Topel theorizes. "Sure, realistic movies are good too. But it's odd that there are so few movies that aren't, except for maybe science fiction and horror. Making sense is the death of creativity. *Hudson Hawk* has no such limitations. In addition to musical numbers and editing tricks, there are cartoon sound effects, Andie MacDowell making dolphin noises, and heroes surviving calamity far beyond typical action heroics. It's happy, funny, exciting, and fun."[10]

Douglas Davidson, founder of and head writer for the pop-culture website Elements of Madness, finds himself on the same page. Trying to make sense of the critical backlash against *Hudson Hawk*, Davidson wonders,

> I'm curious what audiences and critics thought it was supposed to be. What expectations did they have going in? Maybe it's because I watched Hawk alongside Blind Date and Howie Mandel-led films Walk Like a Man and A Fine Mess that I view Hawk with a similar expectation of just enjoying myself. . . . Is it (Willis's) best performance in a film? I don't think there's much in the way of evidence that Willis stretches himself to play Hudson, but a lot of the film's charm comes from Willis's natural comedic timing, both in vocal and physical delivery. This charm is what makes Hudson endear himself. Plus, the script from Steven E. de Souza and Daniel Waters is insanely quotable and the mixture of wise-ass and genuineness as delivered by Willis elevates Hudson from a character to be mocked into one we root for.[11]

—5—

After Willis contemplated the critical reaction to *Hudson Hawk*, he came to the conclusion that the audiences weren't ready, and the critics had no interest in trying to embrace the experiment.

"We had a lot of problems, production wise, shooting it. But I've stopped thinking about the response to the film in the media because I don't think the response that the film got in the media had anything to do with the film," he said. "I think it was my turn to catch a beating in the press. And when it's your turn, it's just your turn. It can be a good film or a terrible film, and it really doesn't have anything to do with the content. It's just, sometimes it's just your turn."[12]

Willis does accept that the stinging rebuke to *Hudson Hawk* convinced him to "take a step back from this whirlwind four or five years, from *Moonlighting* to that time. I was able to take a step back from it, from having rocks thrown at me and rocks thrown at the film, going through that and walking through the fire and coming out the other side and realizing I was still employable. Still able to work.

"It allowed me to not take my work so seriously," Willis continued. "Because up to that time, there was no line between my work and my life. And it was right around that time that I'd just gotten married a couple of years earlier, I had kids now, so I started to see that while this is my job, this is my family, so it helped me in that sense."[13]

As expected, the once-maligned (and still divisive) *Hudson Hawk* eventually found some supporters. The Blu-ray release in September 2022, and the reviews that it received, provided modest vindication for the vanity project, and justice for a type of film that Willis made just to make people laugh.

"*Hudson Hawk* is absolutely silly stuff with some very weird transitions (that are) part of the film's charm. All the actors play their roles like cartoons, and I can appreciate that more now," Marc Ferman wrote for *The Film Junkies*. "While not considered a Bruce Willis classic, *Hudson Hawk* is definitely a one-of-a-kind big studio action film that would never get made today."[14]

He's correct. Too few movie stars in the early 2020s, if any, have the clout and industry currency to push a goofy vanity project like *Hudson Hawk* through the production pipeline. Hollywood trades in proven IP now, and takes precious few risks on unproven ideas, even with a celebrity of Willis's stature attached.

So Willis managed to get a special movie made at the exact right time, and has no interest, still, in apologizing for having it on his résumé. "I thought it was funny then," he said. "I think it's funny now. I think it holds up. People are still watching it. We're both still around. Nobody chased us out of town (or) banished us from the kingdom. We're still doing it."

Just doing it differently, and perhaps a bit more conventionally, because *Hudson Hawk* was so roundly rejected by his fan base.

CHAPTER THREE
DEATH BECOMES HER

Director: Robert Zemeckis
Cast: Meryl Streep, Goldie Hawn, Bruce Willis, Isabella Rossellini
Release Date: July 31, 1992

> *Wrinkled, wrinkled little star. Hope they never see the scars.*
> —Madeline Ashton (Meryl Streep) in *Death Becomes Her*

—1—

Critics reviewing Bruce Willis's movies over the years would describe the actor a dozen different ways. Handsome, self-confident, stoic, sarcastic, tough, contemplative—all those words fit the bill. Few, if any, probably used the term *chameleon* when writing about Willis, however. That adjective was reserved for dramatic and comedic performers who relied on tools of the trade to transform their physical attributes in service of a character. Think of *Saturday Night Live* veteran Mike Myers disappearing into the roles of Austin Powers, Dr. Evil, Fat Bastard, and Goldmember over the duration of his *Austin Powers* spy spoofs. Or Eddie Murphy portraying every member of the Klump family around the dinner table—and helping his makeup team win a well-deserved Academy Award—in the 1996 remake of *The Nutty Professor*. Prosthetics, extreme weight gain (or weight loss), accent changes, and visual effects have helped chameleonic actors such as Peter Sellers, Daniel Day-Lewis, Emma Thompson, Gary Oldman, Tilda Swinton, and Christian Bale masquerade their movie-star looks for the benefit of a part.

Willis hardly ever took that route. Outside of the occasional hairpiece applied for a character, Willis typically presented a slightly altered physical variation of his real-life appearance at the time of filming. *Armageddon*, as an example, delivered "Bruce Willis on an asteroid," with blonde highlights sprinkled through his remaining hair, and the hint of a Texas twang. *The Whole Nine Yards* offered "Bruce Willis as a dapper gangster." Robert Altman's *The Player* and Steven Soderbergh's *Ocean's 12* each earned sizable laughs by casting Bruce Willis *as* Bruce Willis—the role you could argue he was born to play.

"Like Toshiro Mifune and Clint Eastwood—both of whom he was aptly compared to in a 1996 article in *Rolling Stone*—his stardom has been predicated almost since the beginning on a strategic minimalism," Adam Nayman wrote in a Willis profile for the *New Yorker*. "The bald, bullet-headed look that he cultivated over time gave the impression of an actor carved from granite, a sleek solidity fissured only by one of Hollywood's great hairline smirks. In his best roles, Willis chips meticulously away at his charisma until he reaches something rough-edged and elemental underneath."[1]

A major exception to this unspoken rule could be found, however, in the 1992 farce *Death Becomes Her*. Then again, everything offered up in *Death Becomes Her* flew in the face of what audiences had come to expect from Willis on screen.

—2—

Director Robert Zemeckis's jet-black satire of the inevitable aging process was unlike anything Willis had done to that point in his career. It marked a rare detour into the supernatural genre. *Death Becomes Her* also gleefully concealed Willis's toned physicality and stripped away the rugged masculinity he innately brought to the screen in the *Die Hard* series, *Hudson Hawk*, and *The Last Boy Scout*. Gone were the actor's heroic traits or leadership qualities. He willingly replaced them with a mousy and emasculated demeanor, a flaccid posture, and the high-pitched scream of a bona-fide coward, which Willis would emit to outstanding comedic effect.

"He's the damsel in distress in this movie," film critic and podcast host Wynter Mitchell Rohrbaugh wisely pointed out about Willis's placement in the story.[2] It wasn't a position in which Willis allowed himself to be situated before, and he wouldn't accept the opportunity to play a part as submissive and weak as this ever again.

Death Becomes Her producer Steve Starkey believes the collaboration with Zemeckis brought out this browbeaten side of Willis's personality. "I think when Bruce feels that the show's in control, he feels very comfortable in his acting space. And he'll try different stuff, he'll be funnier, he'll say, 'What if I tried this?' He can be more experimental knowing he's being well taken care of by the director," Starkey said. "And so we were fortunate enough, because we had Bob as the director, to have a Bruce that was feeling really good about being there, about going to work, working with [his costars], working with this director, and showing a lot of sides of his acting chops that you may not normally see because of that."[3]

It's unfortunate Willis didn't invest in more of these types of collaborations because *Death Becomes Her* features the frequently solemn star at his most loose, most frazzled, most unpredictable, and most zany. The film applies the same Looney Tunes–level of slapstick that Willis conjured in *Hudson Hawk*, only it's in service of a smarter story. Willis and his costars fully commit to the macabre exaggerations required of the body-comedy spoof, and his no-holds-barred participation ensures that *Death Becomes Her* ranks as one of the funniest movies found on his résumé.

—3—

Death Becomes Her isn't Willis's movie. David Koepp and Martin Donovan's acerbic screenplay instead focuses on longtime rivals Madeline Ashton (Meryl Streep) and Helen Sharp (Goldie Hawn). The former is a fading star of stage and screen who's obsessed with her physical appearance, which she fears is in decline. The latter lives her life in Ashton's shadow, peppering her longtime competition with empty platitudes—right up until the moment Ashton steals the heart of Sharp's frumpish fiancé, plastic surgeon Dr. Earnest Menville (Willis). This betrayal triggers a multiyear war between the women that involves magic potions, reanimated corpses, and a half-naked sorcerer (Isabella Rossellini) who tempts these ladies with the dangerous promise of eternal youth.

Koepp explained his inspiration by confessing, "I was always kind of fascinated and revolted by Beverly Hills, which I just found to be an alien landscape filled with strange people who did strange things to their bodies."⁴ → landscape filled with strange people who did strange things to their bodies."[4] In exploring this abnormal community, Koepp landed on the idea of a story about a man who murders his wife, who happens to be a witch. He murders her *because* she's a witch, and he can't tolerate being with her anymore. From that germ grew the script that would become *Death Becomes Her*.

"[The movie] was so much more than what I was picturing when I wrote the script. Martin and I had seen it as a smaller movie. But of course there's such grandiosity in Beverly Hills, and in these people and their conceptions of themselves," said Koepp.

The story's scope only expanded in the hands of whiz-kid Zemeckis. His *Back to the Future* trilogy, as well as the frantic *Who Framed Roger Rabbit*, demonstrated his knack for merging resplendent comedic performances with cutting-edge visual technology to achieve his unusual visions. "Bob has a way of always going as far as he can possibly go, and it's always beyond wherever I'm at," said Rick Carter, *Death Becomes Her*'s production designer and a two-time Academy Award winner. "He's somebody who, in that era, was like the big bang theory, personified. You would talk with him, and everything would turn into something more than you could possibly imagine."[5]

This explains how *Death Becomes Her* became a witty rebuke of celebrity culture that nimbly dances from ghoulish body manipulations to potshots aimed at the vainglorious entertainment industry. As the hunger for beauty consumes Madeline and Helen, Zemeckis invented ways for Streep to act with her head twisted around 180 degrees, and for Hawn to take a shotgun blast to the stomach that blew a hole through her torso. At every step, the *Death Becomes Her* cast matched their director's imagination, his spirit of ingenuity all but validating their enormous performances.

"The characters were big," Koepp admits. "They were really on the edge of believability. Earnest isn't just sort of henpecked and sort of an alcoholic, he's horribly alcoholic, and horribly dominated. And Madeline isn't just a nasty person. She's Cruella de Vil. So it called for things being stylized, and larger than life."

—4—

Willis wears the part of the wallflower from the moment he shows up in the film, hooting and hollering from the audience of Madeline's failed Broadway production of "Songbird!" before slinking into her dressing room. There's an irony to Willis's character being a plastic surgeon, because he spruces up corpses while ignoring his own appearance. Almost every decision made in creating Earnest Menville tones down his impact in the given scene. His hair (what's left of it) is constantly tussled. His nondescript eyeglasses rest right above his generic mustache, which looks like it belongs to an Alburquerque science teacher who's about to start cooking meth. Costume designer Joanna Johnston drapes Earnest in earth-toned and forgettable suits. They're paired with beige and gray shirts that blend in with the colors of the walls of his doctor's office or mansion. Hawn and Streep, in contrast, positively pop in fire-engine red dresses, elegant white ball gowns, sequined stage costumes (feathery boa included), and, finally, funeral attire.

"Bruce was a joy to work with on this movie. He completely understood this broken, alcoholic character that Earnest was," said Zemeckis. "We both had a great time when we were doing scenes with Earnest because Earnest was just so henpecked by these two women, and he was just so trapped in these dysfunctional relationships that we just relished every moment of what Earnest had to do in this movie."[6]

And what he didn't have to do. Because *Death Becomes Her* isn't Willis's vehicle, he wasn't required to carry it, and he didn't need to overplay his hand to ever steal focus from his magnificent costars. Look for Earnest in most of his *Death Becomes Her* scenes, and he's typically slinking in the background, hoping no one notices him. This opportunity arrived at a stage, early in Willis's career, when the actor remained content to alternate starring roles in the *Die Hard* pictures or *The Last Boy Scout* with potentially rewarding supporting roles opposite proven actors he respected, working for filmmakers he admired. He'd do *The Bonfire of the Vanities* with Tom Hanks and Melanie Griffith if it meant he could work for Brian De Palma. He'd show up for the 1991 biographical gangster drama *Billy Bathgate* because it let him trade lines with Dustin Hoffman and Steve Buscemi.

And in a movie brimming with physical comedy, Willis was allowed to sit back and support two gifted comedians who were encouraged by their director to go for broke. "We have a fight scene that actually had a little accident," Hawn recalled about a sequence where she and Streep use shovels like swords during a heated exchange. "Because one of those shovels fell off onto my face and created a gash on my face. Oddly enough, I was fairly heroic about it. And I said, 'Oh, never mind, never mind. It's OK!' And I still have a scar from it."[7]

Imagine asking an audience member which of the three leads would emerge from *Death Becomes Her* with a facial scar incurred during a fight scene. Nine out of ten folks likely would select Willis, the experienced action star. The movie is better because it didn't need him to lean on the traits for which he had been typecast.

Death Becomes Her was selected eighteenth during the Planet Hollywood episode of the popular *Screen Drafts* podcast, released on August 23, 2021. The show recruits film experts for the purpose of "drafting" movies that fit a given topic, building in essence the strongest possible list of films that can be selected by an equitable panel. Participants on the Planet Hollywood episode of *Screen Drafts* were allowed to choose any films starring restaurant-chain investors Willis, Arnold Schwarzenegger, and Sylvester Stallone. And they debated long and hard over the films that would best reflect the contributions these men had on the film industry.

In choosing *Death Becomes Her*, film journalist and podcast host Jordan Crucchiola wanted a Willis feature that reflected the few times he allowed himself to be zany on screen. "He's so funny," she said. "He's such a perfect foil for these stronger women around him in this film." And in her explanation as to why *Death Becomes Her* deserved placement on the Planet Hollywood list, Crucchiola nailed Willis's ability to convincingly be an actor who is "able to be a John McClane, but somebody who will take this role, read this script, this premise, and go, 'Oh yeah, I'm there. I'm going to show up. I'm going to deliver.'"[8]

The *Screen Drafts* panel eventually got around to a talking point regarding Willis that needs to be highlighted, which is his ability to succeed in roles his Planet Hollywood counterparts couldn't pull off.

"It's just an incredible performance because I don't know a lot of actors who would have taken that role," Rohrbaugh added to the *Screen Drafts* debate. "Schwarzenegger wouldn't have done that. Stallone would have been, 'Absolutely not!' Stallone would have wanted to play Isabella Rosselini's part."[9]

There were moments over the course of their respective careers where the Planet Hollywood partners almost were considered interchangeable by studio executives. Stallone and Schwarzenegger both were offered the John McClane role before it went to Willis. Schwarzenegger famously tricked Stallone into accepting a role in the failed comedy *Stop! Or My Mom Will Shoot* by leaking a rumor that the *Terminator* star was considering the project. These rivalries extended to the box office, as when Stallone's *Rambo: First Blood Part II* went after the same audience as Schwarzenegger's *Commando* in 1985. But Willis, far more often than his action colleagues, took chances on character-driven assignments that made excellent use of his blue-collar relatability and his unflappable comedic timing.

Screen Drafts drafter Drew McWeeny, film critic for the *Formerly Dangerous* newsletter, raved about the *Death Becomes Her* selection and concluded, "It's an amazing performance. [A] great movie. And for Willis, one of the greatest pure comedy performances he ever gave. I think he is in remarkable control here. . . . You can see in this movie that he came to play with Robert Zemeckis. And Zemeckis is at the height of his whiz kid, play-with-my-toys, 'I'm going to do this technical thing that nobody else can do. I'm going to make a Looney Tunes cartoon in live action, and I'm going to do it in a way that actually has cartoon physics, and do things you can't do.' And Bruce Willis gave himself to that.

"It's one of the most engaged things he ever did," McWeeny continued. "And because it is so different, you get a real sense of range from him. It's a moment where you go, 'Bruce has so much gas left in the tank.' This is right after *Hudson Hawk*. He's reclaiming [the fact that], 'No, no. I'm hilarious. And I don't have to be the star.' Which, boy, that was a moment."[10]

—6—

The moment didn't last very long. As McWeeny pointed out, *Death Becomes Her* arrived in theaters a little more than a year after the equally exaggerated and comedic *Hudson Hawk*, meaning Willis plunged into projects buoyed by that silly and exaggerated tone as he flexed his comedic chops. Both movies received lukewarm critical receptions, and while Willis wasn't the sole reason for the tepid response, it's hard not to imagine him drawing the conclusion that mainstream audiences preferred him in straight action as opposed to the broad, entertaining comedies that launched his career.

Death Becomes Her does hold one distinction that possibly no other Willis movie can claim. Over the years, Zemeckis's effects-heavy bite at the Hollywood hand that feeds has been embraced by the LGBTQ+ community who now consider the film to be a touchstone of queer culture.

Drag impresario and filmmaker Joshua Grannell, who goes by the stage name Peaches Christ, touched on the film's unexpected impact on the queer community during a retrospective Q-and-A held for the movie's thirtieth anniversary. "There's this rich history of queerness attached to monster movies. But then they make this [movie] really overtly queer by casting two of our favorite icons of all time: the great actress Meryl Streep and the great, iconic comedy legend Goldie Hawn, and make it all about transformative beauty and magic with relationship to glamor. And it being ultimately about our desire to stay young? Let's face it, gay men especially have this issue. It's actually a real issue. It's a real darkness in our community where we don't talk a lot about the ageism that exists among us. And it's a real thing."[11]

Grannell points out that *Death Becomes Her* thrives as gay cult classic because the queer community embraces the chance to laugh at the darkness reflected in the film, particularly the inability for either female or queer performers to grow older in the entertainment industry. But Grannell particularly loves the fact that Willis lent his star power to the production while also degrading his appearance.

"I give him a ton of credit for that movie. In fact, I think it's his best performance ever," Grannell said. "The way he plays the sort of straight man—no pun intended—against those two women, he's so generous and so good at what he's doing. And I think when the movie came out, much like all great cult movies, it was queer people who immediately loved it. But the world didn't love it. It wasn't some huge phenomenon. It was queer people who kept it alive and showed it to their friends. And now it's considered a cult classic."

If only the film's impact could have been felt sooner, Willis's career arc might have reflected the appreciation he eventually received for his comedy. His choices in the years following *Death Becomes Her* pulled him away from comedy and placed him in his comfort zone of action and drama, leading to features like *Striking Distance* (1993), *Pulp Fiction* (1994), the third *Die Hard* movie (1995), the somber *Last Man Standing* (1996), and his first steps toward big-budget science fiction in *12 Monkeys* (1995) and *The Fifth Element* (1997). Willis didn't completely abandon comedy, as you'll see in our next chapter. But it's not too much of a stretch to conclude that the movie about death that Willis made with Robert Zemeckis ended up being a nail in the coffin of the broad, manic, and comedic subsect of Willis's filmography.

CHAPTER FOUR
THE WHOLE NINE YARDS

Director: Jonathan Lynn
Cast: Bruce Willis, Matthew Perry, Rosanna Arquette,
Amanda Peet, Michael Clarke Duncan, Kevin Pollak
Release Date: February 18, 2000

> *I was probably the most nervous on this movie. . . . I think because everybody around me was so funny that I was a little perplexed how funny people were. I mean, [Amanda Peet's] hilarious. Big Mike's hilarious. Matthew Perry, hilarious. Kevin Pollack, hilarious. I was way behind. I was way, way, way behind.*
>
> —BRUCE WILLIS TO LARRY KING ABOUT *THE WHOLE NINE YARDS*

—1—

Looking over Bruce Willis's comedic work, dating back to his launch in *Moonlighting*, two things become abundantly clear. First, Willis was capable of being the funniest person on screen in any given scene. His dry wit, impeccable comedic timing, magnetic presence, and unlimited number of facial expressions permitted Willis to take over most situations and wrap a movie or television episode around his finger. Even in a busy scene, your eyes drew to him, waiting to see what he'd do. Movie stars possess that quality.

But Willis didn't feel the need to perpetually be the brightest, shiniest star on screen, and frequently preferred to surround himself with proven scene stealers off which he could playfully bounce. Throughout his debut feature *Blind Date*, straight-man Willis skillfully lobbed comedic softballs toward a fumbling Kim Basinger and a furious John Larroquette, allowing them to earn most of the movie's biggest laughs. An unseen Willis let his lively voice provide the belly laughs while Kirstie Alley fell in love with John Travolta through two *Look Who's Talking* movies. Even with 1991's *Hudson Hawk*, a starring vehicle for Willis by design, the actor made sure to pair his singing cat burglar with a charming partner (Danny Aiello), a love interest (Andie MacDowell), two colorful convicts (Richard E. Grant and Sandra Bernhard), and three assassins named after candy bars.

Adam Sandler (*Happy Gilmore, The Wedding Singer*), Jim Carrey (*Liar Liar*), and Mike Myers (*Austin Powers*) stood front and center in the comedies they made around this time. They were the draw. Willis meanwhile flourished inside comedic ensembles, the kind that carried Jonathan Lynn's witness-protection comedy *The Whole Nine Yards* to $106 million in worldwide tickets sold in 2000.

Mitchell Kapner's *The Whole Nine Yards* screenplay first caught the attention of producer David Willis, who decided he wanted his A-list older brother to anchor the cast. Bruce agreed to play Jimmy "The Tulip" Tudeski, a ruthless Chicago contract killer hiding out from vengeful mob boss Janni Gogolak (Kevin Pollack) and his crew. Sequestering himself in the Montreal suburbs earns Jimmy no peace, however. His estranged wife (Natasha Henstridge) still wants him dead so she can collect on their life insurance policy. His ex-partner, Frankie Figs (Michael Clarke Duncan), plays both sides of the crime war so he can climb the ranks. Finally, a fledgling contract killer (Amanda Peet) follows Jimmy around like a puppy dog, begging him to share some tricks of his lethal trade.

These supporting characters orbit Jimmy like satellites throughout *The Whole Nine Yards*, setting him up for funny and frequently violent confrontations as he fights—often literally—to maintain his anonymity. But the movie required an energetic foil for the ice-cold Jimmy, a chaotic jolt of energy that would counter Willis's calm demeanor. And Lynn plucked his preferred co-lead Matthew Perry from—where else?—another incredibly famous Hollywood ensemble: the cast of NBC's smash-hit sitcom *Friends*.

—2—

Unless you experienced first-hand the heyday of NBC's Thursday night "Must-See TV" lineup, you can't fully comprehend what a behemoth *Friends* was for the network, the audience, its six main stars, and pop culture in general. For ten complete seasons that spanned 236 episodes, *Friends* infiltrated several aspects of our daily lives. Because of the weekly antics of these single, white, trend-setting Manhattanites, fans sang silly songs about smelly cats, scouted out comfortable couches in neighborhood coffee shops, and argued over whether or not Ross (David Schwimmer) and Rachel (Jennifer Aniston) were "on a break." The show's creators, David Crane and Marta Kauffman, influenced hairstyles (someone you know paid to get "The Rachel" at some point between 1995 and 2004), turned the pop-rock duo the Rembrandts into one-hit wonders, manipulated college graduates into believing they could afford the New York City lifestyle, and altered the way a generation of TV viewers spoke. Perry's sarcastic character, Chandler Bing, theoretically might ask about his show's success, "Could this sitcom be any more influential?"

Writing on the *Friends* legacy in 2019, in honor of the sitcom celebrating its twenty-fifth anniversary, *USA Today* reporter Kelly Lawler pointed out that the sitcom's expansion onto streaming platforms like Netflix and Peacock allowed a fresh wave of millennials and Gen Z audiences to binge reruns and acquaint themselves with this flawlessly cast ensemble of beautiful misfits.

"The unique legacy of *Friends* is not going to change in another 25 years, because there will never be another show like *Friends* again," Lawler concluded.

> TV has already changed irrevocably from the heyday of NBC's "Must-See TV" Thursdays, and the upcoming streaming surge, as Apple, Disney, HBO Max and NBC Universal all get in the game, will change it yet again. . . . The TV industry is unlikely to produce 236 episodes of a broad, genuinely funny sitcom full of talented, beautiful actors with effortless chemistry that feels fresh and new. But there almost certainly won't be a finale watched by 52.5 million viewers. So while our collective obsession with *Friends* may seem a bit over the top, it's also a singular experience we're desperately trying to hold onto as the world changes. Streamers come, streamers go, but we'll always have our *Friends* to keep us company.[1]

It's a comforting and accurate assessment. But it also makes the cold hard fact that TV audiences rarely followed *Friends* stars to the movie theaters a total shock.

—3—

"Show me an acclaimed and successful TV star and I will show you a frustrated wannabe movie star," the late Matthew Perry wrote in his 2022 memoir *Friends, Lovers, and the Big Terrible Thing*.[2] He spoke from experience. From 1994 to 2003, the six *Friends* leads arguably were the most acclaimed and successful television stars in the industry. But audiences so closely associated these actors with their beloved sitcom characters, it made it incredibly difficult for the cast to shed that baggage and transition to the big screen while the show was in its prime.

The female *Friends* fared better than their male costars in this regard. Courteney Cox can brag about her contributions to the *Scream* franchise. Lisa Kudrow will always have the cult classic comedy *Romy and Michele's High School Reunion* on her résumé. And Aniston is the lone *Friends* costar who parlayed the show's popularity into a lasting movie-star stint. An attractive girl next door, Aniston mostly appeared in generic romantic comedies while juggling *Friends*, playing a slight variation of her sitcom girlfriend role—the attainable love interest, the fetching ingenue, the inspiration—opposite fellow comedians Jay Mohr (*Picture Perfect*), Paul Rudd (*The Object of My Affection*), Jim Carrey (*Bruce Almighty*), or Ben Stiller (*Along Came Polly*). And while she never abandoned rom-coms completely, Aniston detoured post-*Friends* into raunchier comedies (*Horrible Bosses, We're the Millers*), critically lauded indie films (*The Good Girl, Cake*), and well-calibrated tearjerkers (*Marley and Me*). With more than $3 billion in worldwide movie tickets sold, Aniston by far ranks as the most successful "friend" on the big screen.

The least successful? Using box office as the measuring stick, it was Perry—only because David Schwimmer struck gold through the animated *Madagascar* franchise, where he voiced the neurotic giraffe Melman in multiple installments. Perry appeared in ten films over the course of his career. Only one—*17 Again* with *High School Musical* sensation Zac Efron—banked more than $100 million worldwide. Which means his biggest hit wasn't even the movie his manager told him "could be pay dirt" at the time, the gangster comedy *The Whole Nine Yards* that already had Willis attached when it landed in Perry's lap.

—4—

Willis is the biggest star in *The Whole Nine Yards*, but Perry's the movie's lead, the central character whose mundane existence gets flipped on its head because an infamous hitman (Willis) has moved in next door. And he's perfectly capable in the role, even funnier than expected. Perry claims responsibility for adding pratfalls and comedic collisions to Kapner's script.

"I said things like, 'I think this is a great opportunity for physical comedy, and I'd be more than willing to fall down a flight of stairs and leap down some mountaintops to work with Bruce Willis,'" Perry recalls. He astutely pointed out in his memoir that the role required very little acting on his part. "All I had to do was act scared of Bruce—which was easy—and act in love with Natasha Henstridge, which was even easier," Perry said.[3]

The "scared" aspect marked a notable shift for Willis. Somewhere around the release of Michael Bay's 1998 blockbuster *Armageddon*—where a squinty-eyed Willis assumed the role of an overprotective parent, and chased a handsome Ben Affleck around an oil rig—the actor transitioned away from the quippy blue-collar smart aleck with whom you wanted to share a beer, and started playing frightening figures with a low tolerance for the dweeby young costars standing in his way. Intimidation became a tool in Willis's repertoire that he often employed. The moment we first meet Willis's Jimmy in *The Whole Nine Yards*, he's berating his professional movers for working too slow. He gets so angry about Perry's character getting mayonnaise on his hamburger that he throws a piece of luggage fifteen feet, screaming, "I swear to God, when they start slapping that mayonnaise on there, I could kill somebody!"

This new on-screen persona could have been the result of a seasoned, jaded Willis growing a thicker outer shell around his characters, perhaps due to the intense scrutiny his private life faced off set. Perry tells stories of Willis flying him to Turks and Caicos during a three-day break on *The Whole Nine*

Yards, and the *Friends* star noticing that his A-list colleague also purchased every property surrounding his oceanfront abode "so that paparazzi couldn't get their shots."[4] The rest of this new Willis side simply comes off as disdain that the perpetually cooler actor had for the nebbish, submissive actors passing for movie stars at the time.

Film critic Roger Ebert of the *Chicago Sun-Times* picked up on this menacing vibe, writing in his *The Whole Nine Yards* review, "Willis has played countless hit men. This one simply has to stand there and suggest the potential for painful action. 'It's not important how many people I kill,' he explains to Perry. 'What's important is how I get along with the people who are still alive.' Willis glows as absurdities revolve around him."[5]

It's also interesting, when analyzing Willis's comedic output, that *The Whole Nine Yards* finds him coming full circle from *Blind Date*, his first foray into feature films. Similar to Perry, Willis at the time was looking to make the leap to leading-man roles, graduating to the movies with the hope of leaving his television safe haven behind. Willis completed the jump. Perry, not so much. He actually blamed the atrocious *Whole Nine Yards* sequel, *The Whole Ten Yards*, for killing off his movie career.

"We were all given too much freedom, and it sucked," Perry said of the sequel. "The jokes felt stale. . . . It was so bad that a while later, I called my agents and said, 'I'm still allowed to *go* to movies though, right?'"[6]

Parallels could also be found in the plots of *Blind Date* and *The Whole Nine Yards*, illustrating the subtle differences in the approach of each actor. Willis, for example, spent *Blind Date* playing the innocent bystander, bumbling and stumbling through a series of escalating disasters and using pratfalls as punchlines. Perry assumes that portion of the formula for *The Whole Nine Yards*, and it works well enough. With Perry, however, we sense the forced exertion whenever he runs headfirst into a sliding glass door or slinks into a bean bag chair, searching for a laugh. Willis made his lunacy look effortless.

But Willis appeared to believe less and less in his comedic abilities, and chose very few straight comedies after *The Whole Nine Yards* and its putrid, uninspired sequel. Willis instead spent the 2000s flexing his macho muscle in military thrillers (Antoine Fuqua's *Tears of the Sun*), a tense adaptation of Robert Crais's bestseller *Hostage*, Robert Rodriguez's black-and-white gangster noir *Sin City*, and the 2007 revival of his *Die Hard* franchise, *Live Free or Die Hard*. Nary a comedy could be found, which is a shame. Because when Willis committed to comedy, he lit up. And others—like his *Whole Nine Yards* costar Perry—saw in Willis the potential that he frequently squandered.

Perry confirms an urban legend about Willis in his memoir that has picked up steam over the years. As the story goes, Willis didn't believe that *The Whole Nine Yards* would find an audience. So Perry, feeling confident, made a bet. If the movie was a hit, Willis had to come on *Friends* in a cameo role. Willis took the gamble. Then he watched *The Whole Nine Yards* open to number one at the box office and remain there for three consecutive weekends. So Willis made good on his promise. He appeared on three episodes of *Friends* in the show's sixth season, playing the intimidating father of a younger girl that Ross (David Schwimmer) was dating.

Willis had nothing to prove by appearing on *Friends*. He'd stamped his signature on the television format through *Moonlighting* and was at one of the highest points of his movie-making career in 2000. The line separating television and movie stars has currently blurred, but it was uncommon to see silver-screen personalities returning to their TV roots in the pre-streaming age.

Willis was the anomaly. In the years following his Emmy-winning run on *Moonlighting*, the A-lister played himself in standalone episodes of *Roseanne* (1989) and *Mad About You* (1997), and appeared as Dr. Nickle in a 1999 episode of the FOX comedy *Ally McBeal*. Maybe he missed the rigors of the television format? Perhaps he was just paying off a harmless bet he made with Perry. But the *Friends* stint offered a fuller arc for the actor, requiring multiple appearances that allowed him to flesh out an actual character. And he clearly had fun dancing circles around the *Friends* cast as he terrified the nervous Schwimmer, charmed Phoebe (Lisa Kudrow) and Monica (Courteney Cox), then romanced the attractive Rachel (Jennifer Aniston).

Also, he was funny. He reminded audiences that he had the ability to step into the hottest program on network television and steal scenes from the main cast. And perhaps more important, he proved to his industry colleagues that this action sensation still had the razor-sharp comedic chops that put him on their radar in the first place, because his *Friends* performance won him his second Emmy Award.

CHAPTER FIVE
OCEAN'S 12

Director: Stephen Soderbergh
Cast: George Clooney, Brad Pitt, Julia Roberts, Matt Damon,
Catherine Zeta-Jones, Don Cheadle, Carl Reiner, Bruce Willis
Release Date: December 8, 2004

> *"We're looking to come off this baby thing strong. You know, that little statue on the mantle starts smirking at you after a while, you know what I'm saying?"*
> *"Not really, Glen, no."*
> —LINUS (MATT DAMON) TO BRUCE WILLIS IN *OCEAN'S TWELVE*

—1—

Julia Roberts has been sentenced to death.

OK, not the Oscar winner herself, but a character she's playing on screen. A priest sits beside Roberts in a sparse prison cell, reading the Last Rites while Susan Sarandon, Peter Falk, and Paul Dooley observe the pending execution from nearby seats. Guards eventually escort Roberts to the gas chamber, secure the doors, then strap her to a chair. Her eyes dart around the room as lethal amounts of poisonous gas begin to fill the space. She holds her breath, to no avail. Once the toxic fumes overwhelm, her chin falls to her chest.

Suddenly, a nearby guard listening in on a telephone screams in panic, "What?" Down a long corridor, Bruce Willis appears and starts sprinting toward the chamber. Sensing that time nearly has run out, Willis snatches a shotgun from the hands of a startled officer and fires a round into the window pane that protects the observers from the gas. The execution attendees gasp, then race to cover their mouths and noses. An undeterred Willis leaps into the room, undoes Roberts's straps, and carries America's sweetheart to safety.

"What took you so long?" Roberts asks Willis, lovingly stroking his cheek. "Traffic was a bitch," he replies before breaking into his signature smirk.

This scene isn't from an actual movie, so don't feel bad if you can't remember it. The corny sequence served as the audience-friendly storybook ending for an Oscar-baity prestige picture being produced by Griffin Mill (Tim Robbins) and Larry Levy (Peter Gallagher) in Robert Altman's *The Player*, a scathing rebuke of a studio system to which Altman never felt beholden. The maverick filmmaker secured his auteur status in the 1970s courtesy of the critically acclaimed war satire *MASH*, the revisionist Western *McCabe and Mrs. Miller*, and the politically charged country-music ramble, *Nashville*. Altman's films attracted elite talent. The Academy of Motion Pictures Arts and Sciences nominated him for Best Director five times before finally bestowing him with an Honorary Award in 2006 that recognized his reinvention of the art form. Altman was one of the first filmmakers to employ an immersive audio technique that captured overlapping dialogue on set, forcing the audience to decide which snippets to absorb, and which conversations to follow.

Altman would never end one of his own pictures with such an artificial "happy" ending as the one found in *The Player*. And yet, the director viewed the Willis and Roberts interplay as one of his film's most important sequences. It's the punchline at the end of a very long set up, a self-aware jab at Hollywood's risk-averse approach to moviemaking. This manufactured ending, we are told in the story, owed its existence to test screenings, where feedback from Joe and Jane Public could convince a studio to alter a filmmaker's vision. But it's a sellout, and studio executive Bonnie Sherow (Cynthia Stevenson) knows it. Upon seeing Willis save Roberts from a grim death, Sherow immediately grills the screenwriter about the movie's original, more downbeat ending—the one that rang emotionally true, but would likely prove divisive.

"What about the way the old ending tested in Canoga Park?" the writer (Richard E. Grant) spits back, vehemently. "Everybody hated it. We reshot it, now everybody loves it. That's reality."

The high-and-mighty writer sacrificed his principles and caved. His artistic values were compromised. And that compromise was personified by megawatt stars Willis and Roberts agreeing to appear on screen.

"[*The Player*] was about Hollywood. It was about making movies," Altman said. "And I thought we'd pump the reality of the whole project up by having these people appear as themselves. . . . Julia did it because she and Tim Robbins were friends. And Bruce did it because Bruce just does that kind of thing."[1]

The scene, while brief, carried additional significance outside the needs of Altman's story. It demonstrated that Hollywood superstars Willis and Roberts—each red-hot at the box office and capable of choosing whichever project they desired—were willing to take themselves down a few pegs for the benefit of an inspired comedic bit. Altman's ending ridiculed the Hollywood system that built Willis and Roberts up. Their participation served as a ringing endorsement of the director's stinging commentary.

Also, it was funny. So funny, the duo would attempt something similar, though far more intricate, twelve years later. Once again, Willis and Roberts would play realistic caricatures of themselves on screen in what I consider to be Willis's funniest on-screen performance, for Steven Soderbergh's heist comedy *Ocean's 12*.

—2—

The *Ocean's* franchise itself contains a comical number of A-list movie stars being impossibly stylish, sophisticated, and cool in the sexiest international locations.

"These movies are kind of like parties to me," Soderbergh said, "and I'm trying to set up a party that looks like you'd want to attend, at the end of the day."[2]

Soderbergh's guest list for his 2001 franchise launcher consisted of some of the biggest celebrities on the planet at the time: George Clooney, Julia Roberts, Brad Pitt, and Matt Damon were surrounded by industry veterans (Elliott Gould, Carl Reiner) and respected character actors (Don Cheadle, Andy Garcia, Bernie Mac, Eddie Jemison, Casey Affleck, and Scott Caan). Soderbergh's sequels sufficiently increased the star power every time new characters joined the fray—Catherine Zeta Jones as a Europol detective in *Ocean's 12*, Al Pacino as a sleazy casino mogul in *Ocean's 13*. Guest stars needed to do something memorable in an *Ocean's* movie to steal focus away from Soderbergh's glamorous cast. And that's exactly what Willis managed to do with his nearly nine-minute surprise appearance in *Ocean's 12*.

Soderbergh's second *Ocean's* movie shifts the action from Las Vegas to Europe, where Danny (Clooney), Rusty (Pitt) and their crew attempt to pull off a series of elaborate heists. By the time Willis enters the twisty *Ocean's 12* story, Europol agent Isabel Lahiri (Zeta-Jones) has detained half of Ocean's team in a Roman prison, preventing them from stealing a Fabergé egg from the Galleria d'Arte di Roma. Crew members Linus (Damon), Basher (Cheadle), and Turk (Caan) manage to evade capture, though, and are forced to hatch a replacement plan to complete the mission. They need a celebrity who can help them enter the museum and get close enough to the egg. So they recruit Danny's wife, Tess (Roberts), because of her uncanny resemblance to Julia Roberts.

"I remember talking to Carl Reiner after we shot (those scenes), and him coming over and saying, 'I think she nailed this.' He said, 'It's a weird thing to do' and he felt . . . if you're going to play it, she played it exactly the way it should be done," said Soderbergh.[3]

And she held it together when the situation grew weirder. As Linus and Basher struggle to convince an extremely reluctant Tess to pretend to be *Pretty Woman* star Julia Roberts for the afternoon, into their hotel suite walks Willis, who spotted Tess—which he assumed was Julia—entering through the lobby. This ingenious mistaken-identity equation allows Soderbergh to stage a bonkers sequence where Roberts has to play Tess playing Roberts, interacting with the real Bruce Willis, who hopes his famous "friend" can help him retrieve his daughter Tallulah's SpongeBob Square Pants blanket from Roberts's home in Taos, New Mexico.

It's a joke inside of a joke. Linus and Basher needed a celebrity to distract the museum guards. But Soderbergh needed a bigger celebrity to distract the audience from his *other* celebrity. The minute Willis appears, he disrupts the con and raises the stakes. The challenge no longer is, "Can Tess convince museum workers that she's Julia Roberts?" It has become, "Can Tess fool Julia Roberts's close friend, Bruce Willis?" The script asks Willis to become the focal point of a calculatedly chaotic scheme, and he's so magnetic in his movie-star mode, you can't take your eyes off of him.

Salon critic Stephanie Zacharek reveled in Soderbergh's Hollywood shell game in her 2004 review.

"The whole of *Ocean's 12* is an inclusionary in joke—it winks at us and at itself, sometimes pretty broadly, yet there's nothing tediously self-referential about it," she wrote. "Soderbergh has the good sense to realize that Julia Roberts is such a recognizable presence that it's almost crazy to ask an audience to believe in any character she plays. So he finds a way to meld everything we think we know about Roberts with everything we don't know about the character of Tess. . . . Soderbergh makes Tess seem even more 'real' than Julia Roberts, a feat I wouldn't have thought possible."[4]

The entire curveball seems impossible, yet it works remarkably well because of Willis's radiant personality and sharp comedic timing. He exudes charm throughout his *Ocean's 12* romp, playfully flirting in Italian with a gorgeous admirer before bounding into Tess's hotel suite unannounced, sending the *Ocean's* crew scrambling. (Damon and Roberts are masterful at hysterically reacting to Willis's arrival while fighting to maintain the Julia ruse.) Willis knows so much about Roberts, personally, that his line of interrogation about everything from her husband, Danny Moder, to their obstetrician keeps the con artists on their heels.

"Julia and Bruce (use) 'Here's the name of my assistant,' or 'Here's how many horses I have,'" screenwriter George Nolfi said. "We just used their real lives."

More important, the scenes rely heavily on jokes that mercilessly mock Roberts and Willis. And the duo leans directly into all of them. Multiple characters reveal to Willis that they figured out the twist ending of his massive hit *The Sixth Sense*. Linus assures Tess that she doesn't even need to speak when she's pretending to be Julia Roberts in the museum—just smile and wave. "That's all she ever does," Turk throws in as a subtle dig. And Linus, pretending to be a studio publicist, explains to Willis that Julia is trying to spin some positive press out of her pregnancy situation because "that little [Oscar] statue on the mantle starts smirking at you after a while." Willis, who somehow never even sniffed an Oscar nomination, can't relate.

"That's the kind of thing you can get away with on this movie because these guys are willing to do it," Nolfi said.

"Bruce was a great sport about this," Soderbergh added.

—3—

Willis owes his inspired cameo to Roberts but also, indirectly, to Topher Grace. Grace is best known for playing loveable square Eric Forman on the popular FOX sitcom *That '70s Show*. He also appeared as himself, hysterically spoofing the concept of clueless young Hollywood, in Soderbergh's original *Ocean's 11* for a scene where Brad Pitt's Rusty tries to instruct a Brat Pack of fresh, famous faces how to play poker. Soderbergh wanted Grace to return in *Ocean's 12* in some capacity. One idea the creative team considered would have found him playing a prestigious royal figure.

"I know for a while, there was an iteration of the movie in which Julia was not playing Julia, but was going to impersonate a princess that had some connection to the Romanoff family, and that's where the whole Faberge egg came from," Soderbergh explained. "And at that point, I think when we were discussing the princess idea, Topher was going to show up in essentially the Bruce Willis role as the complicating factor. Then, when we settled on the 'Julia as Julia' idea, we decided, 'We've got to find a real movie actor who is understood to have some relationship with Julia.'"[6]

Soderbergh asked Roberts to pick someone with whom she'd feel comfortable, preferably a movie star with whom she shared a rich personal history. She chose her screen partner from Altman's *The Player*, so Soderbergh made the call to recruit.

This weirdly wasn't Willis's first brush with Soderbergh's *Ocean's* franchise. In an alternate universe where production schedules lined up differently, Willis would have been the leader of Soderbergh's merry band of charismatic con artists in 2001's *Ocean's 11*.

"Bruce Willis turned down the first [movie]," George Clooney told *Time* while promoting the 2007 sequel *Ocean's 13*. "He was supposed to be Danny Ocean. And he did end up doing the second one. I think he regretted not being in the first."[7]

He might have regretted it at the time, but accepting the lead role in *Ocean's 11* and staying on for the subsequent sequels would have tied up

Willis's calendar from 2000 to 2007—potentially keeping him out of M. Night Shyamalan's *Unbreakable* (2000), Antoine Fuqua's *Tears of the Sun* (2003), and Robert Rodriguez's *Sin City* (2005).

—4—

Naturally, the funniest scene in the entire film—dare I suggest, in the entire trilogy—almost didn't happen because studio executives balked at the concept, fearing that mainstream audiences wouldn't understand it.

"There are some people for whom this idea was too much," said Soderbergh. "I think the concern on the part of the studio was, 'It's too inside. It's too self-referential. This is going to antagonize more people than it's going to please.' . . . I think the concern [was], 'Is it going to tear the fabric of the movie apart?'"[8]

The director believed he had Hollywood history on his side. He countered the studio's argument with a pioneering scene from Howard Hawks's 1940 screwball comedy *His Girl Friday*. At one point in that film, Cary Grant—playing a fast-talking newspaper editor—asks a beautiful blonde to head downstairs to a waiting taxicab and distract a man named Bruce Baldwin, played by the Oscar-nominated character actor Ralph Bellamy.

"What does he look like?" the lady asks Grant.

"He looks like that fellow in the movie. You know, Ralph Bellamy," Grant explains.

Soderbergh rationalized, "This is a movie that is made in 1940. That's a pretty crazy joke to throw in. (But) it totally works. It's one of the biggest laughs in the movie. And it convinced me this can work. . . . I don't know. I guess, at the end of the day, it was just our gut feeling that it was a fun idea."

And the actors clearly appear to be having fun playing with the idea on screen. Willis comprehends that he needs to embrace all of the preconceived notions of his celebrity persona to sell the idea, so he makes a handful of small, hysterical choices that can go unnoticed unless you analyze the scene. Watch him glare at Linus when Damon dares to put a hand on Willis's shoulder, portraying the expected tough guy. At the same time, he's also putting forth the parental concern that would come with being Bruce Willis, father and husband. He questions why Roberts has flown to Rome, despite being eight months pregnant. He begs Dr. Simon Leopold (Reiner) to slow down their pace as they sprint through the museum, fearing for the health and safety of his pregnant friend. And in a seemingly improvised moment, he plucks "Julia's" sunglasses off of her head and instinctively starts cleaning them with his handkerchief—a gentleman gesture that gets a good laugh.

Soderbergh calls *Ocean's 12* his favorite of his trilogy, lovingly comparing it to another famous middle chapter of an iconic three-part saga, *Star Wars: Episode V—The Empire Strikes Back*. "The things about this movie that people had issues with end up being, for me, the things that I like about it," he said. "First of all, I think visually, it's the best of the three films. But the weirdness of it, the oddness of it, is the very thing that I like about it. It doesn't work the way movies like this usually work."[9]

And as for the concept of repeat viewing, where I point out that an audience likely will pick up on the subtle comedic moves that Willis and his costars included to push the envelope on the absurdity of their situations, Soderbergh has advice when it comes to that, as well.

"I think if you watch [*Ocean's 12*] over and over again, which I encourage everybody to do," he continued, tongue planted in cheek, "keep watching it until [you] like it. If you didn't like it when you saw it, you just didn't watch it enough."

SECTION TWO
BRUCE WILLIS IN THE ACTION GENRE

"Since it's the '90s, you don't just smack a guy in the face.
You say something cool first."
"Like, 'I'll be back?'"
"Only better than that."

Official movie poster for Tony Scott's *The Last Boy Scout*,
starring Bruce Willis. *Author's Collection*

Die Hard was a blessing and a curse for Bruce Willis. John McTiernan's airtight action thriller turned Willis into a global superpower overnight. He graduated from affable television personality to bankable movie star. On the flip side, Willis's complete ownership of the John McClane role meant that he'd spend the next three decades fielding offers to play slight variants of the blue-collar, underdog action hero in multiple copycat features.

Willis didn't start out looking to be Hollywood's next action sensation. For one thing, he lacked the hulking bodybuilder frame of his action-movie counterparts. Also, the former drink slinger and frequent musician seemed to prefer bellying up to a bar in a Blues club, not hitting the gym at the crack of dawn.

"I don't really like to exercise that much," Willis once admitted. "I kind of see it as a burden of vanity. You take your shirt off in a film, and you are going to worry about it. There's nothing that's going to get you in shape faster than [having to] take your clothes off in a film."[1]

But Willis understood, in the post–*Die Hard* era, how convincing he could be in physically demanding action roles, and those who collaborated on pictures of this ilk tended to agree.

"The neat thing about Bruce is that he is physically active, he's a good athlete, (and) he can perform a lot of his own stunts within the parameters of good conscience," said legendary stuntman Terry J. Leonard, who served as stunt coordinator on McTiernan's sequel, *Die Hard with a Vengeance*.[2]

As this book demonstrates, Willis specialized in numerous genres and wasn't afraid to explore heady sci-fi, slapstick comedy, serious adult fare, or grungy genre films as he searched for rewarding stories. Associating him with only one genre would be dismissive. Willis varied his projects, successfully avoiding the industry's efforts to pigeonhole his talent.

"I try to keep myself interested. Again, I could have just stuck at *Die Hard*, and we'd be sitting here talking about *Die Hard 14*," Willis once told Charlie Rose during a 2002 interview. "I've gotten to a point, actually right around the time I did *Death Becomes Her*, I started really taking more chances. And accepting roles that I didn't necessarily know, when I said yes to the role, how I was going to actually do it. How I was going to be funny, or how I was going to play it. And it's scary! Like going out on the ice, and you don't know if it's thick enough to hold you. When the chances for failure are higher, it's just more exciting."[3]

Those risks provided us, the audience, with so many rewards. However, when all is said and done, Willis forever will be associated predominantly with the action genre, where he routinely played beat cops, private investigators, police lieutenants, soldiers and—once—the pilot of a speed boat in the *Pittsburgh River Rescue*.

The genre proved extremely lucrative for Willis. Five of his ten highest-grossing films were pure action stories. Two more of them, *Armageddon* and *The Fifth Element*, were sci-fi blockbusters with a heavy emphasis on action set pieces. His signature *Die Hard* franchise produced five films that earned $1.431 billion in worldwide box-office grosses. And the action genre provided Willis with a safety net to which he could always return if and when an experimental movie missed its mark.

"The action genre, in general, provides a vicarious opportunity for the audience to experience the thrill of these big, larger-than-life things," Willis once explained. "It's entertainment, I guess is what I'm saying. And we provide that, without having to watch the news, or go jump off a big bridge yourself."[4]

Basically, you can't encapsulate Willis's body of work without analyzing the six movies in this next section, all of which showcase the dependable qualities that helped make Willis an all-time action superstar.

CHAPTER SIX
THE LAST BOY SCOUT

Director: Tony Scott
Cast: Bruce Willis, Damon Wayans, Chelsea Field, Halle Berry, Bruce McGill
Release Date: December 13, 1991

Nobody likes you. Everybody hates you. You're gonna lose. Smile, you fuck.
—JOE HALLENBECK (WILLIS), *THE LAST BOY SCOUT*

—1—

Buddy cop movies, my own personal favorite action subgenre, thrived in the 1980s and 1990s, when Bruce Willis navigated his post–*Die Hard* stardom and all of the opportunities that movie presented. Walter Hill's 1982 action comedy *48 Hours* didn't invent the subgenre. James Caan and Alan Arkin test drove the formula for the 1974 black comedy *Freebie and the Bean*. That same year, Eliott Gould and Robert Blake played Los Angeles cops forced to team up in the crime drama *Busting*, which inspired the creation of the 1975 television drama *Starsky and Hutch*.

But *48 Hours* seamlessly solidified the template for conventional buddy cop stories, and connected so squarely with the mainstream audience (thanks to a star-making turn by Eddie Murphy) that it acted like a springboard for multiple projects pitched in its wake. *Tango and Cash* with Sylvester Stallone and Kurt Russell, *Running Scared* with Billy Crystal and Gregory Hines, and even the dreadful *Collision Course* with Jay Leno and Pat Morita owe their existence to *48 Hours*. Hollywood powerbroker Joel Silver, a self-professed fan of this genre, shepherded some of the greatest examples of these movies to multiplexes after receiving a producer credit on *48 Hours*. He refined the formula over the years and delivered *Lethal Weapon*, *Action Jackson*, *Demolition*

Man, *Assassins*, *Kiss Kiss Bang Bang*, *Sherlock Holmes*, and the 1991 Willis vehicle, *The Last Boy Scout*.

"People say, 'Is this like Butch and Sundance?' And I say it's more like Abbott and Costello," Silver said. "But these movies are not comedies per se. They are thrillers, mysteries, dramatic stories that also are very funny. In all the movies I've done, even movies like *The Matrix* and *Die Hard*, there's always gotta be humor. . . . When you put humor in, it makes the movie even more effective because it's a counterpoint to the drama and the mystery."[1]

Chicago Sun Times film critic Roger Ebert coined the phrase "Wunza Movies" when reviewing the 1998 Jackie Chan–Chris Tucker buddy cop film *Rush Hour*. The slang term described the pairings that were central to each story. As Ebert expertly phrased it, "Wunza legendary detective from Hong Kong, and wunza Los Angeles cop. And wunza Chinese guy, and wunza black guy. And wunza martial arts expert and wunza wisecracking showboat. Neither wunza original casting idea, but together, they make an entertaining team."[2]

Willis, however, never found a permanent Riggs to match his Murtaugh, or a Cash to consistently run with his Tango. He didn't launch a buddy-cop franchise during this prolific period, even though studio heads were eager to milk any successful pairing for multiple sequels. This subgenre, after all, produced four *Lethal Weapon* movies, three *Rush Hour* films, *Another 48 Hours* and *Another Stakeout*.

Willis's aloof demeanor and condescending attitude made him an awkward fit in buddy cop stories. By the end of a buddy cop movie, the protagonists who started out as antagonists often discovered they were in fact equals. But Willis's persona, codified in *Die Hard*, matched that of a lone wolf. His characters often prided themselves on not playing nice with others. Even when director John McTiernan loosely applied the formula to the dependable *Die Hard* franchise, pairing Willis opposite Samuel L. Jackson for the action-packed *Die Hard with a Vengeance*, their chemistry was rooted in racial tensions, bubbling over into frustration, and eventually to anger.

"You got some fucking problem with me because I'm white, Zeus? Is that it?" John McClane exploded at his reluctant partner (Jackson) after the two butt heads over a perplexing puzzle involving water jugs. "Have I oppressed you? Have I oppressed your people somehow? I'll tell you what your problem is. You don't like me because you're a racist."

"What?" Zeus replies, incredulous.

"You're a racist! You don't like me because I'm white," McClane accuses.

"I don't *like* you because you're going to get me killed," Zeus corrects.

After *Die Hard with a Vengeance*, Tony Scott's slick and violent *The Last Boy Scout* qualifies as the only other conventional buddy cop movie found on Willis's résumé. (I'm actively ignoring Kevin Smith's dreadful 2010 outing, *Cop Out*, because Kevin Smith himself would want me to ignore the movie he publicly denounces.) And *The Last Boy Scout* dutifully checks every box on an imaginary "Wish List" any producer might have referenced when seeking to create the perfect buddy cop thriller. Mismatched duo? Check. Ribald humor? In abundance. High-concept, borderline-ludicrous action sequences? Damon Wayans rides a horse across a football field in the middle of a game, racing to prevent an assassination, so yes.

But *The Last Boy Scout* leads this book's action section because it also offers the purest distillation—outside of the *Die Hard* franchise—of the quintessential Willis action antihero: A burned out, beleaguered, hungover, chain-smoking, self-loathing punching bag who has been dealt a shitty hand, but doesn't understand the meaning of the word *quit*.

—2—

Willis's action persona differed from his counterparts in the genre at the time. In 1991, the year Warner Bros. released *The Last Boy Scout*, an indestructible Arnold Schwarzenegger raced tractor-trailer trucks around Los Angeles and survived shotgun blasts to the chest as he muscled *Terminator 2: Judgment Day* to the top of the box-office charts. The following year, superheroes continued to strengthen their hold on the industry with Michael Keaton's sequel *Batman Returns* holding the box-office pole position with $162 million in domestic tickets alone.

Willis generally avoided playing the immovable object or the unstoppable force. And despite the popularity of the comic-book genre, he never tried on spandex or a cape to join one of Marvel or DC's lucrative franchises (though he'd dabble in graphic novel adaptations for two series launched by *Sin City* and *Red*). Willis's heroes stood out because they were vulnerable and flawed. They could bleed, and often did—a lot. *The Last Boy Scout* contains a lengthy, painful sequence where criminals repeatedly punch a kidnapped Willis in the face every time he asks for a light of his cigarette. He pauses long enough after each hit to spit blood before delivering his next one-liner.

"I think those are my favorite kinds of characters in films. Guys who are just regular guys," Willis once said. "I just find myself leaning towards that. There are certain roles that I don't think I would be good at playing, that are much better left to other actors that are trained in a different way than I have been. I'm far more interested in guys that have problems, and have obstacles to overcome."[3]

Joe Hallenbeck, the private detective Willis plays in *The Last Boy Scout*, fits that description. When we first meet this tough-talking, streetwise investigator, he's sleeping in his car and remains so hungover from the previous evening that he doesn't even notice the dead squirrel thrown on his chest by some prankster kids. Bill Simmons and Chris Ryan, cohosts of *The Rewatchables* podcast, gave Hallenbeck the nickname "Drunk McClane." That fits perfectly. Hallenbeck's a self-proclaimed low life, sporting three-day stubble and delivering this defeatist pep talk to himself before heading out on a job: "Nobody likes you. Everybody hates you. You're gonna lose. Smile, you fuck."

The private detective begrudgingly pairs up with washed-up NFL quarterback Jimmy Dix (Wayans) as they get drawn into an unfolding criminal scheme involving political bribery aimed at legalizing gambling in California. Someone hires Hallenbeck to shadow a topless dancer named Cory (Halle Berry), who may have overheard damning evidence while on a job. Dix invests in Hallenbeck's investigation because Cory was his girlfriend. Also, she gets killed almost immediately, prompting Dix to seek revenge.

Both men carrying *The Last Boy Scout* suffer personal pains that stem from past failures, and we root harder for them because they're defined as underdogs. Fallen hero Hallenbeck once took a bullet for the president of the United States while working for the Secret Service. Later, he jeopardized his professional reputation by leaving his post to assist a woman who was being physically abused by a corrupt senator. At home, Hallenbeck's foul-mouthed daughter (Danielle Harris) reminds him regularly how much she hates his guts. As the icing on the cake, Joe's wife Sarah (Chelsea Field) cheats on him with his best friend (Bruce McGill), whining that her spouse is never around to satisfy her needs.

Dix's life isn't any better. He was unfaithful to Cory, masking his humiliation at no longer being in the league by popping pain pills and sleeping around. As his investigation into Cory's murder expands, he learns that she was blackmailing some L.A. powerbrokers—not for cash, but to get Jimmy another roster spot on an NFL team. She died trying to help him, and that guilt haunts his conscience while compelling him to proceed with the case.

They're a mismatched pair, as the formula dictates. Their backs are against the wall. A small army of very powerful people block their path to victory. But Joe and Jimmy refuse to stop because they know that allowing the bad guys to get away with something just isn't right.

Or, as the movie's deliciously cheesy tagline promises, "They're two fallen heroes up against the gambling syndicate in pro sports. Everyone had counted them out. They're about to get back in the game."

—3—

The Willis fans who champion *The Last Boy Scout* likely appreciate the Pro Bowl level of Hollywood talent collaborating behind the scenes on this thriller. The names tied to *The Last Boy Scout* were responsible for the most popular genre films of this era. Producer Joel Silver, as mentioned, helped bring *Lethal Weapon*, *Die Hard*, and *Predator* to the big screen. He hired a red-hot director in Tony Scott, who solidified his style of fast-paced, attitude-driven action in the blockbuster hits *Days of Thunder*, *Beverly Hills Cop II*, and *Top Gun*. But the wild card ultimately responsible for *The Last Boy Scout*'s success—or failure, depending on your opinion of the film—was wunderkind screenwriter Shane Black (*Lethal Weapon*).

Here's a fun piece of trivia: when Black first pitched this story of a grizzled old detective and a younger partner, his original spec title was *Die Hard*. Silver loved the idea, but asked the writer if he could transfer that title to another project he was working on at the time with Willis. And that's how

John McTiernan's adaptation of Roderick Thorp's novel *Nothing Lasts Forever* came to be known as *Die Hard*.

Black's script accurately reflected the cynicism and corruption that coated action movies at that time. With that came abrasive insults and misogynistic jokes that passed as mainstream entertainment in this less politically correct era but feel jarring and tone deaf in 2024. The film's cinematography and production values have aged much better. Two decades after its release, *The Last Boy Scout* still looks terrific. Scott and cinematographer Ward Russell (*Days of Thunder*) achieved a rumpled and smoky appearance that mirrored the personalities of the film's beaten-down leading men. They shot wet, neon-drenched alleyways in the evening, flooded their daytime sequences with an artificial California sunlight you could almost feel burning off of the screen, and amplified the sound design of their weaponry so that handguns came off like cannons.

Willis, for his part. excels at playing a washed-up private eye with one foot in a 1940's film noir gumshoe tale and the other foot in a sleazy 1980s late-night cable staple. Hallenbeck doesn't stand shoulder to shoulder with *Die Hard*'s McClane, another blue-collar law enforcement agent with marital issues, a taste for cigarettes, a penchant for being at the wrong place at the right time, and a stubborn streak that prevents him from giving up. Hallenbeck does, however, belong in the same conversation when discussing influential action heroes who played against type in a genre that's rich with cliches.

—4—

The Last Boy Scout wasn't well received upon release. Desson Thomson called it "the filmic equivalent of a hate crime" in the *Washington Post*, condemning the script's misogyny and grotesque violence.[4] The *Miami Herald*'s Bill Cosford claimed *The Last Boy Scout* was "a perfect example of what's wrong with Hollywood."[5] He also remarked, in the same review, that Willis's career hinged on *The Last Boy Scout*, and the superstar's asking salary was sure to plummet once this movie bombed. So maybe let's take Cosford's informed opinions with a grain of salt.

It's possible the industry had sharpened its daggers for Black, who broke a Hollywood record by selling his *Boy Scout* treatment at auction to the David Geffen Company for $1.75 million—unheard of in 1988. Critics also likely were losing patience with a subgenre that, by the end of the 1980s, was pairing Tom Hanks (*Turner and Hooch*) and Jim Belushi (*K-9*) with dogs for partners.

The negative reviews, however, overlooked all of the period-specific elements that *The Last Boy Scout* got right. And over time, *The Last Boy Scout* earned back its reputation. Popular geek online magazines such as *JoBlo* and *Birth.Movies.Death* have published retrospective pieces saluting the film's nonstop pacing and credible attempts at character development, fleshing out Joe and Jimmy's broken histories to humanize them in between the requisite explosions. I also think Black gave birth to the modern-day concept of cinematic Easter eggs the moment he wrote the scene of Hallenbeck returning home to find his daughter Darian watching the Mel Gibson torture scene from Black's *Lethal Weapon*. Self-referential inclusions weren't the norm in 1991. Black helped to make them cool.

It would have been easy, and undoubtedly tempting, for Willis at this stage of his career to keep accepting scripts like *The Last Boy Scout* that traded on his action-star reputation, collecting paychecks for less rewarding fare. He experienced the heat of critical scorn courtesy of *The Bonfire of the Vanities* (1990) and *Hudson Hawk* (1991), and probably retreated to the safety of *The Last Boy Scout* to lick his wounds in a familiar genre. He could have stayed here, ordering his agent to negotiate for more Hallenbeck stories, or seek similar stories that catered to Willis's well-established skill set as an action star. Instead, Willis followed *The Last Boy Scout* with an amusing cameo in Robert Altman's 1992 Hollywood satire *The Player*, a supporting role opposite Meryl Streep and Goldie Hawn in Robert Zemeckis's zany black comedy *Death Becomes Her* that same year, and, eventually, a pivotal role in Quentin Tarantino's landscape-changing masterpiece *Pulp Fiction*. As Willis said, he enjoyed challenging himself and forcing himself to try new things. Those movie choices were the actions that backed up his words.

And in hindsight, given the sheer volume of lazy, tedious, disappointing cop stories that would conclude Willis's career, *The Last Boy Scout* stands head and shoulders above the pack. In my humble opinion, it serves as the Gold Standard for the type of movie Willis could have made in his sleep, if he didn't dream of accomplishing more.

CHAPTER SEVEN
16 BLOCKS

Director: Richard Donner
Cast: Bruce Willis, Mos Def, David Morse
Release Date: March 3, 2006

> *I was trying to do a good thing.*
> —DETECTIVE JACK MOSLEY (WILLIS), *16 BLOCKS*

—1—

Near the beginning of Richard Donner's dutiful New York cop story *16 Blocks*, David Morse tells Bruce Willis's weary, overmatched police detective Jack Mosley that it's "just the wrong time and the wrong place for you today."

The sentiment will sound familiar to Willis's lifelong fans.

Die Hard hero John McClane came to the same conclusion during his confrontation with Hans Gruber (Alan Rickman) in John McTiernan's masterpiece. "Got invited to the Christmas party by mistake. Who knew?" McClane heard it again, like an echo, when John Amos's intimidating Major Grant barked at the frustrated cop in *Die Hard 2: Die Harder*, "You're the wrong guy, in the wrong place, at the wrong time."

"Story of my life," our hero laments.

Willis bolstered his career by playing characters caught in this unfortunate situation. Even outside of the *Die Hard* franchise, Willis carried action-packed stories that took flight once fate placed his character somewhere he didn't belong. Perfect specimen Leeloo (Milla Jovovich) crash-lands into his taxicab at the start of Luc Besson's *The Fifth Element*, sending our hero on a planet-saving adventure. Willis's small-town police chief steps out of a trailer at the exact wrong moment in 2022's aptly titled *Wrong Place*, witnessing a murder and thereby putting his life in danger. And in *16 Blocks*, worn-out NYPD veteran Mosley has a foot out the door at the end of a grueling overnight shift when his lieutenant hands him one final assignment: transport a witness named Eddie Bunker (Mos Def) sixteen blocks from a detention center to a courthouse so he can testify against a band of crooked cops. Mosley wasn't supposed to pull the gig. Only, the officer tabbed for the task got stuck in traffic. Wrong guy. Wrong place. Wrong time.

When discussing Willis's action staples, *16 Blocks* doesn't receive the same attention or praise as *Die Hard*, *The Last Boy Scout*, or *Looper*. The film sits at 56 percent Fresh on the review aggregate site Rotten Tomatoes, while noted critics alternate between calling the film "cliched," "formulaic," or "a sturdy little cop thriller . . . even when it stretches the bounds of plausibility."[1]

That's a crime. This emotional cop drama from 2006 has aged well in my opinion, and deserves recognition, first and foremost, for being the lone collaboration between Willis and Donner, a titan who contributed classics in multiple film genres—including *Superman* (1978), *The Omen*, *Lethal Weapon*, Bill Murray's *Scrooged*, and Mel Gibson's *Maverick*—over the course of his career. Their pairing produces a spellbinding ticking-clock thriller built around a recognizable Willis character blessed with multiple moral shades and problematic flaws, allowing the versatile leading man to slowly peel back Mosley's engrossing layers and explore the darker corners of a tainted white knight. Or, as Roger Ebert wisely wrote, "The bedrock of the plot is the dogged determination of the Bruce Willis character. Jack may be middle-aged, he may be tired, he may be balding, he may be a drunk. But if he's played by Bruce Willis, you don't want to bet against him."[2]

—2—

Willis turned fifty on March 19, 2005—eleven days after Millennium Films and Equity Pictures officially signed him for Donner's *16 Blocks*. Other actors of Willis's age would be searching for ways to look younger on screen, to cheat Father Time and extend their career. Willis of course went against the grain, embracing a project that required him to appear ten to fifteen years older. Daily two-hour makeup sessions added graying hair, deep facial creases, and an unkempt mustache to his character, Detective Jack Mosley. He vaguely resembles Willis, only exhausted.

This weary, lived-in performance provides such a welcome change of pace from Willis's usual action-movie heroism. Mosley isn't super-cop John McClane. This law enforcement agent's best days are behind him. When the story begins, and a team of cops need a fourth-stringer to babysit a dormant crime scene until help arrives, the lead officer literally asks, "Who's downstairs [that] we don't need?" The seemingly valueless Mosley becomes the default answer.

Willis communicates Mosley's weariness by moving stiffly through the film's action, stumbling along with a slight limp, and a slouched posture indicating too many years on the force. Rumor has it Willis kept a pebble in his shoe to help maintain his consistent limp. The main takeaway is that the smallest moves require great effort. In a moment of defeatism, Mosley admits to a convict, "Life's too long. Guys like you make it longer."

This man's exhaustion, his alcoholism, and his physical limitations are distractions, however, from the real reason Donner sought Willis to play this character. For underneath those obstacles rests a noble man still willing to go above and beyond to do what is right. A resilient underdog whose resolve gets tested once the cops in jeopardy of going on trial show up to prevent Mosley's witness from making it the sixteen blocks to the courthouse.

There are a handful of shocking moments throughout *16 Blocks* where Donner manipulates his audience's perception of reality to prove that Mosley hasn't completely lost his abilities, and can remain one step ahead of his pursuers. Outside of a liquor store, when we are convinced a thug is about to shoot a handcuffed Eddie Bunker, a gunshot rings out . . . but it comes from Mosley, snapping out of his fog in order to protect his charge. And in this moment, Willis's stance, his outstretched arm pointing a discharged weapon, resembles the one he'd used in numerous cop thrillers, but was dormant up until that point in this movie. Donner employs the same trick later in the film when David Morse's dirty cop, Frank Nugent, corners Mosley and Bunker in an empty restaurant. Nugent's preparing to frame Bunker for murder, and is positioning a fatal gunshot when suddenly, Mosley emerges from behind the bar with a sawed-off shotgun and manages, again, to keep his pursuers on their heels. In these courageous beats, Willis's signature action hero shines through Mosley's malaise, looking coherent, sharp, and lethal. It's a gear into which Willis is always ready to shift.

Donner's *16 Blocks* feels like a spiritual cousin to John McTiernan's *Die Hard with a Vengeance*, the third chapter in the *Die Hard* saga. Both are gritty, sweaty, race-the-clock thrillers staged within the congestion of New York City's streets. Both McTiernan and Donner frame their action tight and keep their foot on the gas, manifesting a claustrophobia, fear, and sense of urgency that grips each of Willis's heroic leads. There's an unmistakably chaotic energy that comes with films set in New York—even ones that are filmed in Toronto, like *16 Blocks* was. Traffic disrupts car chases. Overcrowding limits movement on the avenues. Sirens, slamming doors, car horns, and other sounds of the city constantly distract our protagonist. But Willis, to his credit, looks at ease in the agitated tension of Manhattan, both in *16 Blocks* and *Die Hard with a Vengeance*. Urban elements that would rattle another character become tools in the actor's acting arsenal. That East Coast, blue-collar grit and determination is yet another card that Willis keeps up his sleeve until necessary, and it's on display here.

When Donner allows the noise and bombast of *16 Blocks* to die down, Willis finds spectacular character moments in the quiet. Over the course of the story, Mosley accepts the critical mistakes he has made, difficult as they are to swallow, and Willis expertly conveys both the weight of guilt that burdens this man, and the release that comes with penance. During a pivotal scene, Mosley's trapped on a bus and surrounded by cops. He thinks that the day's sprint finally has ended, and he'll pay for his mistakes with his life. Mosley takes a tape recorder from his pocket and begins a forgiveness speech to his estranged wife, one that's reminiscent of the bathroom confessional McClane makes to Sergeant Al Powell in *Die Hard*. "Tell her that she is the best thing that ever happened to a bum like me," Willis's McClane asks Powell to communicate to his wife, Holly. "She's heard me say 'I love you' a thousand times.

She never heard me say I'm sorry. I want you to tell her that, Al. I want you to tell her that John said that he was sorry."

Willis makes these moments of weakness and vulnerability plausible. He's one of the few action stars who can riddle a body with bullets in one scene, then credibly bare his soul to the audience in the next. When Willis wants to, he can earn sympathy for his characters by using a wounded look, an encouraging line of dialogue, a shake of the head, a simple shoulder shrug, or an emotionally packed exchange—like the moment Mosley finally solves Bunker's riddle about a sick old lady, a best friend, and the girl of your dreams waiting at a bus stop.

Willis credits his costars for the film's success. "This film really didn't come together until we got Mos Def and David Morse," he said. "It wasn't until all three of us got in the same space together and started working together that the chemistry that you see in the film started to come out. . . . Mos showed up with that character, and it was such a treat, because it gave me and David so much to play off of. He had such great ideas. Mos is such a creative character. That's not him! He doesn't talk like that. I'm sure that that's just some guy that he used to know, and he made it this guy."[3]

But *16 Blocks* ultimately resonates as one of Willis's action classics because it reflects how compelling, challenging, and rewarding the actor could be in the hands of the right director. Donner joins Tony Scott, Quentin Tarantino, Terry Gilliam, Wes Anderson, and Rian Johnson on the list of filmmakers who got one crack at a Willis collaboration, and ended up making something special.

Donner's last directorial credit ended up being *16 Blocks*, though he'd continue to produce until his death in 2021. I'm thankful he and Willis got one chance to work together. Each man, in their own way, helped shape and refine a prosperous genre of action comedies and studio blockbusters through the *Lethal Weapon* films, the *Die Hard* series, *Maverick*, *Assassins*, *Hudson Hawk*, and *The Last Boy Scout*. Their efforts here led to the creation of a stirring cop drama with elements of a classic Western weaved into Donner's direction, with Willis assuming the role of the responsible sheriff standing in defiance to an outlaw gang. Donner even staged the final standoff between

Willis and Morse in an alley outside the courthouse as a traditional Western showdown.

Willis's love for cowboys, and the lawmen of the western frontiers, was well recorded. "I was always kind of partial to Roy Rogers," Willis jokes to Alan Rickman in *Die Hard*, trying to get under his antagonist's skin. "Really liked those sequined shirts." In *16 Blocks*, he relishes the rare opportunity to play a contemporary version of a cowboy savior, the kind Rogers himself might have embodied back in the day.

CHAPTER EIGHT
RED

Director: Robert Schwentke
Cast: Bruce Willis, Morgan Freeman, Helen Mirren, John Malkovich, Mary Louise-Parker, Karl Urban, Brian Cox, Richard Dreyfuss
Release Date: October 15, 2010

> *Here's the thing, Cooper. With age . . . comes a certain perspective.*
> —Ex-CIA operative Frank Moses (Willis)

—1—

In 2023, an elder statesman of Hollywood attempted the improbable. Harrison Ford blew the dust off his high-crowned sable fedora for *Indiana Jones and the Dial of Destiny*, the fifth installment in the Indiana Jones adventure series. "Improbable" because the actor celebrated his seventy-ninth birthday in the midst of filming on the sequel. James Mangold's *Dial of Destiny* required Ford's Doctor Henry Jones Jr. to globetrot through England, Scotland, Italy, Morocco, and the United States in pursuit of a mysterious and powerful device that former Nazi soldiers (led by Mads Mikkelsen) wanted to use to correct Adolph Hitler's mistakes. Ford's character, ever the adventurous archaeologist, leaps back and forth between racing cars; runs across the top of a speeding locomotive; skydives while clinging to costar Phoebe Waller Bridge; and rides a horse through a ticker-tape parade in New York City.

Ford rarely acted his age. This is a man who suffered a near-fatal injury on the set of 2015's *Star Wars: Episode VII—The Force Awakens* when a Millennium Falcon door came crashing down on his seventy-one-year-old leg. But even by the actor's durable standards, the Indiana Jones revival was impressive. It solidified Ford as the exception that proves the rule that after a certain age, offers to appear in stunt-driven blockbusters start drying up, and audiences stop taking actors seriously in these parts.

There's good reason for such skepticism. Arnold Schwarzenegger's last attempt at franchise superstardom, 2019's ill-fated *Terminator: Dark Fate*, used so much computer-generated imagery to cover up the "Governator's" age (he was seventy-two), the feature might as well have been animated. That same year, seventy-three-year-old Sylvester Stallone tried to revive his single-minded Vietnam veteran John Rambo in the gory but pointless *Rambo: Last Blood*. Critics decimated the sloppy sequel, while ticket buyers barely pushed the film's worldwide grosses over $90 million. Dreary results for a once-muscular franchise.

These superstars likely were feeling their ages, and sought to capitalize on one more story in their signature film series before Hollywood turned out their metaphorical lights. But, according to Ford, there's a right way, and a wrong way, to address the elephant in the room.

"In [*Dial of Destiny*] there were a lot of old jokes in the script. We took them all out," Ford explained to the *Hollywood Reporter* during the run up to the film. "There is a moment where he observes himself in this situation and says, 'What the fuck am I doing in here?' But I hate what I call 'talking about the story.' I want to see circumstances in which the audience gets a chance to experience the story, not to be led through the nose with highlights pointed out to them. I'd rather create behavior that is the joke of age rather than talk about it."[1]

Bruce Willis's professional choices around 2009 and 2010 lead me to believe he was contemplating similar sentiments about his age, and the inevitable stage of his career when the action movies that served as his bedrock would stop coming. Willis couldn't have predicted the steady stream of direct-to-video action efforts that would pad his résumé toward the end of his career. Additionally, his humorous performances around this time in the satirical *What Just Happened?*, Disney's family-friendly *The Kid*, and the gangster comedy *The Whole Nine Yards* proved that Willis didn't need deafening firefights and explosions to sustain his career.

But the irony of Willis appearing in two action-heavy feature films in 2010 that poked fun at the advanced ages of both him and his supporting cast members shouldn't be overlooked, because they likely tell us something about where his head was at during this time period, and how he sustained success by leaning into the humor of the situation, as Mangold suggested for Ford in *Indiana Jones and the Dial of Destiny.*

—2—

Willis joined Sylvester Stallone and Arnold Schwarzenegger in August 2010 for one pivotal scene in *The Expendables*, Stallone's attempt at blending beloved action icons of his day with the younger pups who'd moved on his territory. Willis did very little in the movie. His character, the mysterious Mr. Church, hires Stallone's team of mercenaries to overthrow a fanatical dictator, setting the wheels of the plot in motion. Stallone charged into battle alongside Jason Statham, Jet Li, Dolph Lundgren, and Terry Crews. Willis waited patiently for the sequel, where his contributions increased significantly. We'll analyze Simon West's *The Expendables 2* in the next chapter. But Willis's appearance in the initial *The Expendables* helped to sell the movie's primary marketing hook: Buy a ticket and find out how many action veterans Stallone could pack into these excessively violent and unapologetically silly combat movies.

Ten weeks later, with *The Expendables* still drawing crowds, Willis showed up in another action-driven vehicle reliant on the gimmick that the lead characters, in the profoundly wise words of *Lethal Weapon*'s Roger Murtaugh, had gotten too old for this shit. Only, in Robert Schwentke's *Red*, Willis's gun-toting costars weren't bankable action superstars. They were names you'd expect to hear on the call sheet of an Oscar-baity prestige picture.

Red adapts the well-reviewed DC Comics limited series created by Warren Ellis and Cully Hammer. Willis didn't do comic-book movies, but *Red* marked his second stab at a graphic-novel adaptation. (*Sin City* and its sequel being the other.) The title *Red* is an acronym for "Retired, Extremely Dangerous," a designation applied to ex-CIA Black Ops agent Frank Moses (Willis).

"He has retired drug lords, terrorists . . . hell, he toppled governments. He was truly gifted," a paper pusher known only as the Records Keeper (Ernest Borgnine) explains to William Cooper (Karl Urban), a hungry CIA agent

trying to bring Moses down. The Keeper was cautioning Cooper, emphasiz-
ing how dangerous Moses used to be.

"Why was he retired?" Cooper asks.

"He got old," the Keeper spits back.

Willis wasn't old in comparison to his costars. But age became the running joke of *Red*. As Willis's character treks around the country avoiding
corrupt government higher-ups who'd like to punch his ticket, he rekindles relationships with former colleagues who, by action-movie standards,
should have been sent to pasture. Morgan Freeman provides his usual calm
demeanor, but also a spark of mischief, as Moses's CIA mentor, Joe Matheson.
Moses catches up with Matheson at a retirement community, leading to this
humbling exchange between the once virile soldiers of fortune.

"I never thought *this* would happen to me," Matheson sighs.

"What?" asks Moses.

"Getting old," his mentor replies. "I mean, Vietnam, Afghanistan . . .
Green Springs Rest Home? Go figure."

In the voices of each man, you can hear the sobering acceptance that the
industry (be it the CIA in the story, or the film industry in general) doesn't
attempt to use them the way that they used to.

The eccentric John Malkovich, meanwhile, brought his quirky bag of
tricks to the part of Marvin Boggs, a paranoid, delusional former agent who
was experimented on by the CIA and injected with daily doses of LSD for
eleven straight years. Brian Cox joined the fun as Ivan Simonov, a Vodka-
swigging Russian ally who pines for Victoria, a sleek and lethal ice queen
played by Helen Mirren. And Richard Dreyfuss surfaces late in the story as a
sniveling, spineless, bureaucrat arms dealer.

These movie stars were playing against type. A short four years earlier,
Mirren won the Best Actress Oscar for deftly portraying a conflicted Queen
Elizabeth II in the weeks following the tragic death of Diana, Princess of
Wales. *The Queen* fit snugly into the type of picture Mirren thought her audience wanted to see: 1994's *The Madness of King George*; 2001's *Gosford Park*;
the winning comedy *Calendar Girls* in 2003; and the 2005 television miniseries *Elizabeth I*. She knew *Red* marked a distinct left turn, and confessed that
the job offer gave her pause.

"I jumped into this film open-armed and open hearted," she said. "But a little bit of my brain was going, 'I wonder if the people who go to see *The Last Station* or see me as this serious actress are going to feel that I've betrayed them by being in a genre action movie?'"[2]

Her concerns were viable. Mirren hadn't yet joined the *Fast and Furious* franchise by this point, which allowed the Dame the chance to flex her action muscle on a regular basis. So, she ultimately clarified, "I like to shake it up. And for me, the idea of being in an action movie—me, Helen Mirren, in my little world—was an incredibly exciting idea."

—3—

Too bad *Red* isn't very good. It glides by on perfect casting, and the novelty of seeing serious thespians engaging in mindless, violent shenanigans. The trailer's button, or final scene, showed Mirren in a ball gown firing a Browning M2HB machine gun. It tells the audience, "This is exactly what you are signing up for when you purchase a ticket." But the gimmick wears thin rather quickly. The cast occasionally infuses their dialogue with confidence and swagger, but Schwentke's action scenes are pedestrian, outside of one impressive visual-effects sequence that lets Willis step out of a spinning police car so he can fire shots at Urban's pursuing agent. These older actors mostly talk their way out of complicated situations, or scramble for cover during generic firefights. Schwentke flip-flops between grounded espionage and zany comic-book physicality, when embracing one would have been preferred. Otherwise, the pockets of absurdity (like when Malkovich successfully fires a bullet into the head of an oncoming missile, causing a premature explosion) feel like they belong in another, deliberately exaggerated story.

Throughout *Red*, however, we get treated to several aspects of Willis's "Action Star" mode, while also showing off his evolution from Hollywood superstar to "glue guy." The Urban Dictionary defines a "Glue Guy" as "[t]he guy who helps everyone work together; the leader on the team. Not always the best player, but still a guy with a leadership role." Sports reporters typically use the term to praise a contributor on the field or court who doesn't rise to all-star status, but still proves invaluable in a winning effort.

Willis filled this role more often than you'd expect an undisputed A-lister to do over the course of his career. He appeared just as enthusiastic to be part of an exquisite ensemble as he was being a leading man. And within those talented casts, Willis did whatever was necessary for the project to succeed. Several of the actor's highest-grossing movies, from *Armageddon* ($554 million worldwide) and *G.I. Joe: Retaliation* ($375 million worldwide) to *The Expendables 2* ($311 million worldwide), surrounded Willis with ample talent and allowed him to play straight man to their antics. You'd see this in comedies such as *Moonrise Kingdom*, *Ocean's 12*, or *The Whole Nine Yards* and its sequel. You saw it in his acclaimed independent sensation *Pulp Fiction*.

In multiple interviews done to promote *Red*, Willis heaped praise on his costars, and what each brought to the table. He smirked whenever Mirren told journalists that she joined *Red* because of the insatiable crush she had on the *Die Hard* hunk. He gushed over the rare opportunity to share a scene with Borgnine, who was ninety-three at the time of filming. "They had led us to believe that we [had] to go fast because we have to finish Mr. Borgnine by a certain point. But he was ready to shoot all day," Willis remembered. "He's a really sweet guy, and we just sat around all day and shot the shit about *Marty* and *From Here to Eternity* and films like that."[3]

Red also showcases a Willis trait that doesn't get enough attention when analyzing his acting approach. His eagerness to allow an actress to steal scenes from him dates back to his debut feature film *Blind Date*, where a drunken Kim Basinger provided him with a nightmare evening to remember. Since then, Willis frequently found ways to use his inherent charm and sensitivity in service of exquisite performances by Goldie Hawn and Meryl Streep in *Death Becomes Her*, Amanda Peet in *The Whole Nine Yards*, Julia Roberts in *Ocean's Twelve*, Maria de Medeiros in *Pulp Fiction*, Cate Blanchett in *Bandits*—hell, his earliest days on *Moonlighting* with Cybill Shepherd.

In *Red*, when he isn't dispensing antagonists with ease, Willis woos the delightfully spacey Mary-Louise Parker, a gifted comedienne who's right at home in the chaos of the story, playing a kidnapped human resources representative named Sarah who dreams of any life beyond her boring cubicle. Frank Moses gives a very thin excuse for why Sarah needs to join his adventure. You get the impression that Schwentke realized how much of a spark existed between Willis and Parker, so he just decided to write her into the rest of the movie. Their relationship gives a beating heart to both this movie and its 2013 sequel, *Red 2*.

Finally, after the disappointing sci-fi experiment *Surrogates* (2009) and the humorless dud *Cop Out* (2010), *Red* returned Willis to his comfortable spot in the center of the action-hero pedestal. When we meet a retired Moses at the film's start, the malaise and repetition of his daily routine has dulled his edges—on the surface, at least. Because once he's attacked—in the opening seven minutes of the film—Willis makes it clear that Moses's skills remain incredibly sharp, a stark contrast from the Jack Mosley character we just addressed from *16 Blocks*. He single-handedly eliminates a heavily armed assault team without breaking a sweat. He dodges bullets with Malkovich while running around a dock, eventually firing a hand grenade that turns his enemy to pulp. And as mentioned, Willis pulls off that incredibly cool sequence of stepping out of a spinning cop car and firing back at Urban, in one fluid movement. It's easily *Red*'s most memorable action beat.

"I'm very proud of that scene," Willis said. "It's a scene that has never been in a film before. It's never been done. When we were rehearsing the film, I said, 'Wouldn't it be cool if, while the car is still spinning, I just step out of the car and just start firing the gun?' And the stunt guys all got up and said, 'We can't do that, because you won't be safe.' And they ended up being able to do it with digital filming. So it does look cool, but I don't think I was ever in any danger."[4]

—4—

Willis zeroed in on a thought-provoking theme running through the characters who Moses recruits for his mission, after his life is threatened by the organization for which they all used to work.

"Everybody has their own version of being kicked off the old team," the actor said. "And now, they don't really have that much to do. And they miss it."[5]

Willis might have been feeling the same longing for the glory days of his action supremacy, explaining his willingness to work on *The Expendables* and *Red* back-to-back. His return to the *Die Hard* franchise for 2007's bone-crunching *Live Free or Die Hard* probably convinced him he still had a few more bare-knuckle fight scenes left in him. And the action sequences Willis stockpiled in the years following *Red* largely relegated him to the background, where he'd stand still and fire a weapon from a distance, hardly getting down and dirty for the benefit of a fight. Without him realizing it at the time, *Red* and its sequel represent the end of an era for this physically gifted action icon.

Which means his knock-down, drag out fight with Urban in the CIA's offices might qualify as the last great hand-to-hand battle Willis filmed. And the scene delivers. Willis says he and Urban trained for it for months, choreographed it for weeks, and spent nine days filming the fight, which Schwentke wisely set to Aerosmith's grinding rock track, "Back in the Saddle." The scene finds a bloodied Willis trading punches, getting body slammed through filing cabinets, kicking Urban through a glass table, and dislocating his opponent's shoulder.

"They kept saying, 'Well, we're going to cut it down. This film is not about action and fighting.' And then they went back and put some more of it in. But contact was made. I mean, we tried to be as safe as we could, but we did beat each other up a little bit."[6]

Worth it. If even for a moment, the action star—as Aerosmith frontman Steven Tyler screamed it—was back in the saddle again, where he belonged.

—5—

Almost everywhere Willis went to promote *Red*, he faced questions about the cast's age, or his opinion regarding respected character actors slumming it in a genre film. Speaking to why movies like *Red* and *The Expendables* struck a chord with mainstream audiences, Willis said, "I think because science has been able to extend their lives way past sixty-five years of age. People are still vital, and still should be able to do their job. And can do their job. And want to do a good job."[7]

Willis's stated belief pushed back against an industry that often hurried veteran performers off the proverbial stage in favor of the fresh crop of talent that arrived in Hollywood on a daily basis. Not that the *Red* star faced any immediate danger of losing jobs. In fact, in the wake of *Red*, Willis would go on to enjoy a critical and commercial hit in *Looper*, collaborate with Wes Anderson for *Moonrise Kingdom*, return to the *Die Hard* franchise for a fifth installment, and finish M. Night Shyamalan's *Unbreakable* trilogy with the ambiguous and uneven *Glass*.

That didn't stop reporters in 2010 from repeatedly asking Willis if, like his *Red* character, he was on the verge of retirement. "I certainly don't feel ready to retire," Willis said during a press conference in Berlin. "I think actors get a break that not many people in the world get, and that is, you get to work past the time that you are sixty-five."

Maybe even until they are eighty, like Ford in the fifth Indiana Jones movie. Yet, even in *Dial of Destiny*, Mangold employed a relatively new digital technology that effectively de-aged his leading man for the duration of the film's opening sequence, which was set in the past. The result, while not a pristine representation of a forty-year-old Ford in his prime, worked well enough. The visuals even convinced the admittedly skeptical curmudgeon of a film star.

"I never loved the idea until I saw how it was accomplished in this case—which is very different than the way it's been done in other films I've seen," Ford said. "They've got every frame of film, either printed or unprinted, of me during 40 years of working with Lucasfilm on various stuff. I can act the scene, and they sort through, with AI, every fucking foot of film to find me in that same angle and light. It's bizarre, and it works, and it is my face."[8]

Theoretically, AI technology could extend a performer's life span indefinitely. Lucasfilm, as Ford mentioned, has four decades of footage in its archives. They could potentially bring him back for as many future feature films as needed. The visual-effects pioneers at Lucasfilm headquarters in San Francisco played with this innovation for years. Thanks to similar tech, the late Peter Cushing and his *Star Wars* character Grand Moff Tarkin returned to the screen for the 2016 film *Rogue One: A Star Wars Story*. And the smash hit Disney+ series *The Mandalorian* de-aged a roughly sixty-nine-year-old Mark Hamill for its Season 2 finale, allowing a stand-in actor to resemble Luke Skywalker circa *Star Wars: Episode VI—The Return of the Jedi*.

Eventually, Willis found himself at the center of this somewhat controversial tech. Willis, through his agents at CAA, broke the barrier between his true identity and an artificial recreation in 2022. Allegedly, Willis's reps allowed a Russian Deepfake company called Deepcake to create a digital twin of Willis by superimposing his face on another actor's body. The digital recreation of the *Die Hard* star then made it look like Willis appeared in a Russian commercial for a cellular telecom company, Megafon. In the ad, Willis and another man are strapped to a bomb, complete with a digital clock that's counting down to detonation. Only, Willis never set foot on any set, and never shared space with his costar. An artificial neural network placed Willis's likeness on the face of another performer, giving Willis the opportunity to act without having to act.

This innovative technology is both thrilling and terrifying. And immediately after reports about the Willis commercial surfaced, his reps discredited the idea that Willis sold the rights to his likeness. "Please know that Bruce has no partnership or agreement with this Deepcake company," his team told the BBC, while Deepcake covered its own bases by clarifying, "The wording about rights is wrong. . . . Bruce couldn't sell anyone any rights. They are his by default."[9]

For now. This story of Deepfake technology is ever evolving, and the debate over AI created a significant sticking point when the Screen Actors Guild went on a 118-day labor strike in 2023. Its ramifications will impact all methods of artistic expression for decades, from acting and writing, to dance and song. And if the industry ever perfects it, the actors once deemed too old for *Red* might fulfill Willis's wish of working long past the age of sixty-five, for better or for worse.

CHAPTER NINE
THE EXPENDABLES 2

Director: Simon West
Cast: Sylvester Stallone, Jason Statham, Jet Li, Dolph Lundgren, Jean-Claude Van Damme, Chuck Norris, Liam Hemsworth, Bruce Willis, Arnold Schwarzenegger
Release Date: August 17, 2012

> *Sometimes it's fun to run with the pack.*
>
> —CHUCK NORRIS AS BOOKER

—1—

Toward the end of Simon West's *The Expendables 2*, with their shared adversary and his accompanying army successfully eliminated, CIA operative Mr. Church (Bruce Willis) presents his hired gun Barney Ross (Sylvester Stallone) with a gift. It's a vintage Antonov An-2 biplane, a Soviet crop duster designed for agricultural use that the Russian government assimilated into military duties during the Korean War.

The aircraft, on its own, could be a metaphor for the careers of the men in the cast—character actors once hired to complete routine Hollywood jobs who eventually found their true calling, brandishing high-powered weapons for the benefit of on-screen conflicts. Similar to the Antonov An-2, Stallone's *Expendables* colleagues had been repurposed by the film industry and sent off to war. On the other hand, the biplane could have just been a prop that impressed West, prompting him to include it in a shot. Regardless, Church tells Ross he's free to use the plane to fly his band of soldiers—nicknamed "The Little Rascals"—back to the United States.

Stallone's character gives one look at the craft and, with a bemused smirk, surmises, "That thing belongs in a museum."

"We all do," replies his fellow mercenary Trench, played by fellow action movie icon Arnold Schwarzenegger.

There are few better ways to describe the *Expendables* franchise. Stallone, who directed the original 2010 film, used these blood-and-sweat endeavors to establish a cinematic museum that would honor the Founding Fathers of the action genre. The first film adequately captured the bare-chested, mud-caked grit (and razor-thin character development) of most 1980s combat dramas. Think of jungle-set classics like *Rambo: First Blood Part II* and John McTiernan's *Predator* as obvious touchstones for Stallone's first go. The eventual *Expendables* sequels, though, applied a glossy studio polish that had become more prevalent in the 1990s for movies like *Demolition Man, Total Recall, Speed,* and *The Rock.* And like those films, this series lured its audience in with some unsophisticated bait. All it did was create new, though largely meaningless, missions for old Hollywood stars who'd brought both firepower and star power to this genre for decades. If your name and face graced the cover of a VHS box in the action/adventure section of a mom-and-pop video rental store, there's a good chance Stallone's *Expendables* series offered you the opportunity to enhance your retirement nest egg with a paycheck gig.

Willis didn't need to appear in a film like *The Expendables* at this stage in his career. He still enjoyed the freedom to pick and choose his projects, and any actor could have capably played his *Expendables* part without exerting much effort. Plus, if Stallone is to be believed, neither Willis nor Schwarzenegger were financially compensated for the six hours they spent filming a one-scene cameo for the 2010 movie.

At the same time, *The Expendables* movies didn't really need Willis to play along, either. Stallone had already recruited a murderer's row of global action superstars for his ensemble. The veteran director, who had helmed four *Rocky* sequels and *Staying Alive,* believed that fans of the genre would pay the price of admission to watch Jason Statham, Jet Li, Dolph Lundgren, Randy Couture, and Terry Crews kick enemy tail in the jungle, whether Willis was in the picture or not. For the record, he was correct. *The Expendables* opened near the end of the summer season (on August 13, 2010) and tallied an impressive $274.4 million in global ticket sales against a reported $80 million budget.

But leaving Willis out would have been interpreted as an insult, given what he meant to the action genre to which Stallone was paying tribute. Plus, both men—who were savvy veterans of a fickle industry—probably recognized the *Expendables* franchise for what it was: a chance to deliver something cool to their lifelong fans, and an excuse to recapture the fading light of their glory days. As Chuck Norris's lone wolf, soldier-for-hire Booker confesses in *The Expendables 2*, "Sometimes it's fun to run with the pack."

—2—

The kernel of the idea at the core of this mega-team-up franchise could be found in the only memorable scene from Stallone's original *The Expendables*—an otherwise monotonous and pulverizing barrage of bullets, mortar blasts, and body parts. The sequence in question isn't remarkable for its content. In fact, it could easily be overlooked if not for the men who appear in it.

This three-minute conversation takes place inside of a church, where a manipulative CIA operative offers competing mercenaries a routine job involving "resources" on an island that "people" would like to acquire. Textbook action-movie setup stuff. But this sequence earns its spot in the annals of action-movie lore because it marks the first time that Willis, Schwarzenegger, and Stallone appeared together on screen in a motion picture, an achievement that can't be overstated.

Maria LaScala, the unit publicist on *The Expendables*, was part of the relatively small crew assembled at the First Presbyterian Church of Hollywood on a Saturday morning in October 2009 to capture this anticipated meeting of the action-movie legends. LaScala already had concluded nearly five months of work on Stallone's military thriller, accompanying the filmmaker from Rio de Janeiro to the French Quarter in New Orleans for pivotal scenes. But she'd assumed filming had wrapped on the picture back in July before being called out to a secure location in the heart of Hollywood to oversee the one additional day of pickup filming Stallone had booked—after months of schedule delays—with his longtime colleagues and close friends. By the time LaScala pulled up to the facility at 6:15 a.m., Willis and Stallone already were inside the church running lines. Schwarzenegger would arrive twenty minutes later, chomping on a cigar. Hollywood history was about to be made.

LaScala used the word *atomic* when describing the vibe on set while the stars rehearsed.

"At 8:10 a.m., with three cameras rolling, the biggest action icons of our time went to work. . . . The whole crew was mesmerized as we watched the three of them play off of each other," LaScala documented in a blog post.[1]

The magnitude of the situation was lost on no one. Not even a random passerby, who happened to catch a glimpse of the megawatt Hollywood meeting.

"We had no looky-loos or p'razzi [on set]," LaScala concluded. "I was, however, amused by the guy who drove by as the 3 guys were walking to their trailers—he almost fell out of his car . . . nice."

Shock value was in order. These three actors, collectively, were the face of a popular and highly profitable film genre for the better part of three decades prior to their collaboration on 2010's *The Expendables*. Individually, they had accounted for hundreds of millions of dollars in international box-office receipts, and thousands of hours of mass-market entertainment. But it's Stallone that receives credit for being the first director curious enough to see what these talents could accomplish together.

And he wasn't about to stop there.

Critics weren't kind to *The Expendables*. Most reviewers dismissed Stallone's gritty war picture as little more than an expensive B-movie, and pointed out that by attempting to recreate a bygone era, Stallone basically recycled stale action-movie cliches that had lost their impact thirty years prior. It didn't help that Stallone lacked a firm grasp on the tone of the film until cameras were ready to roll, something he readily admits.

"This started out as a dark comedy. It started out as a satire," the director admitted in a 2009 interview. "Then we thought, 'Let's make a really hard R'—[and] then I go back. It constantly was being just brutally changed. It wasn't until a week before filming that I said, 'Let's just make it this kind of movie.'"[2]

That degree of uncertainty, and the consistent script changes described by Stallone, kept *The Expendables* from realizing its fullest potential. But the box-office receipts told Stallone that his intriguing premise of teaming action stars from the past and present for a string of unapologetically violent missions tapped into the veins of action movie junkies around the globe. And in the sequel, 2012's *The Expendables 2*, all involved parties finally figured out how to mix their steroid-enhanced brew into a palatable, explosive cocktail.

—3—

Few would confuse *The Expendables 2* with a great movie. Even critics who graded it favorably in 2012 couched their praise with cautionary phrases like "just entertaining enough" or "cheesy, fun, disposable action pap." Characters begin extended fist fights by warning, "You wanna man up? I'll man you up," and there's only a slim margin of measurable self-awareness or irony in the delivery.

But replacement director Simon West (*Con Air*, *The General's Daughter*) brought his workmanlike Hollywood professionalism to this excessive sequel, producing a better-executed version of Stallone's tantalizing concept. With an increased budget, an expanded cast of action veterans, and their tongues planted firmly in their cheeks, Stallone and company wound up with a rare sequel—ranked alongside James Cameron's *Terminator 2: Judgment Day*, Sam Raimi's *Evil Dead II*, and George Miller's *Mad Max: Fury Road*—that built upon the lean structure of their predecessors to amplify everything that worked (and some things that didn't) and create the best installment of these ongoing franchises.

The *Expendables* all-star trio understood how difficult it was to produce a hit in Hollywood, according to their director. "I don't think any of the guys would pretend that a lot of the movies [they made] weren't pretty bad. But every now and again, there was a gem in there, and a really good one," West said of the collective filmographies of Willis, Schwarzenegger, and Stallone. "For every great one, there were five or six bad ones."[3]

That ratio plays out in the *Expendables* franchise, which only produced one enjoyable movie—*The Expendables 2*—out of its three. As Stallone would remind his young costars on set, sometimes you make *Rocky*, and other times you end up with *Stop! Or My Mom Will Shoot*.

"He came on the set one day," West remembers, "and said, 'I made the biggest mistake of my life when I came on [the *Stop!* set] wearing a diaper.' I think he keeps that at the back of his mind. 'Whatever you do, don't ever come out wearing a diaper again!' . . . Stallone knows that every film can't be a winner. Like all the guys, he has some that he is proud of, and some he'd rather bury."

Most of the same faces from *The Expendables* returned for the follow-up, including Statham, Li, Lundgren, and Crews. But Stallone's experience plotting out sequels for his beloved Rocky and Rambo characters taught him that escalation powers subsequent chapters. So *The Expendables 2* added new faces (Liam Hemsworth, Nan Yu, Scott Adkins, and Chuck Norris), upped the body count, increased screen time for gun-toting Willis and Schwarzenegger, and culminated in a pulverizing but satisfying shootout in an abandoned airport terminal.

One simple distinction separates *The Expendables* from *The Expendables 2* at their creative core. The first movie takes itself seriously, which is a mistake. As mentioned, Stallone flirted with the idea of making a broad satire before retreating into the stasis comfort of action-movie cliches. The second film, however, understands the inherent comedy in the premise and leans into it whenever appropriate. Jet Li dispenses a room full of armed guards using only a frying pan. A platoon of enemy soldiers is eliminated by an unseen assailant—who also takes out a tank with what appears to be a rocket launcher. You're meant to assume a small army did the damage, but no, it was Chuck Norris, all by himself. Finally, Willis yells at Schwarzenegger in the midst of a deafening battle, "You've been back too many times. *I'll* be back." To which the *Predator* star mutters under his breath, "Yippee ki yay."

West and his crew apply a lighter touch to the carnage, milking the larger-than-life personas of the action icons for well-earned laughs. In perhaps the film's best visual gag, Willis and Schwarzenegger tear the doors off of a pint-sized Smart Car and begin to race around the terminal trading quips. "My shoe is bigger than this car," Trench complains. "Shoot something!" Church replies, and the duo does just that. *The Expendables 2* makes excellent use of the charismatic personalities of its tough guy leads, and asks them to twist the humor by being in on the joke. Jean-Claude Van Damme literally plays a villain named Vilain. How much more proof do you need?

Willis's part in *The Expendables 2* was small but mighty, limited in time but unforgettable in terms of scope and impact. This is Stallone's franchise, ultimately. When Willis's Church arrives for the big finale, he tells Barney, "I heard there's a party in town." To which Ross corrects, "Yeah, but it's *my* party." West, however, figured out how to balance screen time for the excessive number of action veterans he had on the call sheet, making it worth everyone's time and talent.

In the end, he approached the daunting task like a mathematical equation.

"There were two big puzzles. One was getting everyone's schedule together. Can you imagine having 12 big stars, and trying to get them all available on the same day, so that you can have some scenes where they are all together?" West explained. "Then the second puzzle is, when you *do* get all of these people together, you have to make sure there is enough time in the movie for everyone to have a great couple of moments. There is a big mathematical equation to making that work."[4]

Take all of that into consideration, and Willis's two appearances in Stallone's bombastic and silly nostalgia play of an action franchise finally begin to add up.

CHAPTER TEN
G.I. JOE: RETALIATION

Director: Jon M. Chu
Cast: Dwayne Johnson, Channing Tatum, Bruce Willis, Adrianne Palicki, D.J. Cotrona, Ray Park, Jonathan Pryce, Elodie Yung
Release Date: March 28, 2013

> *"Try not to scratch her up. [She] idles a little rough in neutral."*
> *"I ain't gonna be in neutral."*
> *"Hooah."*
> —GENERAL JOE COLTON (BRUCE WILLIS) AND ROADBLOCK
> (DWAYNE JOHNSON) PREPARING FOR BATTLE IN *G.I. JOE: RETALIATION*

—1—

Because Bruce Willis worked so consistently during his decades-spanning career, the movie star included more than enough features on his résumé that would prompt even his most ardent fans to ask, "Wait, why is Bruce in this?"

At the pinnacle of his *Die Hard* phase, Willis lent his voice to a toddler for not one but two *Look Who's Talking* comedies, as an example. The A-lister popped up in the modern-day adaptation of *Nancy Drew* (starring Emma Roberts) for one scene where he played himself on the set of a 1940s detective story. And in 1996, sandwiched between the science fiction showpieces *12 Monkeys* (1995) and *The Fifth Element* (1997), Willis voiced a chain-smoking drunk who offers $10,000 to the animated idiots Beavis and Butthead if they'll agree to murder his wife (voiced by Demi Moore) in Mike Judge's moronic *Beavis and Butt-Head Do America*.

Why? Your guess is as good as mine. And the question likely was asked repeatedly by fans during the final years of Willis's professional career, when he stockpiled direct-to-video drivel from producer Randall Emmett, until his aphasia diagnosis offered some clarity to those decisions. Still, one of the more perplexing selections found in Willis's filmography had to be a sequel few were requesting, for a movie that bombed critically (in which he didn't even appear), that's based on a vintage line of Hasbro children's toys.

Leave it to Willis to get the last laugh, however, because the genuinely exciting and highly entertaining *G.I. Joe: Retaliation* works, and he's a big part of the reason why.

After a lackluster attempt by Paramount Pictures to launch a *G.I. Joe* franchise with 2009's *G.I. Joe: The Rise of Cobra*, this follow-up saw the studio heading back to the drawing board to salvage their viable concept by luring superior talent for almost every creative position. Producer Lorenzo di Bonaventura got off on the right foot by hiring screenwriters Rhett Reese and Paul Wernick, the talk of the town in 2009 courtesy of their wickedly clever script for the horror-comedy *Zombieland*. The duo would go on to pen acerbically vulgar dialogue for Ryan Reynolds in *Deadpool* and its 2018 sequel, but not before figuring out how to construct a stylish and funny adventure set in the G.I. Joe world. Next, the energy and flair that director Jon M. Chu brought to his two *Step Up* sequels, as well as the fizzy Justin Bieber documentary *Never Say Never*, earned him the opportunity to inject life into *Retaliation* (because *The Rise of Cobra* director Stephen Sommers couldn't give that movie a pulse). And *Retaliation* received a significant shot in the arm once proven action star Dwayne "The Rock" Johnson agreed to play the coveted role of Roadblock, the Joe squad's go-to expert for heavy artillery. Johnson's success at reviving the floundering *Fast and Furious* franchise with 2011's *Fast Five*, followed by his commendable turn in this enjoyable sequel, earned the wrestler-turned-actor the nickname "Franchise Viagra." It also cemented his status as a dependable global superstar, setting up a consistent run of prosperous action films (*San Andreas*, *Rampage*), comedies (*Central Intelligence*), animated hits (*Moana*), and resuscitated, nostalgia-play franchises (*Jumanji: Welcome to the Jungle*).

Still, *Retaliation*'s most impressive casting coup came in the form of Willis, the Mack Daddy of action franchise legends hired by Chu to play our country's first "Real American Hero."

"He was always our dream guy to play Joe Colton, the original Joe, [but] I didn't necessarily know if he would ever do something like this," said Chu.

"There is no Joe. But we had this character Joe Colton that we built into the movie that would help bring it back to the basics. That was a big part of the movie—these guys don't have laser guns; they are relearning how to be a soldier on the ground, how to be a leader, how to make moral decisions, all those things, reset it all. And Bruce is the guy [to anchor that]."[1]

Not that convincing Willis to step into Joe's combat boots was an easy task. *G.I. Joe* producer Lorenzo di Bonaventura, who'd previously collaborated with Willis on Robert Schwentke's *Red*, initiated the conversations about having the *Unbreakable* icon play the original Joe. Willis seemed open to the idea, as the supporting role very much was in his wheelhouse: gruff, stoic, armed to the teeth, and ready to lead, with as few words as possible. Still, the actor spent months learning about Chu, about the Hasbro brand, and about the character that Reese and Wernick had created from scratch before fully committing.

"I never really thought it would fully happen until he showed up on set," Chu confessed. "But he came through and he was awesome. I mean, he exudes the tone of the movie because he's so cool, and he's so that guy. But at the same time, [he] doesn't take himself too seriously. He just gives you that little wink, or whenever he says one line, you just get it."

—2—

That explains why Chu and his team wanted Willis. As for the superstar's motivations for wanting to assume the historic role of the original Joe, they appear to have been twofold.

The cynical justification boils down to the obvious attraction for virtually every professional actor: money. According to the *Guardian*, during an abnormally candid interview with the Spanish magazine *XLS* to promote *G.I. Joe: Retaliation* in 2013, Willis admitted, "I am very clear with who I am. I work in all sorts of films, but the action movies are the ones that generate the most revenue. I like to earn lots of money from those, but I do all types [of pictures]: small productions, mega-projects, medium-sized, even science fiction."[2]

There exists, however, a genial and innocent alternate reason for Willis wanting to step into the role of Joe, one that traces back to his childhood experiences with the classic toys.

"We used to launch G.I. Joe into the air, put him on arrows. Sometimes firecrackers were involved," Willis joked as he reminisced about playing with the action figures as a kid. "G.I. Joe could just take it."[3]

That sense of reckless, adolescent play fuels *G.I. Joe: Retaliation*, and sets the sequel apart from its joyless predecessor. Chu's sequel takes itself seriously enough, while consistently embracing the fact that it's inspired by a historic line of Hasbro toys, and decades of campy comic-book storylines pitting the patriotic G.I. Joe squad against the sinister forces of Cobra. At the start of this story, Cobra operative and master of disguise Zartan is impersonating the president of the United States (Jonathan Pryce), carelessly abusing the powers of the office while inching the nations of the world closer to the brink of nuclear annihilation. High-tech gadgetry is used on every mission, tickling the audience's imaginations with explosive firefly drones, aquatic tanks that keep prisoners on life support, and a gravity-defying ninja battle on the side of a snowy mountain.

"The weaponry on this film was just off the charts. It raised the bar, for sure," Willis said regarding the production.[4]

The bulk of that weaponry showed up in Willis's first scene. A small team led by Roadblock, Lady Jaye (Adrianne Palicki), and Snake Eyes (Ray Park) infiltrate General Joe Colton's suburban home, seeking an ally in their pending battle against Cobra. What they find is a world-weary combat veteran who's holed up in a residential fortress that hides guns behind almost every surface. But the sequence is played for laughs, and Willis is encouraged to be funny. For his first line of dialogue, he pretends to order Girl Scout Cookies from Roadblock after sneaking up behind the mountain of a man. As Joe Colton helps the Joes prepare themselves for battle, he comically reveals state-of-the-art rifles, handguns, machine guns, hand grenades, smoke bombs, daggers, and more hiding in his pantry, his cabinets, under his kitchen sink, and beneath the cushions of his couch. It's basically Rambo's retirement home. The chef's kiss moment of this flawlessly executed "arm the troops" sequence occurs when Colton detaches the thermostat from his wall, revealing a hidden keypad. He punches in the code 1776—the year America obtained its freedom from the Brits—and unlocks a closet filled with enough weapons to take down the army of a medium-sized country.

"DoD says I can't come out of retirement," Willis's general explains to Roadblock after the soldier wonders if the original Joe is going to join the fight. However, the action hero shrugs and goes on to say, "They didn't say anything about reenlisting. Reporting for duty, sergeant major."

In that moment, Willis rekindles that spark of rebellion he frequently brought to his rule-breaking antiheroes. Joe Colton reveals himself to be just another hero doing the right thing. To hell with the powers that be who've ordered him not to do that anymore. Willis's status as an action-movie legend made him the ideal choice to play the original G.I. Joe, but it's his decision to infuse the military veteran with arrogance and sarcasm that turn Colton—potentially a disposable figurehead—into a memorable character on the actor's résumé.

—3—

G.I. Joe: Retaliation and *Red 2*, also released in 2013, conclude an arc of films that officially graduated Willis into the veteran leader role, mentoring the next generation of action stars as he brandished king-sized weapons and playfully acknowledged his advanced age. The original *Red* makes nonstop jokes about its cast being past the point of retirement. Same goes for 2013's *A Good Day to Die Hard*, where the once iconic John McClane lumbered around Moscow getting lectured by his petulant kid (Jai Courtney) that the old man has grown too old for this shit. And in *Retaliation*, following a badass sequence where Joe Colton fires a machine gun at Cobra operatives from the back of a 1973 Chevrolet El Camino SS, Lady Jaye (Palicki) asks the retired general if he is OK.

"My cholesterol's a little high," Colton quips in return.

There's a direct correlation between the veteran role Willis played in the *Expendables* movies, and the muscles that he's asked to flex in *Retaliation*. The young heroes do the heavier lifting through both sets of movies before turning to the seasoned pro to bail them out, usually because they've backed themselves into a corner. In the case of Joe Colton, this was the man who blazed the trail, formed the mold, and wrote the playbook that the Joes now follow. Similar to the work that Willis did in the action genre for Dwayne Johnson, Channing Tatum, Lee Byung-hun, D. J. Cotrona, and anyone else daring to call themselves an action hero in a post–*Die Hard* world.

G.I. Joe: Retaliation doesn't have the same body count as *The Expendables*. Chu's film adheres to the boundaries of the PG-13 rating, creating a sleeker, safer, and bloodless adventure. It contains one authentic shock that powers its narrative, however, killing off main hero Duke (Tatum) before the movie's midpoint. Imagine the outrage if Stallone treated Schwarzenegger, Statham, or Lundgren as truly expendable?

But *Retaliation* notches a number of victories, primarily in the addition of the new cast members, making it a more accessible crowd pleaser. Casting director Ronna Kress (*Moulin Rouge, Pirates of the Caribbean: The Curse of the Black Pearl*) might be the MVP on Chu's *Retaliation* team. She handpicked Dwayne "The Rock" Johnson as he was evolving into a bigger screen presence, shedding trivial projects like *Journey 2: The Mysterious Island* or 2010's *The Tooth Fairy* for movies that made better use of his skill set. Yes, Kress inherited Tatum, Park, and Pryce. But she also knew that versatile character actor Walton Goggins would have a field day playing a slimeball bully of a prison warden who's so drunk with power, he verbally challenges Snake Eyes.

And Kress helped add Willis to the *G.I. Joe: Retaliation* mix, which brings us back around full circle to the question that opened this chapter: "Why is Bruce in this?" The answer to Willis's work ethic might be found in the braggadocious exchange between military meatheads Roadblock (Johnson) and Colton (Willis) as they geared up for combat. Colton warns Block that the massive tank he's about to navigate through enemy territory idles a little rough in neutral. That wasn't going to be a problem. Because—as evidenced by the six movies he released in 2012, as well as the three he delivered in 2013—Willis never planned to be in neutral.

SECTION THREE
BRUCE WILLIS IN THE
SCIENCE FICTION REALM

"Negative. I am a meat popsicle."

Official movie poster for Luc Besson's *The Fifth Element*, starring
Bruce Willis. *Author's Collection*

Dating back to the 1940s, science fiction has been a fertile and lucrative genre for Hollywood studios. The American Film Institute, when compiling its list of the ten most influential sci-fi movies, started in the 1950s and chose films from every decade. The list currently includes *Invasion of the Body Snatchers* (1956), Stanley Kubrick's *2001: A Space Odyssey* (1968), the original *Star Wars* (1977), and Sir Ridley Scott's *Blade Runner* (1982). James Cameron's visually spectacular *Avatar*, which transported audiences to the far-off planet of Pandora, remains the highest-grossing movie of all time. And Cameron's 2022 sequel, *Avatar: The Way of Water*, came close to matching its predecessor's box-office success, while still managing to become one of only six films to earn more than $2 billion at the global box office.

Science fiction's popularity rarely wanes, but there was a notable period in the late 1980s and 1990s where action-driven science fiction enjoyed a surge at the box office and employed a number of the heroes discussed at length in this book. Audiences powered Steven Spielberg's adaptation of Michael Crichton's dinosaur theme park adventure *Jurassic Park* to more than $1 billion in global tickets sold in 1993. Rapper-turned-actor Will Smith catapulted to international superstardom following the back-to-back smash hits *Independence Day* (1996) and *Men in Black* (1997). George Lucas revived his dormant Star Wars franchise for 1999's *Star Wars: Episode I—The Phantom Menace*. That same year, Keanu Reeves convinced audiences to swallow the red pill and submerge themselves into Lana and Lily Wachowski's groundbreaking *The Matrix*.

Household action names who came to prominence in the 1980s enjoyed incredible success in the science fiction genre around this time, as well. Whether intentional or not, a pattern began to form around these top earners, a camp into which Willis fell. Arnold Schwarzenegger led the charge with James Cameron's first two *Terminator* films, while also packing theaters for *Predator* (1987), *The Running Man* (1987), and *Total Recall* (1990). The more grounded Sylvester Stallone hung up Rocky's boxing gloves and Rambo's bandana long enough to capitalize on this sci-fi/action phase, toplining 1993's *Demolition Man* and the less-than-inspiring 1995 comic-book adaptation *Judge Dredd*. Not wanting to be left out in the cold, Jean-Claude Van Damme sought out science fiction scripts that eventually led to *Universal Soldier* (1992), *Timecop* (1994), and *Replicant* (2001).

Willis's résumé also reflects an uptick in extraterrestrial interests during this time frame. But Willis, by his own words, wasn't following a trend. Listening to Willis describe his motivations for selecting different projects over the years, you find that it often boiled down to two questions he wanted to have answered. Who would he be working with? And would he have any fun? Other factors would affect his decisions, of course, from the quality of a screenplay to the timing of a production's shoot. But I heard some iteration of those two sentiments more than enough times while listening to Willis pitch his movies to the press in junket interviews, or dissect his process while being interrogated by curious journalists, that I now accept it to be true. If Willis liked a director, and thought he could enjoy himself in the process, chances are he'd sign on the dotted line.

He did, however, appear to be pushing back against his stale, blue-collar typecasting when accepting these detours into the science fiction genre. He flatly admitted, while promoting *The Fifth Element*, that he'd officially grown tired with the repetitive action-movie offers that were crossing his desk.

"People in the media try to identify me and say, 'Well, he's this kind of actor.' Or, 'He's a superstar.' Whatever label they want to put on me," Willis said. "I'm still learning how to act. I learn things about acting from every film I do. It would be very easy for me, and also very boring for me, to just do action movies all the time. I am tired of it. So I try to find other things to challenge myself with. I like to do films that I'm not quite sure whether I'm going to succeed in. So there's always that risk of failure."[1]

This risk seemed predominantly evident each time Willis ventured into the science fiction genre. And again, the four pictures discussed in this section largely were chosen by Willis because of the filmmakers with which he was able to collaborate: Luc Besson on *The Fifth Element*, Terry Gilliam on *12 Monkeys*, Rian Johnson for *Looper*, and Michael Bay with *Armageddon*. Though each movie now holds the distinction of being a classic from Willis's résumé, you'll see that none of the four promised guaranteed success, and they relied on the attachment of "Movie Star Bruce Willis," just so the valuable acting lessons he so desperately craved could be experienced during the shoots.

CHAPTER ELEVEN
THE FIFTH ELEMENT

Director: Luc Besson
Cast: Bruce Willis, Milla Jovovich, Chris Tucker,
Gary Oldman, Ian Holm, Tommy "Tiny" Lister Jr.
Release Date: May 9, 1997

> *"V is good. Some very good words in V."*
> *"Like what?"*
> *"Valiant. Vulnerable. Very beautiful."*
> —KORBEN DALLAS (WILLIS) TO LEELOO (MILLA JOVOVICH)
> IN *THE FIFTH ELEMENT*

—1—

When Luc Besson's *The Fifth Element* opened the fiftieth annual Cannes Film Festival on May 7, 1997, some probably viewed it as an unusual choice. The haughty Cannes typically caters to prestigious international features, stimulating arthouse experiments, and awards hopefuls looking to generate publicity waves. Besson instead brought a gaudy, goofy, sexy piece of pop science fiction, with a $90 million production budget that, at the time, made it the most expensive film in French cinema history.

The Fifth Element's financial ties to France's respected Gaumont Film Company probably made the selection more palatable. Plus, Gaumont chief Patrice Ledoux, a producer on Besson's picture, held two aces up his sleeve when securing this high-profile world premiere slot.

"I brought Bruce Willis and Demi Moore," Ledoux said. "And at that time, if you were to tell the Cannes Film Festival that you could bring Bruce Willis and Demi Moore to the opening . . . let's just say they were enthusiastic!"[1]

With the high-profile celebrity couple came the anticipated film-festival carnival. Gaumont threw a lavish afterparty held in a newly constructed, one-hundred-thousand-square-foot structure on the Croisette. A thousand people packed the venue to watch a futuristic ballet performance, a live concert by singer-songwriter Neneh Cherry, a fashion show programmed by *The Fifth Element* costume designer Jean-Paul Gaultier, and an array of A-listers ready to let loose.

"It was overwhelming," Willis said. "It just bangs you. It just comes at you, and keeps coming and coming the whole time. There's no dead space. It's just a spectacle."[2]

He meant the movie, but he could have been referring to the publicity circus that accompanied a Willis release during the actor's movie-stardom prime. And Willis very much was enjoying a career arc high point when *The Fifth Element* arrived. Critics began appreciating his versatility, praising his performances in *Pulp Fiction* (1994), opposite Paul Newman for *Nobody's Fool* (1994), and in Gilliam's dystopian nightmare *12 Monkeys* (1995). At the same time, Willis flexed his box office muscle by returning to the *Die Hard* franchise for John McTiernan's *Die Hard with a Vengeance*. The sequel's incredible $366.1 million global haul made it the highest-grossing worldwide release in 1995.

A running theme we'll return to often as we analyze Willis's excursions into science fiction is that the unconventional projects toward which he gravitated probably wouldn't exist if he didn't express an interest. Besson made that much clear. Terry Gilliam will echo the claim about the next chapter's subject, *12 Monkeys*. And Rian Johnson was coming off of the independent critical darlings *Brick* and *The Brothers Bloom* when he cast Willis as a time-traveling hitman in *Looper*. Willis's bankability and built-in audience helped these offbeat, intelligent, and nonconformist stories get greenlit.

Willis likely could have chosen any project he fancied in 1996. And as he had done in the past, Willis relied on two important "F" words to steer his decision: the *filmmaker* involved, and the *fun* quotient of the production shoot.

"I did this picture, not so much for the science fiction part of it, but just because I wanted to work with Luc [Besson]. It just seemed like it would be a big, fun ride to go on."[3]

—2—

"*The Fifth Element* actually feels like it was scripted by a daydreaming teenager, but in a good way," *Austin Chronicle* critic Marc Savlov wrote in his review of the film. "That is to say, there's a certain 'gosh, wow' sense of wonder to the whole thing."[4]

Savlov wasn't that far off from the truth. Besson cooked up the outline for *The Fifth Element* at the age of sixteen, then tinkered with his concept over the years while toiling on the critically acclaimed *La Femme Nikita* (1990) and *Leon: The Professional* (1994). He ended up with an unusual film, one that emphasizes style over substance. It's a science fiction hybrid of conventional action, screwball comedy, sleek visuals, and Besson's unique artistic vision, attributable to his hyperactive imagination. As Willis wisely predicted, *The Fifth Element* is a big, fun ride.

After a brief prologue set in Egypt circa 1914, Besson's space opera rockets forward three hundred years, where high priests race corrupt government agents and gnarly reptilian soldiers to retrieve a genetically flawless weapon named Leeloo (personified by Milla Jovovich) that can vanquish a newly resurrected Great Evil (personified as a burning planet). At the center of the adventure lies Korben Dallas, a prototypically arrogant, condescending, yet well-decorated and dependable Willis hero. "The Gary Cooper of the picture," he joked in an interview promoting the film.[5] Dallas also requires Willis to once again play the type of hero thrust into existing chaos who spends most of the movie playing catch up. He's not the film's savior, however. Leeloo is.

"You, no trouble. Me Fifth Element," she assures Dallas. "Supreme being. Me protect you."

Several critics took shots at Besson's simplistic story in their reviews. "To me, most futuristic stories are the same—the world is going to hell and the last regular guy on Earth must save it," the late Gene Siskel surmised in the *Chicago Tribune*.[6] They could not, however, ignore the spectacle on display. Besson's futuristic New York City bustles with flying cars, but still contains drive-up McDonald's restaurants. He conceives of a middle-act location stop aboard an opulent floating hotel hovering over the planet Fhloston, where every vice can be satisfied. The story builds toward an operatic performance by the alien creature Diva Plavalaguna (Maiwenn Le Besco), which alone is a showstopper before Besson transitions it into an up-tempo music video montage accompanying an energetic Jovovich fight scene.

The negative reviews missed, in my opinion, some beautiful messages about the sanctity of life, and the point of existence in the face of extermination. Before saving the world, Besson's characters pause long enough to debate whether their heroism and personal sacrifice is even worth all of the effort. "Humans act so strange. . . . Everything you created is used to destroy," Leeloo says to Dallas. "What's the use in saving life when you see what you do with it?"

Dallas blames human nature, a cynical but largely realistic assessment. When he asks Leeloo if she learned about human nature on the screen she watches to rapidly absorb world history, she tells him she isn't finished yet. She's only up to "V." Like the Roman numeral "V," which represents five. Or the Fifth Element.

"All this stuff was in his head," Willis explained about Besson. "He told me this story at my house five years (before filming). He was trying to explain the whole thing to me, and I couldn't quite follow it. About a year and a half [later], he brings me this script and he goes, 'Well, this is that story I was trying to tell you about.' And I went, 'Damn, okay. This is good. This is really good!'"[7]

—3—

Besson's *The Fifth Element* belongs in the same conversation as George Lucas's *Star Wars*, Sir Ridley Scott's *Blade Runner*, Mike Hodges's *Flash Gordon*, and Paul Verhoeven's *Total Recall* when it comes to avant-garde science fiction world building, without ever borrowing from (or blatantly copying) its predecessors. It boasts magnificent creature compositions, award-winning production design, high-powered action sequences, a steamy romance, and all of the bold choices Chris Tucker made as flamboyant talk radio host Ruby Rhod.

It's also truly unlike anything else on Willis's résumé, even if Willis is playing his familiar, heroic notes as part of the grand composition. "One of the things that I like about what Luc did with the film is that it's three hundred years from now, and yet there's still a modern sense of humor to it, and a modern sense of romance, a modern sense of heroism and saving the world. We save the world!" Willis said. "And all of these fun toys that are maybe out of the realm of the Star Wars genre, but brand-new. Brand-new things, and brand-new images. And all very strange."[8]

Strange is a notable word because Willis didn't do "strange" very often. The actor sustained his career by playing relatable, down-to-earth characters. Even his other dips into the science fiction realm painted him as recognizable men, from a salt-of-the-earth oil driller (*Armageddon*), to a convict (*12 Monkeys*), and a love-struck gun for hire (*Looper*). So in *The Fifth Element*, Willis stepped back while his costars fully embraced the eccentricities of Besson's futuristic creations.

Half of Gary Oldman's head, for example, is shaved, then encased in a plastic dome. What's left of his hair gets styled into a look that befits a 1980s New Wave singer, possibly from a Flock of Seagulls or Kajagoogoo. The fast-talking Tucker alternates his vibrant appearance from scene to scene. Skin-tight, leopard-print leotards and a bleach-blonde coif in one scene. A jet-black evening gown with roses for a collar in the next. Tucker's high-pitched Ruby Rhod—who allegedly was almost played by Prince—only gets eclipsed by the lithe Jovovich, who first appears naked in a tube, then maneuvers around her futuristic environments in an outfit made of strategically placed bandages designed by Gaultier.

Willis, in comparison, doesn't deviate nearly as much from his natural look for *The Fifth Element*. In fact, Willis hardly deviates at all—outside of dying his hair blonde—to bring Dallas to life. I'd call it a missed opportunity, except Willis's stoic presence and rugged humanity actually provides precisely what Besson needed from the character. In an imaginative alien landscape bustling with hulking extraterrestrials, ocean-blue opera singers, shape-shifting soldiers, and precious stones passed down by generations, working-class hero Willis grounded the fantasy by playing a beat-up taxi driver from South Brooklyn caught up in the quest to protect Jovovich's creation. His military background makes him proficient with all kinds of weapons. His flippant attitude brings humor and mild impatience to the madness swirling around him (particularly when his nagging mother calls to complain). And when guns start blazing in the film's explosive final act, *The Fifth Element* ditches its futuristic ingenuity and mimics a routine Willis action vehicle.

Because even three hundred years in the future, Willis understood what his audience wanted out of him and figured out how to deliver.

CHAPTER TWELVE
12 MONKEYS

Director: Terry Gilliam
Cast: Bruce Willis, Brad Pitt, Madeleine Stowe, Christopher Plummer
Release Date: December 29, 1995

> *Maybe means, "Maybe I'm in the next cell. Another volunteer, like you."*
> *Or maybe I'm in the central office, spying on you for all those science bozos.*
> *Or hey, maybe I'm not even here. Maybe I'm just in your head. No way to*
> *confirm anything."*
>
> —A MYSTERIOUS VOICE TAUNTING JAMES COLE
> (WILLIS) IN *12 MONKEYS*

—1—

By 2023, traditional Hollywood "Movie Stars" were extinct, and had been replaced by recognizable IP and name-brand franchises. Instead of heading to the theater to see the latest Julia Roberts, Jim Carrey, Denzel Washington, or Sandra Bullock film, audiences flocked to Marvel Studios movies, nostalgia-driven remakes, and legacy sequels (the ongoing *Scream*, *Transformers*, and *Ghostbusters* sagas are contemporary examples), regardless of who starred in them. Tom Cruise probably holds the distinction of being the last official movie star capable of bringing ticket-buyers to the multiplex. But even then, Cruise chose to play it safe during this stretch by producing prudent *Mission: Impossible* sequels, or returning to one of his defining hits with 2022's *Top Gun: Maverick*.

Willis, in his prime, had the power to open movies in the global marketplace. And not just his signature action films. M. Night Shyamalan's psychological dramas *Unbreakable* (2000) and *Glass* (2019), the animated *Over the Hedge* (2006), Michael Bay's bombastic *Armageddon* (1998), and Robert

Rodriguez's sleazy crime noir *Sin City* (2005) rank among Willis's highest-grossing opening weekends. The superstar enjoyed bankability, a valuable commodity in the film industry. What's remarkable, though, is how Willis used it.

Scan Willis's résumé and you'll find an inordinate number of experimental movies from fledgling directors and avant-garde mavericks operating on the fringe of the studio system. He'd move from a slam dunk like *The Last Boy Scout* to a bit part in a Robert Altman satire, or take an uncredited role in the unconventional *Four Rooms* the same year he released *Die Hard with a Vengeance*. Willis frequently straddled the line between art and commerce, putting his significant box-office clout behind visionary storytellers. It became a defining characteristic of Willis's cinematic legacy.

"I think what you need, when you have this kind of relationship between art and commerce that the movie industry is, you need someone to be a champion for you. That has the ability to protect you as you move through the process," said Shyamalan, who was a relative newcomer with two low-budget indies on his résumé before Willis joined his mournful ghost story *The Sixth Sense* in 1999. "For me, at 25 or 26, Bruce was that person. He used his power, his clout, and just said, 'I believe in this guy. I believe in this kid, and I believe in this movie.' And he let me make the movie. And that protection allowed me to have a really different and unique voice.

"I think we owe a lot of gratitude that someone who everyone wanted to come see in the movie theaters actually believed in independent cinema and in new voices," Shyamalan continued. "It was a big deal."[1]

The *Unbreakable* director was neither the first nor the only director Willis went to bat for because he believed in a story. Quentin Tarantino, Antoine Fuqua, Luc Besson, Rian Johnson, Robert Rodriguez, and *Monty Python* veteran Terry Gilliam all credit Willis with earning a greenlight for risky projects that met studio resistance. Though Gilliam was more established at the time he collaborated with Willis—having helmed *Time Bandits*, *Brazil*, and the Oscar-winning *The Fisher King*—Hollywood still viewed his visionary pictures as significant gambles, and potential financial disasters. This included the dystopian time-travel twister *12 Monkeys*, which Gilliam believes wouldn't exist in its current form without Willis signing on the dotted line.

"It was really only when I got Bruce involved that it became a more viable project," he said. "[Studio executives are] obsessed about things like opening weekend. And somebody like Bruce guarantees an opening weekend."[2]

—2—

Willis boasts a handful of masterpieces on his résumé. Gilliam's *12 Monkeys* ranks as one. Enigmatic and demanding, it's exactly the type of big-swing movie Hollywood producers have come to avoid making, mainly out of fear. Gilliam and his co-screenwriters embrace ambiguity as they tell the story of James Cole (Willis), a prisoner who might be a time traveler sent back from a ravaged futuristic society to warn citizens in 1996 of a deadly virus that's about to wipe most of humanity off the map. Because Cole wakes up in a mental-health facility during his "mission," Gilliam includes endless clues that suggest the dystopian "future" our hero describes—where humanity lives underground and wild animals overtake the planet's surface—possibly exists in his mind. And because the audience only comprehends as much as Cole does on every step of the journey, *12 Monkeys* immerses viewers into a disorientating, frequently exhilarating experience that Gilliam visually enhances with canted camera angles and detail-enriched steampunk sets meant to keep the viewer curious, uncomfortable, and continuously off balance.

"There are relatively few shots in this movie that would look normal in any other film," Roger Ebert observed in his three-star review. "Everything is skewed to express the vision."[3]

It's difficult to definitively name Willis's greatest performance. Opinions are subjective. But there's no arguing that his turn as James Cole in *12 Monkeys* has to be part of any conversation on the topic.

Willis gives himself over completely to a director's singular vision in *12 Monkeys*, and Gilliam makes tremendous use of every tool at the actor's disposal. Willis's resilient physicality makes Cole a natural selection by the scientific panel to endure the jarring time-travel process and collect evidence regarding the virus. But Willis taps into his character's fear and frustration at his predicament, which forces us to feel the absence of that power once it's stripped from him by the battery of medications fed to him by the hospital staff. Rarely does Willis allow himself to be portrayed on screen as helpless or incapacitated. But Gilliam leans into Willis's vulnerability, masterfully employing it during one heart-racing scene that follows a doped-up Cole slowly fighting through a medicinal haze to attempt an escape from the hospital while his newfound friend, the live wire Jeffrey Goines (Brad Pitt), creates a diversion. Willis moves as if he's underwater, and the sheer effort exerted by the A-lister—whom we are accustomed to seeing in finely tuned and fast-moving action choreography—is palpable.

The giddy fun of *12 Monkeys* lies in the unknown. Cole could be dreaming about a virus-riddled future because Jeffrey incessantly ranted in his ear about the proliferation of harmful germs. But if Cole in fact is *not* traveling through time, how did a World War I bullet end up lodged in his thigh? Cole also might believe in the eventual decimation of the global population because he and Jeffrey briefly argued in the institute over whether or not the human race deserves to be wiped out. However, Gilliam also suggests that Cole could have been the one who planted the idea of a devastating virus in Jeffrey's head, indirectly making himself the cause of the disease he is racing against time to prevent.

We stay rooted in this nonlinear story because Willis invests into the credibility of each reality as *12 Monkeys* shifts back and forth between its future and present timelines. He's so convincing in his acceptance that we the audience share his point of view and debate Cole's true circumstance right up until the film's ending. The tension of the story comes from what the audience chooses to believe. There even comes a point where Cole himself starts to distrust which reality is his real one and rejects the knowledge of his doomed future. "I am insane. And you are my insanity," he admits to Dr. Kathryn Railly (Madeleine Stowe), a Baltimore psychiatrist who hears enough possibility in Cole's claims to start to believe that he might be telling the truth (another by-product of Willis forging a powerful emotional connection with a costar he needs to have on his side).

The film showcases a skill set that too often gets overlooked when discussing Willis's strongest performances. Willis is a formidable personality, and fully capable of owning any scene. But he also understands when and how to sit in silence, to listen, and to let others do the heavier lifting if the story requires it. Regarding his approach to *12 Monkeys* in a 1995 interview, Willis observed, "It's much more of an internal performance than it is that I'm generally asked to do. And that is to be the driver of the scene, so to speak. This film, I'm much more reactive, and as things happen, I more respond—or don't respond—to it. It was just fun to work in a different way, to not have to play the hero, and to not have to be in charge or be in control."[4]

What's unfortunate for Willis is that the occasional times that he has embraced a more passive role for the benefit of a story, his costars went on to receive some of the industry's top accolades, even though their performances would amount to little without the bedrock of emotional support Willis provided.

—3—

Brad Pitt received the showier role in *12 Monkeys*. Goines is a hyperactive Jiminy Cricket, nattering away in Cole's ear about nothing of consequence and either navigating the time-traveler forward on his mission or misdirecting him away from a more sinister endgame.

The Academy rewarded Pitt's jittery antics and exaggerated tics with a Best Supporting Actor nomination, the first of his career. Really, though, Pitt is overplaying Goines's paranoia. He portrays clinical insanity with a cartoonish stutter, and manic outbursts that end with him pulling down his pajama bottoms while wrestling with hospital security. Hindsight suggests that the Academy wasn't fully aware of Pitt's commendable range at the time *12 Monkeys* was released. He made an immediate impact through smaller roles in *Thelma and Louise* and *True Romance*, then expanded his visibility with *Interview with the Vampire* and *Legends of the Fall*. But years would pass before Pitt earned his reputation as an esteemed character actor in a leading man's body, and Goines—when compared to Pitt's superior performances—comes off as gimmicky. The nomination today feels more like a visceral response to the radiant star scuffing his polished complexion, and Academy members mistaking that for dramatic heft.

Willis, on the other hand, gives the more subdued and award-worthy performance in *12 Monkeys*, sustaining the film's mystery through his unwavering commitment. He has to believe in his fractured reality at every step, so we can believe it as well. Willis explores his full range as Cole, who can be meek, rageful, courageous, naive, and terrified out of his mind. Willis does so much work with his eyes, which show that he's always rapidly assessing his situation. There's a reason why Gilliam opens and closes the movie with zoomed-in shots of young Cole's aqua-blue eyes. His point-of-view defines the story. And in one of the film's most unexpected scenes, Cole temporarily forgets the impending doom that awaits his future, and celebrates the beauty of the past he took for granted. A giddy, childlike joy washes over Willis as he hangs his head out a car window, breathing fresh air and listening to music of the twentieth century. He's magnificent.

The Academy didn't recognize Willis for *12 Monkeys*. Sadly, the organization never nominated Willis for any of his performances. Instead, *12 Monkeys* joins the short list of films that feature Willis's costars getting nominated, while his work gets overlooked. The most egregious of these has to be Quentin Tarantino's masterpiece, *Pulp Fiction*. The film roared out of the Cannes Film Festival in 1994, where it won the prestigious Palme d'Or. The movie became a box-office phenomenon, and eventually earned seven Oscars, including Best Picture. *Pulp Fiction* arguably has four leading actors—Samuel L. Jackson, John Travolta, Uma Thurman, and Willis. The first three received acting nominations for the film. Willis did not.

He encountered a similar, grievous snub in 1999, when the Academy bestowed the smash hit *The Sixth Sense* with six Oscar nominations, including Picture, Director (for Shyamalan), Supporting Actor (for Haley Joel Osment), and Supporting Actress (for Toni Collette). All of them were deserving of the recognition. Osment deserved to win. But how do you honor every major creative contributor to *The Sixth Sense*, and leave Willis out?

One day, perhaps soon, the Academy will attempt to correct its mistakes with a ceremonial Honorary Oscar for Willis. And it will be because of his work on heralded films such as *12 Monkeys*. Gilliam's masterwork remains one of the riskiest projects Willis ever chose, and it's thrilling to watch him rise to the elevated level of the material.

CHAPTER THIRTEEN
LOOPER

Director: Rian Johnson
Cast: Joseph Gordon-Levitt, Bruce Willis, Emily Blunt,
Paul Dano, Noah Segan, Jeff Daniels
Release Date: September 28, 2012

> *I don't want to talk about time travel shit. Because if we start talking about it, then we're going to be here all day talking about it, making diagrams with straws. It doesn't matter.*
>
> —OLD JOE (WILLIS), GETTING RIGHT TO THE POINT OF *LOOPER*

—1—

For the better part of thirty years, I traveled the globe interviewing movie stars: Tom Cruise in both Vienna, Austria and Paris, France; Tom Hanks in Florence, Italy; *Titanic* and *Avatar* director James Cameron in London; Scarlett Johansson in San Diego; and Paul Newman in my hometown of Charlotte, North Carolina, where Pixar Studios held the world premiere of *Cars*. Quentin Tarantino invited me to his home theater in the Hollywood Hills. We also conducted a live interview from the stage of his movie theater, the New Beverly, when he held a book launch party in Los Angeles.

I recognize how lucky I've been to interview such talents, and don't take these valuable experiences for granted. But for every conversation logged with Clint Eastwood, Meryl Streep, Jack Nicholson, Denzel Washington, Sandra Bullock, Harrison Ford, Eddie Murphy, Angelina Jolie, or Hugh Jackman, you spend an inordinate amount of time lamenting the ones that got away.

Like Bruce Willis.

I never interviewed Willis. It's the question I'm asked the most by people who learn about this book. "Did you get Bruce?" He remains my white whale, and likely will stay that way given his health conditions and retirement from the industry. We did, however, bump into each other once when Rian Johnson's science fiction thriller *Looper* opened the Toronto International Film Festival in September 2012.

The film casts Willis and Joseph Gordon-Levitt (*Inception, 500 Days of Summer*) as the same character—a hitman named Joe, only separated by thirty years. One eliminates designated targets in the year 2044. The other is sent back from 2074 but escapes on his own mission before he can be killed. *Looper*'s entire cast, Willis included, traveled to Canada for press during the festival, and one afternoon, I walked through the spacious corridors of Toronto's Ritz-Carlton, waiting for scheduled interviews with Johnson, Gordon-Levitt, and costar Emily Blunt, just not one with Willis, which happens. Massive stars do as much (or as little) press as they please at film festivals, and typically approve the outlets with which they're most comfortable. Willis scheduled a few *Looper* sit-downs, but not with me.

And yet, as I rounded a corner, there he was—bounding down the hallway with a literal skip in his step, and fast approaching me as I neared Blunt's room. Willis found a break in his day and wanted to pop in to say hello to his *Looper* costar. We arrived at the hotel-room door at the same time, so he looked over at me briefly and offered his reflexive, dismissive smirk before strolling in, saying, "You don't mind, do you?"

I didn't reply. I couldn't. I was starstruck—something I'm proud to say rarely happened during my career. But Willis had that effect.

And not just on me.

"I mean, everyone else's cool factor, I feel, hits the floor the moment Bruce would come into the room," Blunt said.[1]

Gordon-Levitt noticed, and admired, something different about Willis, whom he'd idolized since his childhood. "He's actually, I think, even more impressive in person than he is on the screen, to be honest with you. He's huge! I never thought he was so big," Gordon-Levitt said. "Bruce is actually a really big, broad, imposing dude. Which is interesting because his attitude is the opposite of that. He's the most gentle, understated, just graceful, chilled-out guy."[2]

The duality of Willis—a movie star who possessed the rugged toughness of a paid assassin, and the sensitive romanticism of a lover willing to throw that life away, in the same package. These qualities are essential to Johnson's story, and I'm not convinced *Looper* enjoys the same longevity that it does, or leaves the same cultural footprint, if not for Willis's contributions.

—2—

Johnson really only needed Willis for two pivotal scenes in *Looper*. And neither has anything to do with time travel.

That's because, as Johnson explained, "The movie is really not about time travel. One of the big challenges in writing it was figuring out how to get time travel to lay down so that the audience isn't having to process the rules of it the whole time. The heart of the movie is really in the characters."[3]

Or character, singular, when it comes to Joe. The first necessary Willis scene arguably is the film's most memorable—the initial conversation between Joe (Gordon-Levitt) and Old Joe (Willis) across a table in the roadside diner they frequent. It was the first scene Willis worked on with Gordon-Levitt, and the first time that Johnson showed the two men in profile, selling the mirror-image synchronicity of the plot. The crew spent three days shooting this sequence, with Johnson going above and beyond to guarantee that nothing was missed.

"At various points, we had two cameras going for a lot of it," he said. "Our favorite statistic was, in the course of these three days, we shot more film than we did for the entirety of *Brick*."

Johnson called the diner conversation "its own little movie wedged into the middle of a bigger movie," which also had "a lot of weight on it for a lot of different reasons." Young Joe had the rare opportunity to question his older self about the possible life he would lead. And Old Joe could stare down his disappointing former self, a drug-addled murderer with "a fucking child mentality," and remind himself why he fought so hard to leave this version of himself in the past.

"I knew what I wanted these two to butt heads about, and I knew where I wanted it to end up, but I didn't know much beyond that," Johnson said. "It was a real experience for me to work with a dialogue scene of this length and keep it as engaging as any of the action scenes, which was the goal."[4]

The diner confrontation is crucial. But it pales in comparison to the second sequence that required Willis's emotional expressiveness, and ability to convey the passage of a lifetime through an assortment of glances. Johnson uses a montage to show the audience an alternate timeline during which Joe completes his job, peacefully lives his life, stockpiles thirty years of memories, and arrives at the moment when he's sent back in time to confront his younger self. It's the beating heart of the movie, because during this sequence, Joe moves to Shanghai—and meets his soulmate (Summer Qing).

"She's gonna save your life," Old Joe says in the diner, so Johnson uses the montage to show us exactly how. Every shot of Willis captured by Johnson conveys the joy, surprise, contentment, and love of a life well lived. Willis's acting in these visual snippets is spectacular, made all the more impressive because the montage features no dialogue. Willis and Qing sell the couple's deep emotional journey with gestures and reactions. Words are unnecessary.

These scenes are the reason one hires Willis. Of course the veteran action hero can comfortably carry the requisite gun play that surfaces in the film's explosive third act. But not every action superstar enjoys the emotional range that convinces the audience to buy into his mission, which is ethically complicated and morally questionable.

Gordon-Levitt captured the essence of Willis when he said, "He's the star of *Pulp Fiction*. He's in *Sin City*. He's in *12 Monkeys*. I mean, I don't know how many other huge action stars there are who have also been in some of the greatest movies of recent times. That's Bruce for you."[5]

—3—

Willis appeared in six feature films in 2012, including Wes Anderson's *Moonrise Kingdom*, Stephen Frears's shaggy gambling comedy *Lay the Favorite*, and the overstuffed but entertaining *The Expendables 2*. At the time, he considered *Looper* to be his favorite. "It's better than anything I've ever done," Willis raved in an interview. "Rian did an amazing thing. He conceived an original story. He wrote it, sold it, stuck with it, directed it, and finished it. That's just tough to do in this town. Someone always weasels into the process. That didn't happen here.

"It's more than an original story," Willis continued. "It's a story people are going to talk about, and see twice. And argue about. I was arguing with myself about the story when I read it the first time. That's all Rian Johnson, beginning to end."[6]

Looper starts to show the seeds of what will entertain Johnson as a story-teller. He carries over the film noir attitude that coated his dialogue in *Brick*, just not set in a high school. He grows more comfortable with star-powered ensembles that eventually would show up for his scintillating whodunits, *Knives Out*, *Glass Onion*, and *Poker Face*. And he hints at the antiestablishment, rebellious confidence that allowed him to challenge the old way of thinking on a Star Wars movie, breaking the mold to create something genuine with *Star Wars: Episode VIII—The Last Jedi*. The opposing definitions of heroism and the lengths one must go to vanquish evil can trace back to *Looper*, and those arguments Willis said he had with himself while reading the screenplay.

We've yet to mention the reason Old Joe fights to remain in 2044. In the diner, Old Joe mentions the Rainmaker, a mythological figure his younger counterpart heard rumblings about. This futuristic enforcer somehow managed to single-handedly decimate the five largest crime syndicates. To maintain his grip on the underworld, the Rainmaker is closing all loops and killing all Loopers. His goons killed Old Joe's wife in the process, removing our hero's reason for living yet giving him new motivation to survive: revenge.

TriStar Pictures, at the time of release, marketed *Looper* hard on the mirror-image resemblances of the movie's leading men, and the promise of time-travel thrills. But *Looper* resonates as timeless science fiction because those two gimmicks don't matter. They're window dressing to the emotional motivations pushing Johnson's characters forward. A certain level of textbook Willis heroism definitely exists in *Looper*. He's hellbent on changing his wife's future by altering the past. But Johnson also writes an authentic stubbornness into Old Joe that prevents an easy solution to the problem at hand and gives Willis complex wrinkles to explore. Try to choose a side when Young Joe offers his counterpart a simple, sensical solution. "Show me our wife's picture. When I meet her in our shared future, I'll turn and walk in the other direction. We never meet. We never fall in love. She never dies."

"If you give her up, she's safe," Joe says, and he's right. That's probably what Old Joe should do.

When emotions are involved, though, it's never that simple.

"I'm not going to give her up," Old Joe swears. "I'm going to save her." And by any means necessary. *Looper* goes down several dark moral avenues as it untangles its central quandary. Old Joe's willing to murder three children on the off chance they might grow up to become the Rainmaker. Young Joe even contemplates this option once he meets Cid (Pierce Gagnon) and deduces that he is the kid who'll grow up to reign holy terror down on a futuristic society.

These are the arguments Willis wanted audiences to have. While the film's third act ramps up to the requisite shootouts, explosions, and telekinetic rage that have been promised, these end up being *Looper's* dullest moments when compared with the moral quandaries that are baked into Johnson's premise. *Looper's* biggest gut punches are found in the script, and the answers it provides to some challenging ethical questions, such as "Would you have the intestinal fortitude to kill five-year-old Adolph Hitler if given the chance?" But also, "If a mother could give a child who was destined for horror enough love, could she generate enough empathy to change the course of history?"

The strength of Johnson's screenplay, as well as Willis's performance, is that every time I rewatch *Looper*, my answers to those questions change.

CHAPTER FOURTEEN
ARMAGEDDON

Director: Michael Bay
Cast: Bruce Willis, Ben Affleck, Billy Bob Thornton, Liv Tyler, Steve Buscemi, Will Patton, Owen Wilson, Michael Clarke Duncan, Peter Stormare
Release Date: July 1, 1998

> *Bruce is going to tell the guys that they did a bad job of building the drill tank. He's a salt-of-the-Earth guy. And the NASA "nerdanauts" don't understand his salt-of-the-Earth ways. His rough-and-tumble ways. Like, somehow, they can build rocket ships [laughs] but they don't understand what makes a good tranny!*
>
> —BEN AFFLECK ON THE DVD COMMENTARY TRACK

—1—

Professor Leonid Sokolov believes he knows when life on Earth might end. The Russian astronomer from St. Petersburg State University actually circled a specific date on the calendar: April 13, 2036. That's when Sokolov predicts that the asteroid 99942, also known as Apophis, could collide into our planet's surface, with devastating results.

Three scientists from the Kitt Peak National Observatory in Tucson, Arizona, discovered Apophis in 2004. It's one of several asteroids constantly being tracked by NASA's Center for Near-Earth Object Studies, an organization that computes the orbits of celestial bodies, predicts future movements, and assesses the probability of collision with our planet. But Apophis raised concerns because of its projected orbital path—the rock will pass so close to the Earth in 2029 that NASA claims it should be visible to observers on the ground in the Eastern Hemisphere without the aid of binoculars—as well as its size. The space rock's estimated 1,100-foot diameter makes it larger than the Eiffel Tower (1,060 feet tall), but slightly smaller than four football fields laid side by side (1,200 feet).

In case you are curious what the end result of Apophis's possible impact might feel like, here's a comparison. The last known asteroid of consequence to enter the Earth's atmosphere, the Chelyabinsk meteor, struck Russia on February 15, 2013. It traveled at an estimated speed of 42,690 miles per hour. And though the object exploded over Chelyabinsk while still eighteen miles above our surface, the total kinetic energy generated by the blast was equivalent to 500 kilotons of TNT, or thirty-three times the amount of energy released from the atomic bomb that detonated at Hiroshima.

And Chelyabinsk was only fifty-nine feet in diameter.

You can understand why scientists remain concerned about Apophis. Stanford University's Dr. G. Scott Hubbard, an affiliate of aeronautics and astronautics, raised additional red flags when he told the media in 2013, "If a very large asteroid hit—I am talking about something that is miles across—it would probably create the same kind of disaster that wiped out the dinosaurs. We are not talking about ending Earth. We are not talking about ending everything, all life on Earth. But I am pretty sure it would wipe out civilization . . . certainly civilization as we know it."[1]

And professor Sokolov added, "Our task is to consider various alternatives and develop scenarios and plans of action depending on the results of further observations of Apophis."[2]

By "scenarios," could Sokolov mean sending a team of deep-core oil drillers into outer space so they can penetrate the asteroid, drop a nuclear bomb eight hundred feet into the rock's heart, detonate it, and save the world? Because that's the basic plot of Michael Bay's bombastic summer blockbuster *Armageddon*. And as Charlton Heston warned us in the film's opening narration, "It happened before. It will happen again. It's just a question of when."

—2—

The "when" for *Armageddon* ended up being the July 4th weekend in 1998. Touchstone Pictures (and producer Jerry Bruckheimer) greenlit *Armageddon* in part to compete against a similar asteroid-hits-Earth thriller, *Deep Impact*, being produced by Dreamworks and Paramount. Bruckheimer made sure that his movie landed in theaters in time for the lucrative holiday frame, and the decision paid off handsomely. *Armageddon* opened at number one with $36 million in domestic box-office sales—Willis's highest opening weekend total at that point in his career. The film went on to earn $554.6 million that summer, making it Willis's highest-grossing picture. That impressive record only ended up lasting one year. The only other Willis movie to make more than *Armageddon* was M. Night Shyamalan's *The Sixth Sense*, which was released on August 6, 1999, and finished with a global cume of $672.8M.

The irony of *Armageddon*'s tremendous success is that Willis's involvement stems from one of his biggest professional disasters. The year prior, Willis squabbled with director Lee Grant over the creative vision for *Broadway Brawler*, a romantic comedy described by many as *Jerry Maguire*, but set against the backdrop of professional hockey. Twenty days into production, a frustrated Willis (a producer on the film) fired Grant, her producer-husband, Joe Feury, cinematographer William Fraker, and wardrobe designer Carol Oditz. The power move essentially killed the film's momentum and created a significant financial headache. But Disney chairman Joe Roth came up with a solution. His studio brokered a deal that would wipe clean the millions of dollars owed on *Broadway Brawler*, so long as Willis agreed to a three-picture deal for the Mouse House, at a drastically reduced salary. Willis signed on the dotted line, and *Armageddon* ended up being the first project in the package. And that's how Disney managed to only pay Willis $3 million in salary for *Armageddon*, instead of the $20 million he was commanding per picture in 1998.

Marketing tells us Willis is the star of *Armageddon*. He's really not. The asteroid is the star. The Oscar-nominated visual and sound effects used to create the asteroid, and all its tangential destruction, are the star. Before we reach the ten-minute mark of *Armageddon*, the Space Shuttle *Atlantis* explodes and a meteor shower decimates Midtown Manhattan, concluding with the Chrysler Building being cut in half. The top-dollar VFX, paired with Diane Warren's Oscar-nominated song "I Don't Wanna Miss a Thing," probably helped sell more tickets to *Armageddon* than Willis did.

And finally, the red-hot Michael Bay was a huge draw for *Armageddon* at the time of release. After cutting his teeth on music videos and commercials in the 1990s, Bay transitioned to features and quickly established a reputation for explosive action, a fast-paced and aggressive editing style, and a self-confidence that bordered on arrogance. Fans lovingly described the anarchy in his movies as "Bayhem," which the Urban Dictionary defines as "[t]he cinematic conceit of blowing shit up on a large scale, in slow motion and (usually) at sunset."[3]

Audiences couldn't get enough. They devoured Bay's debut feature *Bad Boys*, which turned TV stars Will Smith and Martin Lawrence into overnight box-office draws. Bay's follow-up, *The Rock*, sent Sean Connery and Nicolas Cage to Alcatraz to prevent a nerve-gas attack on San Francisco. It earned $336 million worldwide against a $75 million budget (meaning studio executives loved Bay, as well). People came to *Armageddon* in 1998 for Bay's form of spectacle, as much as they did the all-star cast.

The challenge facing any actor in a Bay movie is cutting through this "Bayhem" to give an actual performance. And certain *Armageddon* cast members—Willis, included—did figure out how to transcend the noise. *Armageddon* would be a lesser movie without the steady hand of Billy Bob Thornton, fresh off his 1997 Oscar win for writing *Sling Blade* and perfectly cast as a no-nonsense NASA problem solver. Disaster movies require an on-screen expert who's responsible for delivering the exposition that keeps the audience up to speed. It's a rote part, but Thornton finds the exact right tone between being the smartest person in a room, and also a grounded, focused government grunt who will pierce through egos if it helps complete the mission.

Steve Buscemi, meanwhile, collaborated with Joel and Ethan Coen (*Fargo*, *The Big Lebowski*), Quentin Tarantino (*Reservoir Dogs*, *Pulp Fiction*), and Adam Sandler (*Airheads*, *Billy Madison*) prior to working with Bay on *Armageddon*. They all tapped into Buscemi's lanky appearance and flippant comedic delivery to create unforgettable characters. *Armageddon* was no different. While each member of Willis's core-drilling team brought a distinct color to the equation, Buscemi stood out by making his character, Rockhound, a degenerate gambler and probable serial sex offender who's also a genius, and likely smarter than every NASA scientist contributing to the unorthodox mission. Buscemi's rascal personality somehow makes Rockhound likeable, even when his brain succumbs to space dementia and he climbs aboard the nuclear bomb, riding it like Slim Pickens near the end of Stanley Kubrick's *Dr. Strangelove.*

Willis is the third cast member to triumph over Bay's excessive use of visual effects and explosions. But what's remarkable about Willis in *Armageddon* is how unremarkable he has to be to make his mark. Harry Stamper's the undisputed leader of the movie's ensemble, a commander who provides a calm hand in the eye of some very crazy storms. While very much a Hollywood movie star, Willis taps into his blue-collar background for Stamper, and effortlessly assumes the role of father figure to his feisty daughter, Grace (Liv Tyler); his surrogate son, A. J. (Ben Affleck); and the roughnecks that make up his work family. Harry's the man who keeps his team laser focused on its improbable sci-fi mission. And he's the one who's willing to sacrifice himself if it means finishing the job.

"I've been drilling holes in the earth for thirty years. And I have never—NEVER—missed a depth that I have aimed for," Willis's unwavering character tells a mutinous astronaut (William Fichter) when it looks like their space mission might go sideways. "And by God, I am not going to miss this one. I will make eight hundred feet."

As the film's leading man, Willis gets more than a few moments to convey genuine emotion amid the chaos. But he doesn't match the movie's combustible energy with his own histrionics. He's confident, forceful, and efficient when confronting Fichter over a nuclear bomb that's counting down to detonation. He's resilient when switching places with A. J. so he can manually trigger the bomb. And he's sympathetic and loving during his final goodbye to Grace.

And because he's Bruce Willis, he makes the absolute most out of every minute the movie allows him.

—3—

Armageddon is a very good "bad" movie. Actors try (and usually fail) to sell lines like, "Sir, the override . . . it's been overridden!" The science fueling the script is questionable. Bay's affinity for jingoism starts to ramp up here and continues to gain an enormous head of steam in *Pearl Harbor*, his *Transformers* trilogy, *Pain and Gain*, and *13 Hours*. *Armageddon* also suffers the bloat that commonly affects Bay's films.

Affleck went on record as saying the plot of Bay's sci-fi thriller makes no sense, courtesy of a relatively infamous DVD commentary track recorded for the film's Criterion Collection release. During the recording, the costar generously admits the story hinges on "a little bit of a logic stretch."

"I asked Michael why it was easier to train oil drillers to become astronauts than it was to train astronauts to become oil drillers," Affleck said, bringing up a simple logical issue found at the heart of *Armageddon* that—once pointed out—deflates the entire narrative. "And he told me to shut the fuck up. So that was the end of that talk. He was like, 'You know, Ben, just shut up, OK? You know, this is a real plan.' I was like, 'You mean it's a real plan at NASA to train oil drillers?' And he was like, 'Just shut your mouth!'

"Let's face it," Affleck continued, turning his attention to the NASA engineers depicted in the blockbuster. "They don't know jack about drilling? How hard can it be? Aim the drill at the ground and turn it on. 'You think it's just drilling a hole? There's a lot you got to know about . . . when are you going to break, snap off an edge on a tranny and you're on a corner of a hot pipe, and you're gonna get a gas pocket!' Like, 'Yeah, what about when the booster rockets don't fire and you're EVA suit and your zero-gravity. . . . Didn't you see *Apollo 13*, boy?'"[4]

Both men were right. But most audience members didn't care. They weren't buying a ticket to *Armageddon* for its scientific accuracy. And they weren't listening to critics like Roger Ebert, who famously skewered the blockbuster by claiming, "The movie is an assault on the eyes, the ears, the brain, common sense, and the human desire to be entertained. No matter what they're charging to get in, it's worth more to get out."[5]

Armageddon became the highest-grossing worldwide ticket earner for 1998, outpacing Steven Spielberg's *Saving Private Ryan* and Roland Emmerich's *Godzilla* (making that quick joke about a dog attacking Godzilla toys in *Armageddon*'s opening scene that much funnier). And while Willis wasn't the sole reason for the film's record-setting turnout, his participation helped continue his steady stream of international box-office hits that included 1997's *The Fifth Element* ($263.8M), 1995's *12 Monkeys* ($168.8M), 1995's *Die Hard with a Vengeance* ($366.1M), and 1994's Pulp Fiction ($212.8M).

The Harry Stamper role seems tame when compared to Willis's other forays into science fiction. The blue-collar oil driller isn't traveling through time, piloting a flying taxicab through a futuristic city, or battling the younger version of himself so he can prevent the rise of a megalomaniac with powerful telekinetic powers. Instead, *Armageddon* serves to remind us that even in a cosmic setting, Willis can ground a story and captivate an audience simply by showing up, doing exactly what's required for the material, delivering a satisfying experience.

Or, as Affleck might say, aiming that drill at the ground and turning it on.

SECTION FOUR
BRUCE WILLIS AND THE AUTEURS

"Whose motorcycle is this?"
"It's a chopper, baby."
"Whose chopper is this?"
"Zed's."
"Who's Zed?"
"Zed's dead, baby. Zed's dead."

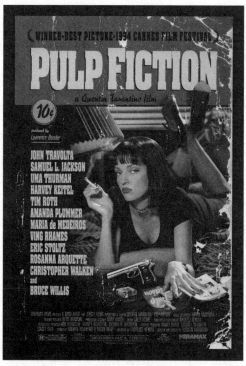

Official movie poster for Quentin Tarantino's *Pulp Fiction*, starring Bruce Willis. *Author's Collection*

Hopefully my forays into Bruce Willis's comedic offerings, his science fiction experiments, and his calculated choice of action projects have proven his versatility and range. This book's main takeaway should be that Willis represented far more than the stereotypical action hero caricature, and his malleability as a performer—incredibly complicated because of his global celebrity—made him an appealing ally for visionaries who were eager to test his boundaries (and benefit from the drawing power of his superstardom).

That application of talent gets displayed in the films of this next section, which follows Willis through some of his most influential collaborations with auteur directors working in the Hollywood system. The term *auteur* applies to a filmmaker whose "personal influence and artistic control over a movie are so great that the filmmaker is regarded as the author of the movie." Quentin Tarantino, M. Night Shyamalan, Brian De Palma, Robert Benton, Robert Rodriguez, and Wes Anderson undoubtedly earn this label. And all six of them coax completely different performances from this multifaceted leading man.

Some of these films worked better than others. Some didn't work at all. But these films all are pivotal chapters of Willis's storied career, solidifying his reputation as a movie star willing to risk failure—or exert his substantial power—when he believed in the vision of a particular storyteller. *Looper, The Fifth Element*, and *12 Monkeys* also permitted me to highlight screenplays and directors who intrigued Willis. But these six films in this next section are, to me, uniquely Willis, and are seminal moments in his filmography. You can't fully appreciate what Willis accomplished over the course of his career without understanding everything that went into his collaborations with these masterful directors. The roles that he took that prepared him for these moments, and the doors that continued to open because of his on-screen contributions to each.

"I think the great leading men, I think it's often overlooked how good [of an] actor they are. And Bruce is a great actor," said Matt Damon, his costar in Steven Soderbergh's comedic *Ocean's 12*. "And he was great in a lot of films. And if you look at his body of work, he did a lot of things that are kind of surprising. . . . And backed a lot of filmmakers. I remember when he went to do *Nobody's Fool* just because he wanted to work with (Paul)

Newman. He knew it was his chance to work with Newman. And he was the biggest star in the world! But he's, like, 'No, no, no. I'm going to go do that supporting role.'"[1]

The only baffling mystery that remains is how Willis never received a single Oscar nomination for his performances in the following films. Further proof that in Hollywood, crimes often are committed in broad daylight.

CHAPTER FIFTEEN
PULP FICTION

Director: Quentin Tarantino
Cast: John Travolta, Samuel L. Jackson, Uma Thurman, Bruce Willis,
Tim Roth, Harvey Keitel, Ving Rhames, Maria de Medeiros
Release Date: October 14, 1994

> *Do you have any idea what he had to go through to get me that watch? I
> don't have time to go into it, but he went through a lot. Now, all this other
> shit, you could set on fire. But I specifically reminded you not to forget the
> fucking watch!*
>
> —BUTCH (WILLIS) TO FABIENNE (MARIA DE MEDEIROS)
> ON BUTCH'S VERY BAD DAY

—1—

Sally Menke's favorite scene that she ever worked on with Quentin Tarantino
was a Bruce Willis sequence from *Pulp Fiction*.

Tarantino knew, going into his directorial debut, *Reservoir Dogs*, that he
wanted a female editor. "I just felt a female editor would be more nurtur-
ing. To the movie, and to me," he said.[1] The director chose Menke, a native
New Yorker and graduate of NYU's Tisch School of the Arts Film Program,
even though Menke's previous editing credits were unremarkable. She honed
her craft on the 1990 live-action *Teenage Mutant Ninja Turtles* movie, cut
the Nick Nolte–led neo-noir picture *Mulholland Falls* for director Lee Tama-
hori, and collaborated with Oliver Stone on one of his lesser features, 1993's
Heaven and Earth.

After reading Tarantino's *Reservoir Dogs* script, however, Menke became
obsessed with landing this gig. While contemplating a possible collaboration with Tarantino, Menke thought of another famous Hollywood pairing

between a prestigious male director and his acclaimed female editor. "[Martin] Scorsese was a hero of mine, especially as he used a female editor in Thelma Schoonmaker," she wrote in 2009, "and this script just had that tone."[2]

Tarantino and Menke's partnership went on to rival that of Scorsese and Schoonmaker, the three-time Oscar-winning editor responsible for *Raging Bull, Goodfellas, Gangs of New York, The Departed,* and *The Irishman.* Beginning with *Reservoir Dogs,* Menke edited every Tarantino movie until her untimely death on a Los Angeles hiking trail in 2010. That list includes *Jackie Brown, Kill Bill, Death Proof, Inglourious Basterds,* and Tarantino's crowning achievement, *Pulp Fiction,* which happens to include a Willis scene that Menke considered to be her absolute favorite.

The scene in question takes place in the back of a taxicab. Fading prize fighter Butch Coolidge (Willis) just won a bout, mistakenly killing his opponent in the process. Butch has fled the scene, however, because he promised the very powerful Marsellus Wallace (Ving Rhames) that he'd throw the fight, earning Wallace a fortune in gambling profits. "In the fifth, my ass goes down," Butch stated to Wallace. But it didn't. And from the back seat of a cab, Butch explains to inquisitive driver Esmarelda Villalobos (Angela Jones) what it felt like to kill another man with his bare hands.

"That was Sally's favorite edited scene," Tarantino said. "She goes, 'Of all the scenes we cut together, that was my favorite, as far as the work I did.'"[3]

Consider the weight of that statement. Menke edited Samuel L. Jackson's emphatic delivery of Ezekiel 25:17 ("And you will know my name is the Lord when I lay my vengeance upon thee!"). She edited Michael Madsen's chilling dance to "Stuck in the Middle with You" by Stealers Wheel. She spliced together Uma Thurman's decimation of the Crazy 88s, and Christoph Waltz's intense interrogation of a terrified French dairy farmer over a glass of fresh milk. And of all those indelible moments from her collaborations with Tarantino, a static two-shot anchored by the commanding Willis ranked as her favorite. That says something about the leading man's magnetism in a scene, the gravitational pull he exerted on the audience, and the amount he could communicate using glances, squints, and pauses in his dialogue.

Tarantino echoed sentiments expressed by numerous Willis collaborators when he said, "Bruce is one of our great movie stars. And not only is he a great movie star, he was a terrific actor. He was a very adventuresome movie star. He used his movie stardom to a really interesting effect. He knew the kind of action movies that he could do, that would really deliver well. . . . But then also, he was very quick to work with different respected directors because he wanted to work with those directors. So he used his movie star to help those directors get those movies made."[4]

Pulp Fiction being one of his finest.

—2—

You can't overestimate the magnitude of the impact *Pulp Fiction* had on the film industry. The 1994 release world premiered at the Cannes Film Festival in May, where it won the event's prestigious Palme d'Or. By October, *Pulp Fiction* had blazed an unexpected path, and amplified the drawing power of independent cinema, when it opened wide to play suburban multiplexes as well as arthouse theaters.

Seeing *Pulp Fiction* in a crowded theater became a mandatory event. I remember seeing it for the first time in an AMC Theatre located in a shopping mall in Northern Virginia. It felt unlike anything else that had been offered at that location before. The audience collectively screamed when John Travolta plunged a needle directly into Uma Thurman's heart. We laughed, to stave off the shock, after Marvin (Phil LaMarr) got shot in the face. We squirmed through Butch and Wallace's encounter with "The Gimp" (Stephen Hibbert). And we marveled at the circular narrative structure of Tarantino's story once it became clear that Jules Winnfield (Samuel L. Jackson) and Vincent Vega (Travolta) were eating breakfast in the same diner being robbed by Pumpkin (Tim Roth) and Honey Bunny (Amanda Plummer) from the movie's electrifying opening scene.

Pulp Fiction bulldozed through an invisible barrier that stood between independent movies and mainstream audiences. The film earned an unthinkable $213.9 million in worldwide grosses—more than any other indie production that came before it. In the wake of *Pulp Fiction*'s success, major

Hollywood studios reflexively established production arms such as Focus Features and Fox Searchlight, which were dedicated to discovering, producing, and distributing independent cinema. And perhaps most shockingly, *Pulp Fiction* redefined the type of people who were allowed to make movies in the insular Hollywood community. Tarantino and his *Pulp Fiction* cowriter Roger Avary eschewed the film-school route of their predecessors. They earned their education behind the counter of Video Archives, a movie-rental shop in Southern California that offered the duo a library of global cinematic offerings, and all the time in the world to sit around with like-minded junkies and analyze the films and directors they admired.

The ripples caused by *Pulp Fiction* can still be felt in Hollywood. The film's dangerous, provocative, and almost forbidden tone inspired a tidal wave of substandard rip-offs, all populated by foul-mouthed and too-cool criminals. These knockoffs continue to surface every few years to this day, though none have come close to matching Tarantino's masterpiece. *Pulp Fiction*, and specifically Willis's participation, encouraged more traditional A-list movie stars to venture into the indie cinema pool, chasing the type of awards attention that potentially followed such risky transitions. And Tarantino himself continues to fuel a cottage industry of insatiable film enthusiasts who absorb, process, and regurgitate his opinions on cinema, past, present, and future. There are endless books and podcasts, some created by the man himself, that can help you better understand *Pulp Fiction*'s seismic impact on pop culture and the film industry.

That's not my goal. My hope here is to apply a scalpel to the repetitive commentary that surrounds the film, and slice directly to the core of Willis's enormous contributions. This is an essential film for Willis, featuring one of his most impressive performances.

—3—

"It is the rarest thing in the world to get a script as well written and interesting as *Pulp Fiction*," Willis said during an interview around the time the movie opened 1994's New York Film Festival. "I told Quentin I'd do anything, whatever part he wanted me to play."[5]

That part ended up being Butch Coolidge, a hard-headed bruiser of a boxer Tarantino says he modeled after 1950s character actors Aldo Ray and Ralph Meeker. After Butch reneged on his agreement to throw the fight, he planned to escape California with his own gambling winnings, and his Kewpie-doll girlfriend, Fabienne (Maria de Medeiros), on his arm. Only, Fabienne left a very valuable item behind in the couple's apartment: Butch's father's gold watch. And the boxer's attempt to retrieve it goes more horribly wrong than anyone could imagine.

Pulp Fiction probably ranks as Tarantino's most quotable movie. His fans still call McDonald's Quarter Pounder "a Royale with Cheese." They know how to answer when you ask what Marsellus Wallace looks like. They might even wince when they remember that Zed's dead, baby. Zed's dead. While *Pulp Fiction* received seven Academy Award nominations, including Best Picture and Director, Tarantino's Best Writing Oscar ended up being the movie's only win.

So it's remarkable that in a movie celebrated for its dialogue, Willis's best scenes are characterized by silence, and the enormous tension he generates by saying next to nothing.

Two minutes and six seconds—that's how much time passes from the moment Al Green's "Let's Stay Together" starts to play until Butch first speaks to Marsellus Wallace in their first shared scene. And that's how long Willis stares into the lens, listening to an intimidating crime boss tell his prideful character why he has no options left, save for betting against himself. An actor has to have extreme confidence in their abilities—and trust in their director—to patiently wait, to remain still, and yet manage to hold the viewer's attention by doing next to nothing.

"It's such a fascinating effect in the film," Willis said. "Because you would think that the question is, 'Is it going to hold? Is it going to be interesting to watch?' And what it does is it just sucks the audience right into it. Because all of a sudden, you just look at my eyes, and see, 'What am I thinking? What am I doing?' And that's right where Quentin wanted you. He wanted you to get inside of my head."[6]

This interaction is an appetizer. The full meal arrives later in the film, when Tarantino saddles Willis with nearly six minutes of wordless action (aside from him whispering, "Looking good, Butch") as the character approaches his Los Angeles apartment building, enters, retrieves his prized gold watch, and suddenly realizes he got the drop on one of Wallace's hitmen. Butch's silence throughout this sequence helps to punctuate the looming threat of the people he has double-crossed. We're waiting for someone to shout his name or recognize his presence, and that apprehension generates an obscene amount of tension. Willis understands that he creates more pressure in the sequence by doing less. There's brilliant economy to the editing and choreography of the gold watch rescue mission, with Tarantino slowly tightening the vice because he's aware of the insanity he's about to unleash on his characters (and the audience) in the basement of a seedy pawn shop.

"I think this is one of the most controlled performances that I've done," Willis said. "There are times when it's completely out of control. The things that I do are really out of control. But for the most part, it's a very romantic role. I don't know how you reconcile romance and violence in the same character. It's a weird combination. I mean, the whole film is that. The whole film is a strange combination of humor and violence . . . but it's like watching a car accident. You just can't help but watch."[7]

Silent film actors used expressive movements and exaggerated reactions as substitutes for dialogue. Their technique began in the theater, and evolved into flexible physical performance through the vaudeville era. Willis goes the opposite route in *Pulp Fiction*. He mentions his eyes in his initial scene with Wallace, and how they serve as internal windows to Butch's conflicted soul. For long stretches of the apartment sequence, though, Tarantino chooses to shoot Willis from behind, giving us a look at the back of the actor's head that robs him of the ability to show us concern, fear, or adulation through his facial reactions. Even when Willis permits some emotion to peek through, it's with subtle mannerisms that we've come to associate with the star. My favorite, easily, is the incredulous smirk that crosses Butch's face when he safely returns to his car with the watch in his possession. For a second, he allows himself to start believing he's going to get away with it.

"That's how you're going to beat 'em, Butch. They keep underestimating you," he whispers.

As you no doubt know, the getaway isn't going to be so easy.

—4—

Numerous actors circled Tarantino's *Pulp Fiction* screenplay, begging for parts. *Reservoir Dogs* established the writer-director as an ascending voice in Hollywood. The hungriest thrill-seekers in town wanted a piece of whatever he chose to do next.

How many of them, I wonder, paused—or even outright passed—once they got to the terms *ball gag* and *The Gimp* in the section of Tarantino's *Pulp Fiction* script titled "The Gold Watch"?

Matt Dillon apparently did. Tarantino wrote the Butch part with Dillon in mind, but rescinded the offer after the *Drugstore Cowboy* star told the director he needed to sleep on the screenplay before committing.

"He didn't 100 percent get it," Tarantino said. "And he didn't want to play that part. He wanted to play the Vincent character. That was almost all the way down the line. Any time I offered somebody a part, they wanted to play somebody else."[8]

Including Willis, who reportedly asked Tarantino for Travolta's Vincent Vega part when they first met to discuss *Pulp Fiction*. Willis might have even thrown his movie-star weight around when he was told no. "Of course, Bruce is, 'What? I'm not going to play the lead?'" recalls Mike Simpson, Tarantino's one-time agent at William Morris Agency, about casting the *Die Hard* star. "'I'm going to be bound up by some hillbilly in a pawn shop so that *John Travolta* can be the lead?'"[9]

The *Pulp Fiction* basement scene in which Willis eventually participated is as shocking and harrowing as it is unexpected, a slice of John Boorman's *Deliverance* transported from the remote North Georgia woods to the populated strip malls of Los Angeles. You initially believe that the man behind the pawn shop counter, Maynard (Duane Whitaker), is endangered by the arrival of a feuding Butch and Marsellus. Instead, this shopkeeper and his accomplices are the actual threat.

Tarantino shuffles through genres repeatedly in *Pulp Fiction*, all in an effort to keep the audience off balance. A sultry and flirtatious date night between a hitman and his boss's wife suddenly transforms into a pulse-pounding, race-the-clock, drug-overdose thriller. A philosophical conversation between two criminals who may have experienced an act of divine intervention ends up becoming a gripping Mexican standoff that has to be diffused by a killer in the middle of a spiritual awakening.

The pawn shop pivot is the film's most extreme. And Tarantino is only able to successfully transition from a shootout in the streets and a vicious fist fight to a vulnerable, helpless situation involving sexual violation because Willis and Rhames are such spectacular actors who ground the reality of this surreal situation. If they are not able to credibly convey the wide spectrum of emotions Butch and Marsellus experience, then *Pulp Fiction* potentially flies off the tracks and descends into camp. "Bring out The Gimp" becomes a punchline, and not a four-word phrase that conjures spine-tingling terror.

Once again, Tarantino asks Willis to do the heaviest lifting without any dialogue, so unusual in a film where almost every other character receives a delicious soliloquy, a memorable passage, or a marketable catchphrase. Some of Butch's silence in the basement scene is attributable to the ball gag Maynard places in his mouth. The rest, though, is a directorial choice, with Tarantino making terrific use of the commanding presence of Willis.

Ignore the rest of *Pulp Fiction*, and the pawn shop scene alone is an Oscar worthy tour-de-force performance by the actor. By the time we reach this scene, we're invested in the underdog boxer, his relationship with Fabienne, and his triumph over Wallace, so we're rooting for his escape. Our eyes zero in on Butch the moment he wakes up in the basement, bound and gagged next to the man who moments ago was trying to kill him. Willis doesn't show panic as he processes the insanity of the situation. He avoids eye contact with Zed (Peter Greene), as if *not* acknowledging him might make the sadist disappear. And Willis even keeps Butch somewhat collected once he frees himself from the chair, knocks out the Gimp, and heads for the shop's exit.

But what follows, I'd argue, is the most extraordinary stretch of acting in Willis's entire career.

Butch reaches the front door. He's about to escape a nightmarish situation. But he stops long enough to look back and processes what's happening to Wallace, who until minutes ago was his bitter enemy. Willis sells the character's moral uncertainty in his pained hesitation. Try as he might, Butch can't leave another man in that circumstance.

Over Butch's shoulder, Tarantino hangs a Tennessee license plate so it appears in frame. It's a deliberate call back to the boxer's Knoxville, Tennessee, roots, and the visit Captain Koons (Christopher Walken) made in a flashback to deliver the gold watch to young Butch (Chandler Lindauer, who, like his adult counterpart, says one word in his entire four-minute and thirty-eight-second scene, predominantly listening). And all of a sudden, this line from Koons takes on new meaning.

"Hopefully, you'll never have to experience this yourself, but when two men are in a situation like me and your dad were for as long as we were, you take on certain responsibilities of the other," Koons said.

Two scenes set in appalling locations: a POW camp, and an S&M dungeon. Two scenes made up of male acquaintances forging an alliance. And two scenes that somehow involve the ass. Tarantino brings Butch's family history full circle. And now he's taking on "certain responsibilities" for Wallace.

You can see this entire transition in Willis's face as he stands in the pawn shop's front door. He's scared. Then he's relieved. Then he's tortured by the difficult decision. And finally, he's resilient, comfortable with the decision to head back down into the sodomy chamber and rescue his killer. But he isn't going empty handed. The parade of weapons Butch test drives before going after Zed and Maynard is both hilarious and horrifying. Willis communicates the boxer's rising confidence by bulging Butch's eyes and lighting up his features as he moves from the hammer to the baseball bat, from the chainsaw to the samurai sword.

The conclusion of the basement sequence marks the closest that Willis comes, in *Pulp Fiction*, to replicating his familiar action persona and falling back on those comfortable tropes. Butch had been portrayed as a lover, not a fighter. The shot of Willis slinking down Maynard's basement steps, his T-shirt soaked in blood and a sword clenched in his hands, fits better inside a *Die Hard* sequel than it did with any scene Tarantino had written for Willis up to that point.

The visceral sight of a bloodied Butch sitting on Zed's chopper is so worrisome, it actually makes Fabienne start to cry. She doesn't recognize the tender man she cuddled and kissed earlier in the film while discussing her desire for a potbelly, and plotting out her breakfast options. So our hero must slip back into his doting, attentive lover mode, the one that sets her at ease. And Willis's ability to play all sides of Butch—the subservient criminal, the blood-thirsty boxer, the sentimental boyfriend, the angry son, the terrified captive, and the vengeful angel of death—makes *Pulp Fiction* his most versatile and awards-worthy role.

All the more reason why the Academy failing to even nominate Willis for an Oscar—while bestowing nominations on costars Jackson, Thurman, and Travolta—is an inexcusable, embarrassing, and shameful omission, and one of many that make it difficult to continue to defend the value of that hollow industry trinket.

CHAPTER SIXTEEN
THE SIXTH SENSE

Director: M. Night Shyamalan
Cast: Bruce Willis, Haley Joel Osment, Toni Collette, Olivia Williams
Release Date: August 6, 1999

> *I see dead people.*
> —COLE (OSMENT) TO DR. MALCOLM CROWE (WILLIS)

—1—

Spoiler alert: Bruce Willis was dead the entire time.

Trust me. No one saw it coming. I sat in a packed theater on opening night for *The Sixth Sense*, not even knowing that a twist ending was on its way. You could actually feel the wave of collective realization surge through the audience the moment everything became clear. Willis was one of the ghosts that Haley Joel Osment had been seeing. His character, Dr. Malcolm Crowe, died in the opening scene from a gunshot wound. M. Night Shyamalan pulled the rug out from underneath his audience, and you couldn't help but feel gratified, exhilarated, and basically in awe as the final pieces of the director's puzzle fell into place.

That celebrated twist ending was only the first of multiple surprises associated with *The Sixth Sense*. Analysts never anticipated that the third feature from an unknown Philadelphia-based filmmaker was going to take the summer 1999 box office by storm. Powered by critical acclaim and strong word-of-mouth recommendations, *The Sixth Sense* spent five consecutive weeks in the number one slot on the box-office charts, and became the first film since James Cameron's *Titanic* to gross more than $20 million each for five weekends.

Most surprisingly, at least for the purpose of this book, *The Sixth Sense* holds two significant financial records for Willis. Shyamalan's thriller earned $672.8 million in worldwide ticket sales by the end of its theatrical run, making it the highest-grossing film of the actor's career. Additionally, because he agreed to a compensation deal worth 17.5% of both the film's profits and its DVD proceeds, *The Sixth Sense* made Willis the first actor to earn more than $100 million in salary for a single film—not an explosive action feature—and not a chapter from his signature Die Hard saga. But rather, it was a quiet, meditative ghost story where he supports a remarkable child performer and rarely raises his voice above a whisper.

The Sixth Sense is a magic trick. It convinces us to look at one clenched fist, where we believe its answers lie. Then, it opens its other hand to reveal the actual truth. And we immediately want to go back to the beginning, watch the trick all over again, and try to figure out how the storyteller pulled it off.

What's amusing is, once all the cards are displayed on the table, the movie is deceptively simple—not unlike the penny trick that Dr. Malcolm (Willis) teaches Cole (Osment) during one of their sessions. When you say the plot out loud, you begin to wonder how you missed all the signs and clues pointing toward the reveal. The film opens with a child psychologist getting shot by a disgruntled former patient. "The next Fall," as we are told, the doctor tries to make amends by assisting his next case, a haunted boy—literally and figuratively—who lives with his single mom (Toni Colette), struggles to fit in at school, and eventually tells his shrink that he sees dead people.

"They don't see each other. They only see what they want to see. They don't know they're dead," Cole tells Dr. Malcolm. "They're everywhere."

Of course Willis's character would be one of them. We watched him get shot in the first scene. And Cole openly tells the audience that the ghosts don't know they have died—which helps explain Malcolm's actions in the film in all the scenes that don't involve Cole. How did we miss these obvious reveals?

Because it didn't matter. Even with the clues laid out in front of us, the ending of *The Sixth Sense* delivered a knockout punch. And even if you know where *The Sixth Sense* ends up, there's so much to enjoy about the ride. It's one of the most satisfying features on Willis's résumé.

The Return of Bruno (HBO, 1988). Shown: Bruce Willis (as Bruno). *HBO/Photofest ©HBO*

Moonlighting (ABC) 1985–1989. Shown from left: Bruce Willis, Cybill Shepherd. ABC/*Photofest* ©*ABC*

Die Hard (1988) Directed by John McTiernan. Shown: Bruce Willis. *Twentieth Century Fox Film Corporation/Photofest* ©*Twentieth Century Fox*

The Bonfire of the Vanities (1990) Directed by Brian De Palma. Shown from left: Bruce Willis, Melanie Griffith, Tom Hanks. *Warner Bros./Photofest ©Warner Bros.*

Death Becomes Her (1992) Directed by Robert Zemeckis. Shown: Meryl Streep, Bruce Willis. *Universal Pictures/Photofest ©Universal Pictures*

Die Hard 2 (1990) Directed by Renny Harlin. Shown: Bruce Willis (as John McClane). *Twentieth Century Fox Film Corporation/Photofest ©Twentieth Century Fox*

Pulp Fiction (1994) Directed by Quentin Tarantino. Shown: Bruce Willis. *Miramax Films/Photofest* *©Miramax Films*

12 Monkeys (1995) Directed by Terry Gilliam. Shown from left: Bruce Willis, Brad Pitt. *Universal Pictures/Photofest ©Universal Pictures*

The Fifth Element (1997) Directed by Luc Besson. Shown: Bruce Willis (as Major Korben Dallas). *Columbia Pictures/Sony Pictures Entertainment/Photofest ©Columbia Pictures/Sony Pictures Entertainment*

Armageddon (1998) Directed by Michael Bay. Shown: Bruce Willis (as Harry S. Stamper). *Buena Vista Pictures/Photofest © Buena Vista Pictures*

The Sixth Sense (1999) Directed by M. Night Shyamalan. Shown: Bruce Willis, Haley Joel Osment. *Buena Vista Pictures/Photofest © Buena Vista Pictures*

Live Free or Die Hard (2007) a.k.a. *Die Hard 4* Directed by Len Wiseman. Shown: Bruce Willis. *Twentieth Century Fox Film Corporation/Photofest ©Twentieth Century Fox*

The Expendables 2 (2012) Directed by Simon West. Shown from left: Arnold Schwarzenegger, Sylvester Stallone, Bruce Willis. *Lionsgate/Photofest © Lionsgate, Photo by Frank Masi*

Looper (2012) Directed ty Rian Johnson. Shown from left: Bruce Willis, Joseph Gordon-Levitt. *TriStar Pictures/Photofest © TriStar Pictures, Photo by Alan Markfield*

—2—

And yet, Willis gives the third-best performance in *The Sixth Sense*. That's not a slight toward him. It's a compliment to the brilliant, compassionate performances by his costars Osment and Colette, both of whom received Best Supporting Oscar nominations in their respective categories. Osment, who was eleven years old at the time of filming, performs beyond his years. He shows a deep understanding of sadness and possesses a grip on melancholy that shouldn't be possible for a boy his age. He also earns sympathy for Cole through the softened and earnest delivery of his dialogue. All you want to do while watching Osment in *The Sixth Sense* is reach through the screen and safeguard this tormented child at all costs.

That's why Colette is so effective as Cole's protective mother. She's the audience's surrogate, trying hard to pierce through her child's malaise and eliminate whatever problems are plaguing him. She's frustrated by an inability to help her child, yet adamant about the fact that her unconditional love for Cole eclipses any impatience she's feeling as a single caregiver. Their unforgettable breakthrough scene in the car while they wait for an accident to clear is the movie's most emotional moment. The devastating scene creates an opportunity for Colette to connect with the spirit of her late mother, and provides the audience with a cathartic release due to Cole and his mom finally communicating about his unique supernatural abilities. This duo plays the sequence perfectly.

Again, this does not diminish Willis's contributions to *The Sixth Sense*. The movie doesn't work unless the actor cast as the child psychologist forges a bond with Osment in which the audience can invest. Willis used performance tools he had developed over the years to supplement Shyamalan's writing. Malcolm possesses an inherent need to save someone, to rescue them from a complicated situation. Willis credibly filled that hero role in the audience's minds, even though Malcolm relies on word games and childlike magic tricks instead of guns and fists, like some of Willis's previous saviors.

"The first thing I told Bruce was, 'I need to see you vulnerable in this movie,'" Shyamalan said. "Because he has such an air about him of, 'No matter what happens, he'll figure it out.' And I wanted to see him hurt and vulnerable."[1]

Also, Willis's work in *Pulp Fiction* (1994) and *12 Monkeys* (1995) educated him on the usefulness of silence in a performance. Willis undoubtedly was the star of *The Sixth Sense*, the name in bold at the top of the poster. But the film exceeds its potential because Willis, the actor, understood the need to step back, listen, observe, and keep the spotlight on his engrossing young costar. There's value in that sacrifice that can't be overstated.

"I work on little things like that, trying to say a great deal with as little effort as possible, as little 'seeing the acting.' I don't want you to see the acting. I just want you to see the behavior," Willis said.[2]

The Sixth Sense also represents, for Willis, a movie and role that arrived at his doorstep at the exact right time. There are characters and parts that are synonymous with certain actors because they brought exactly what was needed to make the movie soar. But if that same person tried to play that same part any earlier, or later, in their career, it might not have worked out as well. Willis needed specific experiences, both on and off of a movie set, to properly play the intriguing facets of Dr. Malcolm Crowe's personality.

Aside from the placidity in Crowe, there's also a playfulness to the child psychologist's paternal tricks, evident in the way that Willis improvises some cartoonish physical flourishes while performing a magic trick for Cole during a session. It suggests that Willis had done something similar for one of his own daughters, who would have been around Osment's age at the time of filming. This was a man right in the middle of being a father off camera, and that parental warmth—as well as a persistent, palpable concern—finds its way into Willis's relationship with Osment on camera in *The Sixth Sense*. The movie is that much better because of it.

—3—

Stepping back to observe the totality of Willis's career, there's a noticeable reinvention of the actor's public persona happening around the time of *The Sixth Sense*. One of the industry's most bankable action heroes was gradually transitioning to "Hollywood dad," with his chosen roles involving more fathers and father figures. Willis would be paired with a nine-year-old autistic codebreaker for the predictable thriller *Mercury Rising* in 1998. That same year, he made audiences sob as he bid farewell to his headstrong daughter Grace (Liv Tyler) at the conclusion of Michael Bay's *Armageddon*. They provided an unexpected emotional throughline in what billed itself as a hollow, effects-driven blockbuster. And two years after that, Willis tapped into his natural parental instincts when he played a selfish corporate executive forced to confront his adolescent self in Jon Turtletaub's charming fantasy, Disney's *The Kid*.

The late Roger Ebert picked up on this trend and identified it as "a nice little sideline" when writing about Disney's *The Kid* for the *Chicago Sun Times*.

"It's a sweet film, unexpectedly involving, and shows again that Willis, so easily identified with action movies, is gifted in the areas of comedy and pathos," Ebert observed. "This is a cornball plot, and he lends it credibility just by being in it."[3]

That's also exactly what Willis did for Shyamalan, and for *The Sixth Sense*, itself a story built around the paternal relationship formed between a childless psychologist and a lonely boy whose father has left. Willis lent the movie credibility by being in it. He went to bat for an unknown filmmaker, helped him get his story greenlit, then fended off studio interference so Shyamalan could retain his creative vision. And, whether he realized it at the time or not, he formed a lasting familial relationship with the writer-director that would go on to span four films in two decades.

"[Willis] was my hero. As a kid I had a *Die Hard* poster up on my wall forever. And when I was writing *The Sixth Sense* and there was this *Die Hard* poster, I thought, 'What about that guy? He could play it.' He is from New Jersey, he grew up basically 30 minutes from where I live, so we were always from the same part of the world," Shyamalan said. "To me, [Samuel L. Jackson] and Bruce are somewhere between a big brother and a father figure. They have that vibe for me—a protector vibe—when I think about the two of them."[4]

Willis's films with Shyamalan stand apart from the movie star's other features because the director dwelt on a subdued, introspective side of Willis the audience rarely got to see. Shyamalan reduced the actor's reliance on physicality to emphasize facial reactions and small, almost imperceptible gestures that communicated more than enough. Watch the actor's first scene from their second collaboration, *Unbreakable*. Shyamalan films Willis on the Eastrail 177 train, and frames the actor's face through seats, so we're only able to see his expressions while he talks to an attractive female passenger. It's an engrossing sequence that limits itself in terms of movement, and visually boxes Willis into a corner, yet still tells us so much about the man's marital problems, his lack of self-confidence, and his inability to communicate—crucial aspects to the character he creates through the rest of the story.

Circle back to the financial stats on *The Sixth Sense*. The mammoth crowd pleaser turned Willis into one of Hollywood's highest-paid actors, and it holds the spot for highest-grossing movie of Willis's career. But when you look at the rest of his top five films, it appears to be an anomaly. They are, from two to five: *Armageddon* ($554.6 million); *Live Free or Die Hard* ($382.2M); *G.I. Joe: Retaliation* ($375.7M), and *Die Hard with a Vengeance* ($366.1M). It's the expected mix of blockbusters, sequels, and Die Hard chapters. Four safe action movies, with *The Sixth Sense* being the outlier.

That's not how I see it. Yes, Willis and all involved in the picture caught lightning in a bottle. The unforgettable twist ending, the career-defining performance by Osment, and the pop-culture fervor that followed *The Sixth Sense* created a legitimate Hollywood sensation, of which Willis was a part. But the overwhelming success of this spellbinding ghost story reminds me that Willis wasn't afraid to take chances. He'd sign on for the latest project by an exciting, unproven director. He'd give himself over to a character if he believed in the material. And when it all clicked, like it did with *The Sixth Sense*, the audience would follow.

CHAPTER SEVENTEEN
THE BONFIRE OF THE VANITIES

Director: Brain De Palma
Cast: Tom Hanks, Melanie Griffith, Bruce Willis, Kim Cattrall, Morgan Freeman, Kevin Dunn
Release Date: December 21, 1990

> *The only movie I would not do again, given the opportunity, is Bonfire of the Vanities.*
>
> —WILLIS IN A 1996 INTERVIEW WITH *PLAYBOY*

—1—

Bruce Willis rode a white-hot success streak through the year 1990. John McTiernan's *Die Hard* had propelled him to superstar status, instantly inserting Willis into any conversation surrounding action-movie greats. Renny Harlin's follow up *Die Hard 2*, released on July 3, 1990, proved to the industry that the original film wasn't a standalone hit, but rather the start of a money-making franchise. Willis was enjoying the spoils of celebrity, but also struggling to process it.

"There's no way that I can explain to you how I feel about what has happened to me in my career," Willis told a journalist in 1990. "There's nothing that I can say. I can tell you, 'Geez, the guy has had a meteoric rise to fame.' But man, what's going on inside of me? I still think of myself as this guy. Just a guy who wanders around and wants to be an actor. . . . I still feel much closer to that guy, to the have-not guy, then I do to finding some kind of acceptance for where I'm at now in my life. It's a strange thing."[1]

The level of scrutiny associated with fame only magnified when, ten days after *Die Hard 2* opened in theaters, Willis's then-wife Demi Moore appeared alongside Patrick Swayze and Whoopi Goldberg in the supernatural romance

Ghost. Willis was actually considered for Swayze's role at one point, but turned it down because he didn't understand the concept, and figured it would fail.

"I just didn't get it. I said, 'Hey, the guy's dead. How are you gonna have a romance?' Famous last words," Willis joked.[2] He couldn't have been more wrong. *Ghost* was a smash hit. It earned five Academy Award nominations, including Best Picture, and scored two wins. By the end of 1990, *Ghost* had become the highest-grossing film released that year—no doubt a cause for celebration for the celebrity couple.

"We were both very surprised," Willis said at the time about the couple's one-two punch. "It's just a fun thing that it happened this way. It certainly makes for good press, that we are now the hot couple in Hollywood. But like you say, it's just a joke. It's just something that we kid each other about."[3]

The laughs died down in December. Willis returned for Amy Heckerling's *Look Who's Talking Too*, but the sequel couldn't replicate the first film's goofy, adolescent charms. To his credit, Willis's sarcastic quips and buoyant delivery were the comedy's saving grace. Then came *The Bonfire of the Vanities*, which marked the beginning of a professional tumble. Willis would spend the next three years toiling on critical punching bags (*Mortal Thoughts, Billy Bathgate*), costly vanity projects (*Hudson Hawk*), and lackluster action vehicles (*Striking Distance*) looking to recapture some of that *Die Hard* heat. It was *Bonfire*, though, that started this rare rough patch in the movie star's early career.

On paper, *The Bonfire of the Vanities* made sense. It adapted a controversial bestseller by celebrated author Tom Wolfe (*The Right Stuff, The Electric Kool-Aid Acid Test*), which remained the talk of the town throughout production. It lured a prestigious director in Brian De Palma (*Blow Out, Scarface, The Untouchables*), who in turn populated his ensemble with high-powered movie stars. Yet, the best laid plans, specifically on a movie set, often go awry. As two-time Academy Award winning director Alejandro Gonzalez Inarritu once said, "To make a film is easy. To make a good film is war. To make a very good film is a miracle."[4]

Bonfire arrived at a time when Willis was still navigating fame, and the media circus that can accompany it. His marriage to Moore generated endless tabloid speculation, and Willis's relationship with the press had grown thornier. "It's just one of the more unpleasant things about being a public figure. They can say anything about you, and they hound you," Willis said. "It's like anything else bad in the world. Air pollution. Car accidents. I know we could probably go out to some newsstand right now and find something shitty that somebody has said about me. It sells magazines."[5]

Which is part of the reason why Willis agreed to play failing New York reporter Peter Fallow in De Palma's *Bonfire*. He viewed the role as a chance to strike back at the media hoards he resented for interfering with his personal life. "I wanted to make this guy a real scumbag," he said of his character. "I thought that this would be a great opportunity for me to take a shot at these yellow journalists who had been coming after me for the last five or six years. (But) I found that that wasn't as important to me as getting inside the dynamic of why an intelligent man who knows the difference between right and wrong will still choose to do the wrong thing instead of the right thing. That was a lot more interesting."[6]

Bonfire is not a good film. It's a miscalculation on almost every level. And the behind-the-scenes horrors that plagued *Bonfire* did in fact make De Palma feel like he'd enlisted in some form of conflict. His troubled production faced ballooning costs. Pivotal shooting locations around New York City kept falling through. Local press outlets published a steady stream of blowback from native New Yorkers who despised Wolfe's book (because they recognized themselves in the caricatures *Bonfire* skewered), while local politicians argued against the book's interpretation of the Bronx to score points with voters.

The entire disastrous affair is chronicled in Julie Salamon's essential read *The Devil's Candy: The Anatomy of a Hollywood Fiasco*. The *Wall Street Journal*'s former film critic received unprecedented access to De Palma's misguided attempt at adapting Wolfe's novel. Reporting from the front lines, Salamon provided a thorough, firsthand account of De Palma's follies. Her bestseller also held a magnifying glass up to the nasty backstage politicking that likely occurs on almost every film set, only they didn't have a journalist on hand to write about every wart.

Salamon's presence on set infuriated Willis. She portrays him as an arrogant, conceited celebrity who ignored her (and others) while mostly camping out in his trailer. And he considered her to be one of the "parasites" who fed off his celebrity. "Brian De Palma chose to have this girl come on the set and write a book about the making of the film. But he neglected to tell the actors about it until she had already been skulking around for about four weeks," Willis complained. "By the time we learned what she was doing, the damage was done. Basically, she decided to take a big shit on a bunch of people she would never get to be in her own life."[7]

It's hard not to laugh, however, at the fact that the movie Willis hoped would humiliate yellow journalists bombed both critically and commercially. And every step of the film's demise was documented by one of the reporters he considered to be part of the problem.

—2—

Anyone compiling a master list of "Things That Went Wrong" with regards to De Palma's *The Bonfire of the Vanities* would have to go pretty far down the list—possibly into the double digits—before they reached Willis and his performance. He deserves credit for reaching outside of the action-movie comfort zone that enveloped him in the late 1980s, and pumping the brakes on the freight train that was the *Die-Hard* franchise to attempt riskier roles in the war-veteran character piece *In Country*, or De Palma's high-profile adaptation.

"This was not necessarily a safe choice for me," Willis said. "There were other things that I could have done that I would have been much more comfortable with, or more sure that I would have done a good job at."[8]

My personal list of *Bonfire* mistakes starts with De Palma, a genre director with a taste for the perverse who was the wrong choice to adapt Wolfe's satirical novel about race and class warfare in a sensationalist version of New York City. Material like *Bonfire* requires a delicate comedic touch, dutifully pointing out the grotesque flaws of practically every character involved. De Palma attempted one comedy prior to *Bonfire*, the unfunny and broadly farcical *Wise Guys*, which paired Danny De Vito and Joe Piscopo as low-level mobsters. It's baffling that any studio executive walked away from *Wise Guys* thinking De Palma was a proper fit for *Bonfire*. Joel and Ethan Coen would have had a field day with Wolfe's biting source material. Deeply cynical movies like *Fargo*, *The Hudsucker Proxy*, and *Burn after Reading* suggest they'd have nailed the necessary tone for *Bonfire*. And damn, now I lament the fact we'll never see Willis and his blistering comedic timing in a Coen Brothers movie.

The Bonfire of the Vanities likely cratered because the driving creative forces didn't fully comprehend Wolfe's source material. "The book was really divisive," Salamon observed. "There were a million essays about what the book was, and what it wasn't. Was Tom Wolf reporting on the realities of class and race? Or was he exaggerating things, making them worse?"[9] Someone needed to answer those questions before an adaptation of *Bonfire* was mounted, because without a definitive stance, you end up with a toothless, marginalized interpretation of a fiery novel.

The poor decisions extended beyond De Palma, though. Celebrated composer Dave Grusin (*On Golden Pond, Tootsie*) concocted a jaunty, playful, soft jazz score that doesn't suit the material. His music felt tailor-made for a heartwarming family story, not a ruthless sendup of the one percent. Too-nice Tom Hanks, meanwhile, didn't quite comprehend how to play the story's main character, Sherman McCoy, a Wall Street baron and self-professed "Master of the Universe" whose life unravels once he's part of a highly publicized hit-and-run accident. And Melanie Griffith hammers away at one obnoxious note as Maria, an oversexed Southern bimbo involved in Sherman's crime.

But I thoroughly enjoyed Willis as failing journalist Peter Fallow, who rides McCoy's coattails to literary success and becomes a media-created monster in the process. Willis's on-screen confidence makes Fallow suave, even when he's supposed to be a starving, hack reporter. He brings that pitter-patter tempo to his dialogue, and even applies some of the self-absorbed aloofness that results from movie stardom to Fallow's opening scene—a stunning unbroken shot through the backstage arteries of a bustling convention center. Willis is terrific as a smooth-talking bottom feeder who chews his way to the top. He understood the assignment, and his nimble performance remains one of the few salvageable aspects of this otherwise disappointing dud.

—3—

"I knew what could go wrong with [*Bonfire*]," De Palma famously told Salamon in confidence. "And the irony is, it still bombed. I made a lot of compromises. And it was a disaster."[10]

But there's value to revisiting *The Bonfire of the Vanities* nearly thirty-five years after its debut. The film acts as an intriguing relic of an overindulgent American culture at the time. And it's sad to admit that so much of what gets lampooned by Wolfe with regard to racial discrimination and invisible societal lines separating the "haves" from the "have nots" continues to be a serious problem today. De Palma and screenwriter Michael Cristofer might have painted with broad strokes in their feature. But the issues of white privilege, white panic, and the threat of civil unrest in the face of judicial injustice are as relevant today as they were the year *Bonfire* opened.

The movie's impact on Willis's career, however, was more of a blip than a lingering strike on his permanent record. The same could be said for all of the major players on the *Bonfire* call sheet. Even though De Palma's movie has cemented its legacy as a flop, it wasn't a career killer. The director returned to psychological horror with 1992's *Raising Cain*, then had back-to-back hits in *Carlito's Way* (1993) and the first *Mission: Impossible*, with Tom Cruise. Griffith never duplicated the success of 1988's smash *Working Girl* in the years following *Bonfire*, but she alternated between interesting film and television roles for the better part of the next four decades. And Hanks rebounded quickly by playing washed-up baseball manager Jimmy Dugan in Penny Marshall's *A League of Their Own*, then enjoyed a spectacular run of starring roles that included *Sleepless in Seattle*, *Philadelphia* (which earned him his first Best Actor trophy), *Forrest Gump* (which earned him his second Best Actor trophy), *Apollo 13*, *Toy Story*, *That Thing You Do!* (his directorial debut), and *Saving Private Ryan*. The *Bonfire* sting didn't linger too long.

The same can be said for Willis. He has his share of stinkers, but *Bonfire* doesn't get mentioned as often—possibly because the following year Willis's pet project, *Hudson Hawk* would bomb with such a thunderous boom it drowned out all criticism of the movie star's participation in *Bonfire*. He became the film critic community's punching bag for a few years thanks to *Mortal Thoughts*, *Striking Distance*, and *Color of Night*. But Quentin Tarantino eventually ended the actor's slide when he threw Willis a metaphorical life preserver in the form of 1994's *Pulp Fiction*. Willis restored his movie-star status and avoided a sustained career drought for the next twenty years.

Revisiting *The Bonfire of the Vanities*, I push back on the notion that Willis was miscast. His portrayal of Peter Fallow might have had less bite than he had hoped, the result of Hollywood executives leaning on De Palma to manifest one likeable character out of Wolfe's novel. "I've been accused of that," Willis joked in an interview. "Of not making him bad enough. . . . My original intention was to make him a very bad guy."[11]

But Willis's work on *Bonfire* can be encapsulated by a line his character delivers in the film: "If you are going to work in a whorehouse, there's only one thing to be. The best whore in the house." That was Willis. The best "whore" in the dilapidated house De Palma built.

CHAPTER EIGHTEEN
MOONRISE KINGDOM /
THE *SIN CITY* FILMS /
NOBODY'S FOOL

—1—

At the risk of sounding like a broken record, allow me to repeat a few important takeaways. From the moment he rocketed to stardom courtesy of *Die Hard*, Bruce Willis frequently used his Hollywood clout to either back riskier projects he believed in, open up doors for fledgling filmmakers, or earn himself a spot in a star-studded ensemble where he happily contributed as much—or as little—as was needed. Collaborations with auteur filmmakers already have been categorized in this book as comedies (Steven Soderbergh's *Ocean's 12*), science fiction thrillers (Terry Gilliam's *12 Monkeys*), and experimental indies (Quentin Tarantino's contribution to *Four Rooms*). As has been discussed, Willis's professional decisions often were determined by the director who'd be at the helm.

The three auteur projects already discussed in this section put Willis front and center, relying heavily on the power, weight, and marketing influence that came with his movie stardom. These next three films I've grouped together, however, provide effective examples of Willis trading his celebrity for a chance to work with exciting voices on coveted materials or share the screen with fellow acting legends he's admired and emulated. These three projects demonstrate how well the versatile Willis could shape his skills to match the need of very unique, and very different, storytellers. Captain Sharp from *Moonrise Kingdom*'s docile island community of New Penzance, for example, has nothing in common with the grizzled *Sin City* cop John Hartigan, who lays it all on the line to protect an innocent citizen in Basin City. And those two officers differ completely from the cocky local contractor Willis plays alongside Paul Newman in Robert Benton's *Nobody's Fool*.

But they are roles shepherded by visionary filmmakers who offered Willis an opportunity to stretch and grow as a performer, as well as to entertain. Benton confirms this notion when he describes the process of luring Willis to *Nobody's Fool* after the duo had worked together before on 1991's *Billy Bathgate*.

"I called Bruce and said, 'This is not like *Billy Bathgate*. There's no money here,'" Benton said when addressing the fact that Willis agreed to work at the scale-rate of $1,400 a week for *Nobody's Fool*, a steep drop from the reported $15 million he was commanding per picture at the time. "I said, 'We're all doing this picture on the lowest possible budget.' He said, 'Don't worry about that. We'll have a good time.'

"You can count the number of actors who do that on the fingers of one hand," Benton concluded. "I think the great thing about Bruce is that if your material interests him, he doesn't care what the money is."[1]

—2—

Wes Anderson's 2012 picture *Moonrise Kingdom* opens with a monologue about the symphony orchestra. It's a fitting analogy to a typical Anderson feature, which often plays as a two-hour, live-action diorama box of comedy. His original scripts are calibrated compositions of quirky dialogue, subdued delivery, and exquisite visual scenery blessed by the filmmaker's love of symmetry. But there's rarely a standout star of Anderson's ensembles, which is by design. Each cast member is an instrument that Anderson, as the conductor, utilizes, his fingerprints found on every aspect of each scene.

Some actors end up being more efficient with the precise rhythms required for Anderson's dialogue. For that reason, the director will rely on a handful of repeat players who understand Anderson's tone: Bill Murray, Jason Schwartzman, Owen Wilson, and Tilda Swinton come to mind. But then there are unexpected performers who sign on for one or two stories, and temporarily plug directly into Anderson's unmistakable tempo: Gene Hackman in *The Royal Tenenbaums*; George Clooney for *The Fantastic Mr. Fox*;

Cate Blanchett in *The Life Aquatic*; Ralph Fiennes in *The Grand Budapest Hotel*; Bryan Cranston in *Isle of Dogs*; and Willis, as Captain Duffy Sharp, in *Moonrise Kingdom*.

Anderson had only met Willis briefly before approaching the movie star to join the troupe on location in Rhode Island. "He was so completely agreeable and into it. His ideas about the character just sounded perfect to me," Anderson said. "We don't have trailers or . . . people aren't really off the set. They're together. And he embraced that like everybody else did."[2]

Moonrise Kingdom is Anderson's warmest movie. He wrings tender emotions out of a first-love teenage romance without sacrificing any of the eccentricities the director's fans appreciate and expect. While it's less than inspiring that Willis agreed to play another variation of a police officer for Anderson, Sharp doesn't resemble John McClane, Joe Hallenback, or Jack Mosley—memorable officers from Willis's filmography.

"I just thought I ought to have somebody who would be unquestionably believable as police," Anderson explained about Willis's casting. "So I liked the idea of him playing a policeman for the Nth time, but being a different kind of policeman from what we've seen him as before. His character is quite passive and depressed, but authority is in his blood."[3]

There's also a sympathetic warmth found in Sharp as he searches for missing Khaki Scout camper Sam Shakusky (Jared Gilman), who we learn is a product of the foster system. Shakusky isn't missing, however. He has run off with Suzy (Kara Hayward), who captured Sam's impressionable heart while they were pen pals.

In *Moonrise Kingdom*, the adults behave like children, and the story's preteen leads conduct their romantic courtship with a patience and maturity that betrays their ages. Sam and Suzy plan an elaborate rendezvous and are more than capable of surviving on their own. Willis's Captain Sharp frequently has to be the adult in the room, trying in vain to de-escalate a complicated situation involving Suzy's eccentric family, the resourceful Khaki Scouts of North America, and an indifferent Social Services officer (played by Tilda Swinton). For all his efforts, Sharp still gets dismissed as "that sad, dumb policeman" by the community members he's sworn to protect.

We learn little about Sharp, and can deduce even less by his measured delivery and standard-issue uniform (which doesn't fit very well in the legs). Sharp's having an affair with a married woman (Frances McDormand), and he says he loved someone once—probably referring to McDormand's character—though she didn't love him back. He temporarily shelters Shakusky once the children are found, and connects with the boy while dispensing earnest advice in Willis's most remarkable scene.

"Look, let's face it, you're probably a much more intelligent person than I am. In fact, I guarantee it," Sharp tells Shakusky. "But even smart kids stick their fingers in electrical sockets sometimes. It takes time to figure things out. It's been proven by history. All mankind makes mistakes. It's our job to try to protect you from making the dangerous ones, if we can."

Conventional emotions and passions rarely surface in an Anderson film. The director usually sacrifices genuine emotion if it means he can achieve a humorous visual payoff, or a line delivery that's so dry, it might snap like a twig.

"What happened to your hand," Sam asks, observing that Suzy's bloody hand is wrapped in gauze.

"I got hit in the mirror," Suzy replies.

"Really? How did that happen?" Sam inquires.

"I lost my temper at myself," Suzy explains.

But Willis manages to slice through the ennui that hangs over the whole of *Moonrise Kingdom* to discover something we don't expect to find in Anderson's stories: relatable humanity. Anderson's films are delicate ships constructed inside bottles. New Penzance is as much a fantasy landscape as Neverland or Narnia. In *Moonrise Kingdom*, we're amused by a curious Khaki Scout named "Lazy Eye," a legal counselor (Bill Murray) who works through his frustrations by drinking wine while chopping down trees, and a rule-bending camp counselor (Jason Schwartzman) who illegally marries two adolescents in a top-secret ceremony.

Amid the tomfoolery, however, Willis creates a character we could actually encounter in the real world. As the other adults worry about frivolous details, Sharp maintains resolute compassion for Shakusky, and eventually shows flashes of the heroism we associate with Willis in the film's final act. Stoic, sad, but competent, Willis makes his bold mark on *Moonrise Kingdom* without upsetting the carefully constructed apple cart or negating the mathematical equation behind Anderson's storytelling. His gentle and resolute comedic performance, his authentic leadership traits, and the empathy that constantly rests beneath Willis's surface serve Anderson's vision to the fullest. And that's the highest compliment one can give.

—3—

Basin City couldn't be farther from New Penzance Island, in every respect. And *Sin City* is as vicious and cruel as *Moonrise Kingdom* is compassionate and sweet. Where Anderson's fictional community looks like a spice rack of carefully curated antique structures, Robert Rodruguez's rain-soaked, crime-infested "Sin City" stinks of rot, decay, and depravity. Stories begin in "a lousy room, in a lousy part of a lousy town," and conclude with deranged rapists being beaten until only "wet chunks of bone" from a yellowed corpse remain. The fact that Willis fits comfortably into both environments says everything about his range and adaptability as a performer.

Sin City thematically matches graphic novelist Frank Miller's other popular works. *The Dark Knight Returns*, *Batman: Year One*, and the Spartan underdog saga *300* all pit flawed and morally ambiguous heroes against the rising cesspool of humanity. Miller described his 1991 neo-noir thriller *Sin City* as "a completely selfish act," filled with all of the things that he personally loved to draw: fast cars, beautiful women, and hulking thugs in trench coats we usually saw in James Cagney and Humphrey Bogart movies.

"It's kinda like the old Rolling Stones song," Miller said, "where every cop's a criminal, and all the sinners are saints. Where the lowlifes would often be heroic, and the most stridently beautiful and sweet women would be prostitutes."[4]

Despite a handful of filmmakers circling possible adaptations of *Sin City* in the late 1990s, it was *Desperado* and *Spy Kids* visionary storyteller Robert Rodriguez who convinced Miller to agree to a collaboration, insisting that the artist come on board as a codirector. "I started really looking at it as, instead of trying to turn [*Sin City*] into a movie, which would be terrible, let's take cinema and try to make it into this book," Rodriguez explained.[5]

To help people understand the way he saw Miller's world coming to life on screen, Rodriguez spent time in his Troublemaker Studio in Austin, Texas, filming a three-minute reel with actors Josh Hartnett and Marley Shelton. It ended up being the first segment of the finished movie, "The Customer Is Always Right (Part 1)." The Customer (Shelton) stands on a balcony overlooking Sin City, her red dress and lips the only color to pop off the sharp black-and-white palette. She's approached by "The Salesman" (Hartnett), a smooth talker who relaxes this femme fatale with empty promises. They embrace. They kiss. And then he puts a bullet in her heart, coldly claiming, "I'll cash her check in the morning."

Rodriguez used this sizzle reel as a proof of concept as he started showing it to trusted colleagues, and possible partners. Fellow director Quentin Tarantino's jaw hit the floor once he saw it. "It wasn't like, 'This will be sort of what it will look like,'" Tarantino said. "This was like 'Boom!' It was ready to play at the Cinerama Dome!"[6] The *Pulp Fiction* and *Four Rooms* director eventually agreed to codirect a portion of the Clive Owen and Benicio Del Toro–led story, "The Big Fat Kill." Rodriguez paid Tarantino $1 for his services. The maverick filmmaker just wanted to be involved. So much so that he broke one of his own personal cardinal rules to always shoot on film, using instead the Sony HDC-F950 digital camera.

Willis signed on to *Sin City* almost as quickly and for many of the same reasons. Rodriguez invited the leading man to Austin, knowing he wanted him to play Hartigan in the vengeance story "That Yellow Bastard." The character is described as a "Dirty Harry" type, which is why the girl he's sworn to protect, Nancy, has the last name Callahan. Hartigan starts "The Yellow Bastard" on the day he's due to retire from the police force. He has a bum ticker and an unhappy wife waiting for him at home. But there's one last loose end he has to tie up before he can hang up the spurs.

Rodriguez believed he needed an iconic actor to play an iconic character like Hartigan. So he showed Willis the three-minute "Customer" reel to illustrate what *Sin City* could look like. One minute into the viewing, Willis pressed pause, turned to Rodriguez, and said, "Whatever I see after this, I just want you to know. I'm in. I want to be in this film."[7]

That, as you'll recall, was Willis's instantaneous response to Tarantino's *Pulp Fiction* script. It didn't matter what the movie was going to become. Willis wanted in on the ride. He wanted to be part of what he thought could be something magical. It proves how passionate this powerful Hollywood star could be when he encountered material that inspired him, challenged him, and excited him—material that stoked his curiosity about the creative process.

"I could not believe what I was watching," Willis said about those three minutes of *Sin City* test footage. "I wanted to know how you did it. How did you make the rain? How did that happen? How did this whole thing happen? Now, to look back at it, it makes us all look like we knew what we were doing. . . . But I was totally baffled by the process and what it was going to look like."

Willis adored having Miller on set as a codirector for the shoot. It allowed him to service two auteurs on one project. "Frank Miller and I talked at length about film noir," Willis said. "I had been a fan of film noir forever. He got that I got it, right away. That's what all of these stories are. Gritty, pulp fiction. In that style. Quentin said the same thing. . . . Think about that book. Think about the tattered, yellow pages. The skanky book that got left in the rain, or in your car."

Sin City and *Moonrise Kingdom* have their differences, but similarities exist in the features, as well. Visuals enhance the storytelling, but script is king, and cadence matters if an actor intends on striking the right tone. For Hartigan, the bulk of the work is done with a pained, raspy whisper of a narration that exudes fortitude, but also exhaustion.

"If you read Frank's writing without looking at the panels, it stands alone just as true film-noir writing," Willis said. "I think all the actors felt that it was our job to not only pay homage to the books, and to film-noir style, but also to Frank's writing.

"I don't think anybody changed any lines. Frank did," Willis continued. "He would suggest cutting a line or changing a line. I would argue with him, and go, 'No, no. Let's do the exact text in the books.'"

Anderson probably overdid it with his twee dialogue on *Moonrise Kingdom*. Rodriguez and Miller were more selective with *Sin City*. Remove Hartigan's weary narration, however, and Willis all but gives a silent performance, relying on his naturally chiseled features and intentionally strained physicality to convey his character's struggles. Rodriguez tells us more about Hartigan with a side profile of Willis set against a brick facade than he would with pages of dialogue.

Sin City marked Willis's first true experience with fully immersive green screen, and Rodriguez's swift process (due to the efficiency of digital photography) awakened a creativity in the actor. Willis worked ten days on *Sin City* but claims the team accomplished the equivalent of five weeks of shooting on a conventional film set. "It was the fastest I'd ever gone," he said. "And it was all green. I remember asking [Rodriguez], we were on the dock, and I asked, 'Well, what's going to *be* back there?' And he said, 'It will be a little bit of the city.' And at the premiere, it's the entire city. The entire city is drawn in.

"Actors had to throw away all their preconceptions about the rules of filmmaking," Willis continued. "The thing that we kept talking about is that it was like *Playhouse 90*. You were shooting a film live with a dock, three actors, and I think a gun. That was it. You had to really trust Robert and know that, 'Okay, we're in your hands now.' And all you have to do is act. Do your work. After a day, I never even thought about it."[8]

Hearing Willis speak so enthusiastically of the minimalism of green-screen work is heartening. There are phases throughout his career where it's suggested that the lengthy filmmaking process suffocated the fun he once had on a movie set. He spoke glowingly about the language of *Sin City* and the efficiency of the admittedly unusual green screen technology, that appealed to him greatly in 2005. "No one knew what it was going to look like. No one knew what it was going to be," Willis said. "And when I saw it, I was just astonished. It was far beyond anything I could have ever imagined."

Unfortunately, while *Sin City* is a technical marvel and a visual masterpiece, the gratuitous violence involving cannibals, hitmen, hookers, and gangsters does more than push the envelope. They make it difficult to embrace the source material. The movie succumbs to unchecked masculinity, and the relentless deviant behavior overcomes the undeniable style. I love Willis's story of heroism fueled by murky motivations. But the rest of *Sin City*—and the entirety of its unnecessary sequel, *Sin City: A Dame to Kill For*—resembles a bloated, vulgar corpse sinking to the bottom of Basin City's waterways.

—4—

Something is missing from the opening credits of Robert Benton's *Nobody's Fool*, a charmingly innocent vehicle for an aging (but still wonderful) Paul Newman. Willis's name isn't listed with the rest of the cast as the film begins—unusual when you consider the mega-star's popularity circa 1994. Newspaper and magazine writers still were championing Willis for Oscar consideration for his role of the washed-up boxer in Quentin Tarantino's *Pulp Fiction* when *Nobody's Fool* released. Movie producers and marketing teams should have been tripping over themselves to showcase Willis's name in the credits of a character piece aimed at the senior-citizen demographic.

But this was all by design.

Hoping to separate himself from the "Action Hero" pigeonhole that hung over so many of his career choices, Willis continued to embrace the dramatic material offered in projects like *Nobody's Fool* and, in this specific case, relished the opportunity to spend valuable time opposite Newman (after briefly serving as an extra in a courtroom scene starring Newman for Sidney Lumet's *The Verdict*).

"[Newman and I] got along famously," Willis recollected to an interviewer in 1999. "All of my scenes were with him. And I did that film because my scenes were with him, and I wanted to hang out with him."[9]

Benton's astounding credits also had to serve as a lure. Over the years, the three-time Academy Award winner helped to write *Bonnie and Clyde* for Warren Beatty and Faye Dunaway, directed Dustin Hoffman and Meryl Streep through *Kramer vs. Kramer*, and helped pen Richard Donner's *Superman*, with Christopher Reeve in the lead.

Here, Benton adapted Richard Russo's homespun novel of the same name. The story's main character, Donald "Sully" Sullivan (Newman), meanders around a humble, Frank Capra–esque town where warm bodies bump into each other over the course of a chilly Thanksgiving week. It's sweet and unsurprising, and makes up in personality what it lacks in plot.

One thing *Nobody's Fool* doesn't lack is star power. Oscar, Emmy, and four-time Tony Award winner Jessica Tandy made her final screen performance in the film playing Beryl Peoples, Newman's former eighth-grade teacher who now rents him a room in her spacious house because she appreciates his company. A young Philip Seymour Hoffman appears as an overzealous cop handing Newman a steady stream of traffic tickets. And the casually flirtatious Melanie Griffith—coming off a string of duds that included the ill-fated *The Bonfire of the Vanities*—made good use of her sexiness as Toby Roebuck, neglected spouse of Newman's archnemesis, Carl Roebuck (played with snark by Willis).

An entitled nepotism brat, Carl owns and operates a construction company that was handed to him by his father. Willis's choices lead us to believe Carl has been a Big Man on Campus most of his life, particularly because he never left the small pond that allows him to be a big fish. *Nobody's Fool* positions Newman and Willis as rivals, despite their obvious age difference. Benton milks easy laughs out of Newman repeatedly stealing Willis's snowblower or wandering over to Toby's kitchen to openly flirt with her and complain that she's wasting her time with the "dummy," Carl.

And in a way, Willis's cocky *Nobody's Fool* performance could be interpreted as the upstart movie star brushing off the fading marquee talent that was Newman. Willis might not have been capable of showing such swagger in front of one of his acting idols early in his career, but by *Nobody's Fool*, Willis had countless blockbusters under his belt. He was sandwiched between 1994's *Pulp Fiction* and the one-two punch of *Die Hard with a Vengeance* and *12 Monkeys* in 1995. There was no question that Willis was the biggest star on the call sheet for *Nobody's Fool*.

And yet the pressure that comes with being a star appears to be off of Willis in this movie, as if he knows that more eyes will be on Newman in any scene they share, allowing him to be playful and loose, which only adds more confidence to his overly satisfied character. He's not intimidated by Newman, going so far as to verbally bully his costar, maintaining the upper hand until his comeuppance arrives. More than anything, Willis shows up. He cares. He's invested in the material, and he rises to the level of his equally famous costars.

As Willis probably could have predicted, every review for *Nobody's Fool* focused on Newman—and rightfully so. "Moviegoing holds few pleasures greater than watching an established star completely inhabit a role that exactly suits his personality and abilities," Kenneth Turan wrote in the *Los Angeles Times*. "And seeing Paul Newman in *Nobody's Fool* defines that pleasure."[10] And *New York Times* critic Caryn James went so far as to call Newman's performance in *Nobody's Fool* "the single best of this year and among the finest he has ever given."[11]

Enough members of the Academy of Motion Picture Arts and Sciences agreed with the sentiment, as Newman earned his ninth Oscar nomination for playing Donald "Sully" Sullivan—and went on to lose to Tom Hanks for his portrayal of Forrest Gump. Benton, Newman, and Russo routinely garnered award considerations during their professional careers. Benton, as mentioned, won screenwriting Oscars for *Kramer vs. Kramer* and Sally Fields's *Places in the Heart*. *Kramer* also earned Benton his lone Best Director statue. Russo would go on to win the Pulitzer Prize for Fiction in 2002 for his acclaimed novel *Empire Falls*. That work later inspired an eponymous two-part miniseries for HBO that earned Newman a Primetime Emmy Award and a Golden Globe Award for Best Supporting Actor in a Series, Miniseries, or Television Film.

But 1994 brought with it a tough lesson for Willis that I've frequently raised: awards distributors might recognize movies he starred in, but they wouldn't recognize him in the process. Worse than that, while his colleagues collected prestigious Oscar nominations, Willis received Golden Raspberry Awards, or Razzies. Of the four movies Willis released in 1994, two were showered with Academy Award nominations (*Nobody's Fool* and *Pulp Fiction*) and two were ridiculed by the Razzies (*Color of Night* and *North*).

Willis had to know he was a longshot for a *Nobody's Fool* nod. That was Newman's picture, and the strongest play of any awards campaign. But the A-lister likely believed he had better-than-average odds at earning recognition for Tarantino's *Pulp Fiction*. Yet, when the Academy announced the seven Academy Award nominations for *Pulp Fiction*, Willis's name wasn't included. Whether intentional or not, the industry's message appeared to be that Willis's peers at that time weren't prepared to accept him as anything more than the action superstar he had become, no matter how many outside-of-his-box, "Carl Roebuck" parts he took.

SECTION FIVE
THE *DIE HARD* FRANCHISE

"You know what you get for being a hero? Nothing. You get shot at. You get a little pat on the back, blah, blah, blah, attaboy. You get divorced. Your wife can't remember your last name. Your kids don't want to talk to you. You get to eat a lot of meals by yourself. Trust me, kid, nobody wants to be that guy."

"Then why are you doing this?"

"Because there's nobody else to do it right now, that's why. Believe me, if there were somebody else to do it, I'd let them do it, but there's not. So we're doing it."

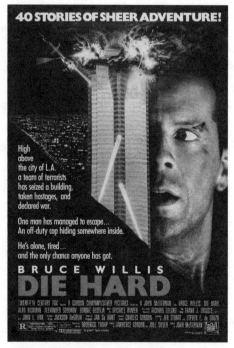

Official movie poster for John McTiernan's *Die Hard*, starring Bruce Willis. *Author's Collection*

Kevin Smith used to tell an unflattering story about Bruce Willis. Several of them, in fact. He'd share them from the stages of national comic book conventions and even included the juiciest ones in his 2021 book *Kevin Smith's Secret Stash: The Definitive Visual History*. Smith called Willis "one of his cinematic idols," praising the actor's uncanny ability to play the everyman hero. Smith also loved that, like him, Willis came from New Jersey. "This motherfucker came from Penns Grove, New Jersey. And now he's John McClane," Smith said. "You could come from New Jersey, and something cool would happen."[1]

But the duo meshed like oil and water on the set of Smith's 2010 studio comedy *Cop Out*, and the director coped with the traumatic experience the only way he knows how. He talked.

Of all the stories I've heard Smith recount over the years, this one stings the most, because it's evident how much Smith cherished Willis. But as the old adage goes, meeting your heroes can come with unexpected and detrimental results. On this particular day, Smith found himself standing next to his leading man on a side street in Brooklyn. Traffic had stopped due to a red light, and two men who were driving a truck happened to look over, spotting Smith and Willis—but mostly Willis. "The [drivers] see Bruce, and go absolutely ape shit," Smith recalls. "They go, 'Whoooo! *Die Hard!*' They don't use his name. They call him by the title of the movie. Which I love! That's how you know a true movie fan."

The men continue to scream from the truck, telling Willis how much they love him. Smith understands—sort of. The director regularly experiences View Askew patrons—loyal devotees of his adolescent comedies—referring to him as Silent Bob as they gush over *Clerks*, *Mallrats*, or *Chasing Amy*. He's built a reputation for interacting with his very vocal fan base, so on this occasion, he beams on behalf of his extremely famous *Cop Out* star. He turns to Willis, in an effort to connect, and says, "That's gotta feel awesome. Isn't that great?"

And Willis reportedly replied, "I hate the ones that scream '*Die Hard*' the most."

Smith's implication is that Willis had come to resent fans who only associated him with his action masterpiece, *Die Hard*. And that's fair. Doing so ignores decades of feature films from numerous genres that teamed Willis with the industry's top filmmakers. Willis is more than *Die Hard*.

But there's no escaping the reality that *Die Hard* is now, and forever shall be, the definitive picture on Willis's résumé. It's the movie that introduced him to a global audience. It launched a cottage industry of copycat films whose simple, one-sentence pitch was, "It's *Die Hard* on a Blank!" The "blank" being a bus (*Speed*), a battleship (*Under Siege*), a commercial airliner (*Passenger 57*), the White House (*White House Down*), and at the Stanley Cup Finals (*Sudden Death*). *Die Hard* went on to become Willis's longest-running film franchise, producing sequels in the 1990s, the 2000s, and the 2010s. During that time, Willis became synonymous with New York Police Department Detective John McClane, and the blue-collar hero's noble character traits were interlocked with the actor's development for the remainder of his career.

And he knows it.

"As it turns out, if you think about John McClane now, you can't imagine anybody but me doing it, right?" Willis once said, commenting on the names of the actors once rumored to have been up for the part. "The thing about the first film you have to understand is I was doing TV, I'd only been in L.A. for a couple of years, I was still really learning how to act. So most of what went into making John McClane from a character standpoint was the South Jersey Bruce Willis—that attitude and disrespect for authority, that gallows sense of humor, the reluctant hero."[2]

As this next section will explain, Willis is *Die Hard*. And *Die Hard* is Willis. Just don't shout how much you love it, should you happen to encounter him on the street. And please, use his name, instead of the title of the movie.

CHAPTER NINETEEN
DIE HARD

Director: John McTiernan
Cast: Bruce Willis, Alan Rickman, Bonnie Bedelia, Reginald VelJohnson,
Paul Gleason, Alexander Godunov
Release Date: July 20, 1988

Welcome to the party, pal.

—JOHN MCCLANE (WILLIS) IN *DIE HARD*

—1—

Let's get this much out of the way: *Die Hard* is a Christmas movie. The
story unfolds on Christmas Eve, where an office Christmas party on the
thirtieth floor of Nakatomi Plaza has gone awry. Thieves have infiltrated
the event, hellbent on breaking into a heavily fortified vault and escaping
with $640 million in bearer bonds. They've planned for virtually every pos-
sible hiccup—save for off-duty New York Police Department officer John
McClane (Willis), who attended the party in hopes of reconciling with his
estranged wife, Holly (Bonnie Bedelia).

Admittedly, cops, crooks, guns, and vaults don't sound like the ingredients for a traditional holiday movie. Carols, eggnog, presents, and families
reuniting at home usually are on the menu. But a steady stream of well-placed
Christmas references underlies the film's action, which begins when a father
travels across the country to be home for the holidays, and concludes with
Vaughn Monroe crooning "Let It Snow! Let It Snow! Let It Snow!" over the
end credits.

Take, for example, limousine driver Argyle (De'voreaux White), who asks
to play Christmas music on his car's tape deck, and Run DMC's "Christmas
in Hollis" blasts through the speakers. Later, a Santa hat sits atop a criminal's

corpse, his gray sweatshirt sporting an ominous warning with a seasonal punctuation, "Now I have a machine gun. Ho-Ho-Ho." When safecracker Theo (Clarence Gilyard Jr.) reaches his final impediment, an electro-magnetic seal placed around the vault, sophisticated criminal mastermind Hans Gruber (Alan Rickman) injects a rare warmth into his tone when he inflects, "It's Christmas, Theo! It's the time of miracles." Finally, *Die Hard* composer Michael Kamen uses Beethoven's Ninth Symphony, a staple of the Christmas season, as the backbone to the movie's score. Try listening to "Ode to Joy" and not thinking about a barefoot McClane climbing through the air shafts of a Los Angeles skyscraper, moaning, "Come out to the coast. We'll get together. Have a few laughs."

The argument over *Die Hard*'s status as a holiday staple may sound superficial. We have more than enough Christmas-themed movies. Who needs another? But once you learn why the brain trust behind this groundbreaking action thriller views *Die Hard* through a Christmas lens, you can fully understand what helps the movie stand apart from (and above) its brawny competition.

"*Die Hard* is definitely a Christmas movie," screenwriter Jeb Stuart said. "I'm out in L.A. now and I can remember writing it years and years ago at Christmas and, coming from the East Coast, I felt a little bit of, 'What am I doing in Los Angeles for Christmas?' And there is a lot of that wrapped up in that script."[1]

John McTiernan, the film's director, takes a more diplomatic approach. "I don't know that it's a debate," he says. "Also, it's not for us to say. It's people. It's for the audience to say. If the audience decides they want to make it a Christmas movie, then it's a Christmas movie. It turns out that way."[2]

—2—

Mind you, *Die Hard* didn't start that way. Stuart originally pitched this treatment to producer Joel Silver as a traditional terrorist film adapted from Roderick Thorp's 1979 novel *Nothing Lasts Forever*. "It was about these horrible, leftist terrorists who come into the Valhalla of capitalism, Los Angeles, and they bring their guns, and their evil ways, and they shoot up on people just celebrating Christmas," said McTiernan. "Terrible people. Awful people. And [the Stuart script] was really about the stern face of authority stepping in to put things right again. It was, 'Are you feeling lucky, punk?'"[3]

Only, McTiernan had no interest in making that type of movie. Any hack could rip off *Dirty Harry* to produce a generic copycat. McTiernan was coming off the 1987 Arnold Schwarzenegger hit *Predator*, though, so he enjoyed some influence over the studio and his backers. He countered Stuart and Silver's predictable concept with an unorthodox interpretation of his own—one that drew inspiration from Frank Capra's 1947 Christmas fantasy, *It's a Wonderful Life*.

McTiernan claims he specifically focused on the Potterville sequence from that film, which paints an alternate reality for the small town of Bedford Falls, the one that might have occurred if corrupt banker Mr. Potter (Lionel Barrymore) got to have his way without Jimmy Stewart's character, George Bailey, interfering in his plans.

"It's the clearest demonstration, and criticism, of runaway, unregulated cowboy capitalism that was ever done in an American movie," McTiernan said. "And I wondered, 'How did that wind up in a Christmas movie?'"[4]

In McTiernan's mind, the terrorists featured in Stuart's script were unapologetic capitalists who possessed no political agenda. They distracted the authorities with empty demands involving the nine members of the Asian Dawn Movement, and sacrificed innocent hostages while pursuing extraordinary sums of money. They're the European equivalent of the greedy Mr. Potter, soiling a Christmas party in search of cash.

"So that's what this was all about? A fucking robbery?" McClane asks, equally shocked and disgusted, during his final confrontation with Hans Gruber.

This made McClane, in McTiernan's analogy, the George Bailey role, standing up against the oppressors despite the adversity because it's the right thing to do. "I went to Joel and I said, 'OK, if you want me to make this terrorist movie, I want to make it where the hero in the first scene, when the limo driver apologizes that he's never driven a limo before, the hero says, 'It's all right. I've never ridden in a limo before.' A working-class hero. And Joel understood what I meant."[5]

So did Steven E. de Souza, the prolific writer and script polisher whom Silver and McTiernan brought in to refine Stuart's final draft. De Souza knew his way around the action template, having worked on the television series *The Six Million Dollar Man* and *Knight Rider* before transitioning to film for *48 Hours* and the back-to-back Schwarzenegger classics *Commando* and *The Running Man*. But it was de Souza's Philadelphia roots and awareness of Atlantic City and its surrounding neighborhoods that helped him bond with New Jersey native Willis on the *Die Hard* set. Willis apparently encouraged de Souza to inject more levity into Stuart's darker treatment, leading to such infamous lines as "No fucking shit, lady, do I sound like I'm ordering a pizza?" as well as, "Now I know what a TV dinner feels like."

De Souza also claims he wrote the most famous line of Willis's entire career: "Yippee-ki-yay, motherfucker." Willis once stated that he improvised the catchphrase in the moment, hoping to entertain the crew. And Stuart jokes, "You could ask the grip on *Die Hard*, and he's going to claim he wrote that line."[6]

Here's the important part: add de Souza to the *Die Hard* Christmas list. He's the one who put "Ho-Ho-Ho" on Tony's gray sweatshirt. He's the one who maintains that because *Nothing Lasts Forever* takes place entirely on December 24, *Die Hard* should be viewed as a Christmas movie. And de Souza feels like he put the argument to rest when he crafted a handy chart comparing *Die Hard* to Bing Crosby's seasonal favorite, *White Christmas*. When it came to Christmas components—takes place during Christmas, number of Christmas songs, Christ-like sacrifice—*Die Hard* topped *White Christmas* in every category.

"And that is how *Die Hard* became [a Christmas movie]," concluded McTiernan. "We hadn't intended it to be a Christmas movie. But the joy that came from it is what turned it into a Christmas movie. And that's really the best I can tell you about it."[7]

—3—

Two people you probably never heard of deserve the lion's share of the credit for Willis starring in *Die Hard*. That would be twin siblings Cyrus Zachariah

Shepherd-Oppenheim and Molly Ariel Shepherd-Oppenheim, born to Cybill Shepherd on October 6, 1987.

If Shepherd hadn't been pregnant with her twins in 1987, *Moonlighting* wouldn't have had to pause production for eleven weeks. If *Moonlighting* hadn't shut down for that span, Willis would have been required on-set for his full-time TV gig. And if Willis had been shooting *Moonlighting*, he couldn't have headlined the sensation that turned him into a global superstar.

Die Hard is a perfect film. It's lightning in a bottle, tightly scripted and expertly cast. The right amount of comedy balances the spectacular action set pieces. Jan de Bont's magnificent cinematography gives nighttime Los Angeles the shiny gleam of a bank vault door. Meanwhile, the combination of Michael Kamen's score and Frank J. Urioste's well-paced editing gives *Die Hard* a propulsive energy that starts the moment McClane's plane touches down at LAX.

In big-picture terms, *Die Hard* changed the film industry. Willis's $5 million salary for the film was unheard of for a television star making the leap to film. Especially a TV comedian trying to pass himself off as an action star.

"The next day, every male actor's salary rose up to $5 million," Willis said. "I didn't get a Christmas card or anything."[8]

Casting Willis off a television show immediately widened the pool of viable candidates for action-movie leads. And his portrayal of McClane broke the mold of the traditional action superstar by reversing gears on the infallible, muscle-bound heroes portrayed by the likes of Stallone and Schwarzenegger at the time. Willis perfectly encapsulated the everyman persona, a beat cop on vacation who must maneuver a lethal situation while barefoot, alone, terrified, but resourceful. He made it incredibly popular to cheer for "the underdog who just refuses to quit and admit when he's beaten," as McTiernan described the character. While promoting *Die Hard* in 1988, Willis corrected a journalist who compared John McClane to Rambo and Superman, or a typical Schwarzenegger character such as the Terminator.

"With *Die Hard*, I chose the role actually because I wanted to play against those other characters you mentioned. I think John McClane is the opposite of a superhero. He's not invincible. He's a very vulnerable guy. He's capable of being afraid, of making mistakes, and of being afraid. And

I think that that's part of the reason the audience has responded so well to (this) film."[9]

You can point to countless scenes throughout *Die Hard* where Willis allows McClane to lower his guard, and remind the audience that he's as human and flawed as they are. Following an argument with Holly about the fractured status of their marriage, McTiernan leaves the camera on Willis, showing him banging his head against the wall and immediately regretting how stubborn he allowed himself to get, after flying three thousand miles to try and apologize to the woman that he loves.

"That's great, John. Good job," McClane says to himself in the mirror. "Very mature."

McClane isn't in control of his situation, and is frequently playing catchup on Gruber and his team. The lone wolf relishes the moments he has the upper hand on Hans. "Ooops. No bullets. What do you think, I'm fucking stupid, Hans?" But he's also capable of allowing Gruber to get underneath his skin, and give in to his short temper. After Hans blows off McClane's pleas to stop firing missiles into the LAPD's armored tank, McClane makes the impromptu decision to drop a brick of C4 down an elevator shaft, eliminating a portion of Gruber's team.

"*Die Hard* is rightly situated as a visceral experience because John McClane becomes such a direct surrogate for the audience; it becomes a 'what would you do' scenario, and an exercise in improvisation," film journalist Jason Bailey wrote for *Vulture* on the movie's thirtieth anniversary. "This was part of the ingenuity of Stuart and de Souza's screenplay adaptation—in *Nothing Lasts Forever*, Joe Leland is a contracted security expert with a specialty in international terrorism, so his actions are informed by his knowledge, research, and on-the-ground experience (he even knows Gruber's background and bio already). John McClane is a street cop, flying through this thing by the seat of his pants, just like we would."[10]

Die Hard's standout emotional scene, of course, is the bathroom confessional over a walkie-talkie between a badly wounded McClane and his partner on the ground, Al Powell (Reginald VelJohnson). Our barefoot hero narrowly escaped certain death by sprinting down a hallway littered with broken glass. In an effort to distract himself from the pain of removing the shards from his feet, McClane asks Powell why he's no longer a beat cop policing the streets. Powell tells him the story of the time he accidentally shot a kid. McClane answers with compassion. He conveys sympathy. Then, against the unwritten action hero rules, he cries while asking this compassionate stranger, once all is said and done, to find his wife, Holly, and to apologize to her.

"[That scene] is unimaginable for a Schwarzenegger or Stallone at the time. They just wouldn't have gone near that role," comments journalist and author Nick de Semlyen, whose book *The Last Action Heroes* analyzed the impact of the films of Willis, Schwarzenegger, Stallone, and their ilk. "In the wake of *Die Hard*, you saw all of these films where the heroes suddenly were more vulnerable. And then you saw Keanu Reeves. You saw Wesley Snipes. You saw these more regular guys who weren't always in the gym bodybuilding become the new wave of action heroes."[11]

—4—

Outside of *Die Hard*'s unmistakable influence on the film industry, the blockbuster also forever altered Willis's professional track, and shaped the type of films he would make for the remainder of his career. He'd alternate action thrillers and comedies, but never again find a project that so flawlessly balanced what Willis could bring to a role—not even in the *Die Hard* franchise.

The original *Die Hard* is a singular event. It came together at a time when Willis still was comfortable being the irreverent smart ass that weekly audiences tuned in to see on *Moonlighting*. His relatable physicality helped sell the idea that McClane could survive the situations presented on screen, while also allowing us to believe we might be able to do the same if we were in his shoes—if he had shoes, that is.

And in the first two *Die Hard* movies, at least, John McClane was a vulnerable protagonist who bled when beaten, who complained of exhaustion, and who realistically made us wonder if he'd actually triumph before the bad guys got the better of him. That vulnerability disappears with *Die Hard with a Vengeance*, and McClane gradually becomes the antithesis of what made the hero special in the first place. It's legitimately suspenseful when McClane stands on the edge of a skyscraper with a fire hose wrapped around his waist and mutters, "I promise, I will never even think about going up in a tall building again." It's far less exciting watching an unstoppable McClane tumble out of an eighteen-wheeler and land on the wing of an F14 fighter jet, leaping to safety seconds before the plane explodes. That's not McClane. And those movies don't understand *Die Hard*.

As *Die Hard* concluded, Argyle jokes, "If this is their idea of Christmas, I gotta be here for New Year's." *Die Hard* in Times Square on New Year's Eve sounds like such a reasonable pitch, I'm surprised that it wasn't used for one of the multiple sequels that followed McTiernan's masterpiece. Instead, we'd see the action shift to Washington, D.C., New York City in the summertime, and even Moscow. But they never matched the miracle success of the first movie. And Willis knows it.

"If I was going to make an action movie today and I hadn't done *Die Hard*, I would totally rip it off," he said. "The claustrophobic building, the good guys, the bad guys, the hostages, everybody's trapped in this building, you put John McClane in all of these little tight spaces, you have him kill or beat the shit out of everybody else, and save his wife—it's really hard to compete with that first film."[12]

CHAPTER TWENTY

DIE HARD 2: DIE HARDER VS. DIE HARD WITH A VENGEANCE

Here's the most controversial statement you'll read in this book: Renny Harlin's *Die Hard 2: Die Harder* is the best *Die Hard* sequel, and a better *Die Hard* sequel than John McTiernan's *Die Hard with a Vengeance*.

"Blasphemy!" you'll scream, but hear me out. I'm not necessarily calling *Die Hard 2* a better movie than *With a Vengeance* (though, by the end of this chapter, that opinion may actually be supported). It's more that, by the purest definition, *Die Hard 2* adheres more firmly to the unspoken rules of a Die Hard premise. What defines "*Die Hard?*" Here's where opinions will start to differ. But to me, a *Die Hard* story follows a skilled, stubborn, street-level hero who faces insurmountable odds but refuses to stop because he hates to lose. Fate places Bruce Willis's beloved blue-collar cop John McClane in the wrong place at the wrong time, and we marvel at his abilities to continuously emerge victorious, even when survival seems impossible.

Discussing his approach to *Die Hard 2*, Harlin explained, "I kept talking about 'replicating the experience' in the sense that when you sit down in the movie theater, you're not faced with a completely new kind of character. You feel that this is the familiar Bruce Willis that you met in the first movie. His attitude, his sense of humor, and his troubles in life are still something you can relate to."[1]

It'd be ridiculous to believe the *Die Hard* franchise could continue to "replicate this experience" in multiple stories with any credibility. As McClane exasperatedly asks himself in *Die Hard 2*, "Another basement. Another elevator. How can the same shit happen to the same guy twice?" Eventually the formula would bend too hard and break, because Hollywood executives weren't about to let the lucrative *Die Hard* series rest. But in my opinion, *Die Hard 2* avoided most of the demands placed on the subsequent *Die Hard* sequels to blow out the action sequences, increase the stakes, and amplify each new villain's motivations.

"That was the approach," co-screenwriter Doug Richardson said. "To come at it from a realistic standpoint, learn how planes fly, how you could put them in danger, and then how you could realistically create a situation where a terrorist was trying to shut down the airport."[2]

Because as the *Die Hard* sequels wandered farther and farther away from what made the original film special, they also forgot who John McClane was, in the process. And to demonstrate that truth, one need only compare 1990's *Die Hard 2: Die Harder* with 1995's *Die Hard with a Vengeance*.

The Stories

Joe Roth, chairman of 20th Century Fox, greenlit *Die Hard 2: Die Harder* immediately—a no-brainer decision. Harlin actually filmed a teaser trailer for the sequel before Richardson and cowriter Steven E. de Souza had written a single word of dialogue. Fox started running the clip in theaters in December 1989, a mere seventeen months after McTiernan's masterpiece dominated the box office and turned Willis into a global superstar.

Yes, *Die Hard 2: Die Harder* largely borrows the original movie's premise, shifting it to the opposite coast. It's Christmas, again. John McClane wants to reunite with his wife Holly (Bonnie Bedelia), again. And terrorists launching a plan of their own stand in the way of a McClane family celebration, again. But there are crucial ingredients present in de Souza and Richardson's script—an adaptation of Walter Wager's novel *58 Minutes*—that help *Die Hard 2* rise to near the level of its predecessor. The action, for example, contains itself to a primary location. The officer tower of *Die Hard* expands to a snowbound airport in *Die Harder*, but the limitations forced on McClane in both situations are similar. Existing law enforcement agents are more of a hindrance than a help, so McClane trusts his gut and acts on his own. As in the first movie, he can't leave the area without endangering Holly, so he must use the scant resources available to him at the moment to outwit his lethal opponents.

There's a powerful ticking-clock urgency to *Die Hard 2*, as well. The "58 minutes" of Wager's title is the amount of time Holly's airplane has before it runs out of fuel and starts plummeting toward the White House lawn. McClane might have been able to wait out the hostage situation in *Die Hard*, or delay his adversaries with strategic tactics. He doesn't have that luxury of time in *Die Hard 2: Die Harder*, and that reality ratchets up the sequel's pace and tension.

It matters, too, that in the setup for *Die Harder*, McClane coincidentally happens to be at Dulles International Airport the same day Colonel William Stuart (William Sadler) and his military colleagues plan to free General Ramon Esperanza (Franco Nero), who is being extradited to the United States. That randomness should be a *Die Hard* staple. An unprepared McClane innocently stumbles on a dangerous situation, then heroically rises to the challenge of preventing it. In *Die Hard with a Vengeance*, the once valiant cop gets dragged kicking and screaming into an unfolding threat, belligerently complaining every step of the way. To me, it's out of character, and deflates some of that film's fun.

Additional problems embedded in the DNA of the *Die Hard with a Vengeance* story prevent it from feeling like a proper *Die Hard* movie. Probably because its screenplay didn't originate as a *Die Hard* project at all.

Originally titled *Simon Says*, Jonathan Hensleigh's script was meant to power a standalone action vehicle for Brandon Lee. Unfortunately, Lee died on the set of 1994's *The Crow* when an uninspected prop gun fired off a live round, mortally wounding the actor. Warner Bros. later purchased *Simon Says* and rewrote it as a potential *Lethal Weapon* sequel for Mel Gibson and Danny Glover. When that failed to launch, 20th Century Fox obtained the rights and started shaping it into the third *Die Hard* movie.

As such, *Die Hard with a Vengeance* works efficiently as a formulaic buddy-cop movie featuring a veteran cop and a mismatched shop owner reluctantly solving a series of riddles to prevent a maniac from blowing up a New York City school. It's a solid premise, executed with fervor by a director who knows how to maximize all his filmmaking tools. But it doesn't feel like a tight-knit, claustrophobic *Die Hard* movie, where every scene is calibrated to wring the maximum amount of tension. Probably because the script was being rewritten on the fly to suit the conflicting needs of its opinionated director and influential star.

With Hensleigh gearing up to rewrite Joe Johnston's *Jumanji*, and trusted script doctor de Souza occupied by *Beverly Hills Cop 3*, the studio brought in *Terminator 2: Judgement Day* cowriter William Wisher Jr. to polish the existing *Die Hard with a Vengeance* draft—which neither Willis nor McTiernan reportedly liked—and deal with issues as they arose. What started as a two-week gig ended up lasting the length of the movie's shoot.

"Basically, I rewrote everything," Wisher said. "We pulled it apart and put it back together many times. I rewrote my own rewrites many times. My job basically was to stay ahead of the first unit. The continuity girl fucking hated me. The continuity script . . . it looked like *Moby Dick*. I was rewriting the script they handed me, and then rewriting my own stuff and adjusting that, and talking to Bruce about what he wanted and what McTiernan wanted."[3]

Die Hard with a Vengeance isn't the first studio blockbuster to be filmed by committee under chaotic circumstances. When Christopher McQuarrie and Tom Cruise rolled cameras on 2018's *Mission: Impossible—Fallout*, for example, they only had a story outline and a 33-page script. Two-hour movies typically have 80- to 120-page screenplays. McQuarrie believes the *Mission* movies benefit from not being tied down to a locked script. "[Typically], the finished screenplay rules. In *Mission*, the finished screenplay does not. The finished screenplay actually confines and limits," McQuarrie said. "Everything that happens in [a] scene is malleable, and it can change so long as it conforms to what's been shot. It does not need to conform to what hasn't been shot. What hasn't been shot is completely malleable."[4]

McQuarrie tends to make that system work. His films *Fallout* and *Rogue Nation* rank as two of the best features in the *Mission: Impossible* franchise. The absence of a concrete vision on *Die Hard with a Vengeance*, however, only clarifies why McTiernan's surging thriller lacks a purpose or direction as it rockets up and down Manhattan island connecting its set pieces, shifts to upstate New York, transports its action even farther north to Canada and, in the infamous alternate ending (that studio executives hated), finds McClane tracking Simon Gruber (Jeremy Irons) all the way to Hungary, where he kills him in a cafe using a rocket launcher.

"There was some amount of discussion amongst, I remember, the studio executives and the producers and John McTiernan, that this sequence made John McClane look too cruel," Hensleigh recalled on a commentary track for the deleted scene. "That his tyranny over Simon Gruber here, his psychological attack on Gruber here, made McClane too cruel and menacing."[5]

That cruelty, frustration, and impatience weren't just a part of this scene. They were baked into the way Willis chose to play McClane in *With a Vengeance* (and each movie that followed), which also felt in stark contrast to the vulnerable, sympathetic hero of the first two films.

How John McClane Is Portrayed

Far be it from me, or anyone, to tell Willis how best to play John McClane. The durable, relentless New York cop is Willis's bread and butter, and his interpretation of the character trumps all. But there's no denying that, beginning with McTiernan's *Die Hard with a Vengeance*, Willis deliberately injected a bitterness into the underdog hero that wasn't present before—and it's jarring.

"I've always made the choice to play him as a guy who doesn't want to be doing what he has to do in these films. And if he had any other choice, he wouldn't do it," Willis explained. "He's in situations where he has absolutely no other choice than to do the one thing that he has to do. Jump onto a train that he knows is about to explode. Climb out of a two-and-a-half-ton cement truck and surf it on a forty-two-foot wave of water."[6]

The primary reason why McClane jumped through those hoops, however, changed in *Die Hard with a Vengeance*. McClane fought against impossible odds to save his family in the first two *Die Hard* movies. He and Holly had separated long enough for her to start using her maiden name, Gennaro. But the couple ended *Die Hard* in a loving embrace, and a brief phone conversation near the start of *Die Hard 2* found John promising his wife a romantic interlude, where they'd "check into a hotel, leave the kids with your parents, order some room service." The McClane marriage appeared stable—strong, even—for the last time in the franchise.

When *Die Hard with a Vengeance* begins, Holly has left John for reasons we're never given. He's estranged from his kids, and suspended from the police force. Lieutenant McClane responds by drowning his sorrows in booze, smoking cigarettes, and watching episodes of *Captain Kangaroo*. He's surly, unshaven, and half-asleep. He's perpetually hungover, which makes him short-tempered. McClane was never a pristine white knight, but the *With a Vengeance* version of the character comes with so many jagged edges, it's nearly impossible for us to embrace him, if not for the established goodwill from the previous two films.

I'd argue that the personal motivations driving McClane in *Die Hard 2* are more relatable than the riddles and red herrings that propel him through *Die Hard with a Vengeance*. The first two features center around a husband and father who pushed himself past his breaking point to preserve his family. It's a sentiment virtually everyone watching can recognize.

"Hey, fuck Monday morning. My wife's on one of the God damn planes these guys are fucking with. That puts me on the playing field," McClane barks back at the contemptuous Captain Carmine Lorenzo (the outstanding Dennis Franz) in *Die Hard 2*. "And if you'd have moved your fat ass when I told you to, we wouldn't be hip deep in shit right now."

Those passionate, emotional stakes don't carry over to *With a Vengeance*, and the decisions—both in the writing, and in Willis's performance choices—start to make McClane prickly, less engaged, and borderline unlikeable. His police colleagues pity him. His disgruntled partner, Zeus (Samuel L. Jackson), largely dismisses him as a loser. Willis and Jackson do share an incredible chemistry that's sparked by mutual disdain, and it evolves into the tangible respect survivors often feel following a traumatic experience. But what's most troubling in *With a Vengeance* is that McClane isn't compelled to defeat the bad guy. He's forced to by a powerful manipulator—one who tortures McClane with wild goose chases and overly complicated kids' games involving jugs of water. Worse than that, it's in *With a Vengeance* where our once vulnerable blue-collar cop jettisons his humanity and becomes the cliched unstoppable machine of an action movie protagonist.

The John McClane Abuse-O-Meter

Another unofficial rule of the *Die Hard* franchise is that by the end of each movie, John McClane should be beaten to a bloody pulp. Whether it be from running across shards of broken glass, ejecting out of an exploding cockpit, falling from a bridge to the deck of a cargo ship, or fist-fighting multiple terrorists, McClane should always limp across the finish line, his body being held together by sheer willpower.

McClane takes his requisite lumps in *Die Hard 2*, ending the picture by getting his bloodied and broken body kicked off the wing of a moving airplane by Colonel Stuart (who impressed audiences earlier in the movie with his naked tai chi). McClane's physical punishments would test a man's boundaries, but he doesn't do anything so extraordinary that it borders on comical, or takes you out of a moment because it's too incredible. Harlin takes the time to show how difficult it is for McClane to lift a heavy grate as a plane's wheel races toward him, or how fast he'd have to move to secure himself inside an ejector seat before a dozen hand grenades ignite. The believable adrenaline, intensity, and fear Willis conjures in the exploding-cockpit sequence help make it one of my favorite moments in the *Die Hard* series.

"I have the same goals in this one that I had in the first one in that I don't want John McClane to be a superhero," Willis said of *Die Hard 2*. "I don't want him to be invincible."[7]

That goal changed between *Die Hard 2* and *Die Hard with a Vengeance*, because in McTiernan's sequel, McClane goes from tough and credibly durable to an unkillable force with exceptional skills. He survives a close-range explosion that's powerful enough to derail a subway car. He single-handedly dispenses with four European terrorists—one of them the size of an NBA power forward—in the cramped confines of an elevator car. With only one remaining bullet, McClane pulls off an impossible shot by hitting an electrical wire in the perfect spot and sending it toward Simon Gruber's helicopter, grounding the chopper in explosive fashion.

With a Vengeance also contains the indisputable "jump the shark" moment in the *Die Hard* series: McClane surfing on the top of a dump truck.

Radio personality Jon Hein coined the phrase *jump the shark* in 1985, and it's been part of the pop-culture lexicon since. Hein was referring to a 1977 episode of the TV sitcom *Happy Days*, which featured the beloved character Arthur "Fonzie" Fonzarelli (Henry Winkler) water skiing in bathing trunks and his signature leather jacket as he jumped over a tank containing a shark. The plot was not a creative highpoint for the show, and so the phrase *jump the shark* started to represent the moment when a television series, movie franchise, consumer product, political movement, or anything with a measurable level of popularity started to backslide from its perceived apex.

When McClane climbs out of the driver's side window and surfs atop his dump truck while thousands of gallons of rushing water overwhelm him in a New York aqueduct, the *Die Hard* series officially jumps the shark and never looks back.

Visually speaking, the sequence looks ridiculous. The torrential stream approaching McClane in the aqueduct looks like a black cloud of digital pixels. While attempting an escape, McClane manages to spin the two-and-a-half-ton truck 180 degrees in one fluid motion, something the most experienced driver could never accomplish. Once McClane realizes his vehicle won't outrun the water, he exits the truck's cab and surfs on top. It remains the lamest visual effect in the entire series. And yet the scene gets remarkably worse. McClane manages to grab hold of an open grate, pull himself into a tunnel leading to the surface, and gets spit out in a geyser of fluid at the exact spot where Jackson's Zeus is driving past at the very moment.

Goodbye, logic.

Nitpicking an action set piece in a franchise that features our hero wrapping a fire hose around his waist and leaping from the top of a thirty-five-story skyscraper sounds silly. But up until the dump-truck surf, the *Die Hard* movies appeared to care about grounding the physical limitations of its hero. McClane endured an extreme amount of bodily damage, but he faced danger we believed he could survive. The crushing disappointment of the overplayed dump truck sequence is that this became the norm for the *Die Hard* series moving forward. The two post-*Vengeance* sequels ignored logical physical statutes so they could stage more spectacular stunts. The hero who found it hard to die eventually became impossible to kill. There's a significant difference between those two, and only one of them makes for gripping storytelling.

Final Verdict

Die Hard with a Vengeance isn't a bad film, but it's a disappointing *Die Hard* film. McTiernan loosened his once-firm grip on the character, encouraging him to sink to a depressing moral depth. Impromptu rewrites involving detours to Yankee Stadium, trivia questions about the twenty-first US president, and serial numbers on the bottom of aspirin bottles deflate the enormous tensions that propelled the first two films in the series. If Willis toplined the picture playing any character not named John McClane, *With a Vengeance* could pass as a slick, gritty, efficient, explosive, far-fetched summer blockbuster with two firecracker leads, some memorable action set pieces, and a third act that overreached its goals. Producers likely would have offered Willis and Jackson at least one sequel, to see if lightning could strike the same spot twice.

But viewed through the *Die Hard* lens, counterintuitive character choices and weaker-than-expected plotting shave crucial value points off *Die Hard with a Vengeance*. It begins the steady decline in quality that would tarnish the remainder of the series. Only *Die Hard 2*, by admittedly replicating the beats of the original, maintained the magical ingredients that made Die Hard special, and marked the last time we saw the selfless, dogged, courageous version of McClane that I recognized as the hero of Nakatomi Plaza.

CHAPTER TWENTY-ONE
LIVE FREE OR DIE HARD /
A GOOD DAY TO DIE HARD

. . . AND THE END OF THE *DIE HARD* SERIES

John, you're a Timex watch in a digital age.
—TECH SAVVY VILLAIN THOMAS GABRIEL (TIMOTHY OLYPHANT)
TO A STUBBORN JOHN MCCLANE (WILLIS)

—1—

"This is not a good idea. . . ." Veteran New York Police Detective John McClane speaks these prophetic words while leaning out the driver's side of a speeding patrol car. The durable but aging hero is preparing to exit the vehicle, hit the pavement, and send the car airborne like a makeshift rocket where, if all goes well, it will take out a helicopter that's hovering outside the entrance of a Washington, D.C., tunnel.

McClane's hasty assessment referred to the deadly stunt, one of many inventive set pieces created from the entertaining sequel *Live Free or Die Hard*. But those six words—which also are a callback to McClane hopping on a moving subway in *Die Hard with a Vengeance*—could equally have represented Willis's internal monologue as the film star contemplated signing on for the fourth installment in his signature *Die Hard* franchise. Willis had plenty of reason to worry. Len Wiseman's *Live Free or Die Hard* opened in theaters on June 27, 2007—just shy of the twentieth anniversary of John McTiernan's 1988 masterpiece. Audiences supported the *Die Hard* sequels over the years, but action movies like *Casino Royale* (2005), *Batman Begins* (2005), and the *Bourne* franchise changed appetites to darker and grittier fare, and there was uncertainty about how the blue-collar McClane might fit in to the post–September 11 landscape.

"Have you done stuff like that before?" McClane gets asked after he brutally takes out a team of heavily armed mercenaries.

"Yeah," he replies, adding, "Not for a long time."

Legacy sequels can work if the intentions are noble and producers assemble the right creative team. Joseph Koskinski and Tom Cruise, for example, returned to the skies over the Top Gun flight school thirty-six years after Pete "Maverick" Mitchell first felt the need for speed. As a result, 2022's *Top Gun: Maverick* tapped into the mainstream audience's affinity for an integral film from their childhoods. They broke box-office records, rejuvenated a post-COVID theatrical exhibition model, and took home an Academy Award for Best Sound.

At the same time, no sequel guarantees success, and you can count on one hand the number of long-running film franchises that improved beyond the third film without recasting (like the timeless James Bond series) or reinventing its central wheel (like the *Fast and Furious* saga, which moved from street racing to high-stakes, international espionage). Hollywood treats nostalgia as a powerful narcotic. Digging up the past can lead to surprising hits (*Jurassic World*, *Creed*, and 2018's *Halloween*), but also embarrassing misses (*The Godfather: Part III*, *The Two Jakes*, or 2021's *The Matrix Resurrections*).

Against these odds, Wiseman's first stab at a *Die Hard* movie worked extremely well, coming up with a timely, feasible, and suitably relentless action thriller tailored to the strengths of the franchise's perpetual underdog protagonist. Like McTiernan's *Die Hard with a Vengeance*, the *Live Free* screenplay started off as a generic action treatment that was fashioned into a *Die Hard* adventure. *Enemy of the State* screenwriter David Marconi came up with the idea for his *WW3.com* script after reading a 2011 *Wired* article about possible cyberterrorist attacks on the US government. Marconi invented the concept of a "fire sale," a targeted attack on our nation's infrastructure that would use computers to shut down America's transportation systems, financial institutes, and utility grids if terrorist demands weren't met. Screenwriters Doug Richardson and Mark Bomback gradually took turns at revising the existing story into a possible *Die Hard* vehicle, which shifted from *Die Hard*

4.0 to *Die Hard: Reset* as it solidified McClane's involvement and made him the central hero.

This should have been the last *Die Hard*. Too bad for all involved, it wasn't.

—2—

Willis thought about bringing John McClane back a few years earlier. The military drama *Tears of the Sun* started out as a possible "Die Hard in the Jungle" experiment before the team pivoted. By the time *Live Free or Die Hard* surfaced, Willis found himself interested in exploring the dynamic between his old-school hero and a new-school style of techno anarchist in Thomas Gabriel.

"When I heard Len's vision of the film, a light went off. I told him my secret goal, wanting to do a film that was as good as the first film," Willis said. "Hearing his point of view, and the technology side of it, bringing the film into the 21st century, but still doing an old-school, real stunts, smashmouth hard core film seemed to be the right thing to do."[1]

Live Free or Die Hard marks the last time Willis appeared invested in portraying McClane on screen. He moved like an agile action star, for one of the last times in his career. He strategized, and reacted on the fly, the way the resourceful McClane did in the previous films. His quips, punched up by *Die Hard with a Vengeance* script doctor William Wisher, were sharper than anticipated. "Is the circus in town?" McClane grumbles when a soldier who's proficient in parkour (Cyril Raffaelli) lands on our hero's windshield.

And the elaborate action sequences conceived for *Live Free or Die Hard*, many of them done practically, justified the franchise's return. Willis couldn't ignore his age (he was fifty-two when the film came out), so he made his crusty detective more jaded, frustrated, and unappreciated by his employers, his family (personified by Mary Elizabeth Winstead playing a grown Lucy McClane), and the computer hacker (Justin Long) he has agreed to protect. But Willis fully committed to the grueling requirements of the film's many stunts, the high point being a visceral fight with the magnificent Maggie Q that concludes with the two stars wrestling inside an SUV that's dangling from cables inside of a tight elevator shaft. "I wanted McClane to look like he could still take whatever's thrown at him," Willis said, explaining why he stepped up his workout regime ahead of filming on *Live Free*. "[It was] just to get my muscles big enough so I wouldn't break my bones diving around the concrete with these young stunt guys."[2]

Wiseman, meanwhile, takes a safe approach to his picture. He might not impress with his technique, but he also doesn't steal attention away from his star by attempting the choppy camera flourishes and jarring edits the *Bourne* movies popularized at this time. Still, *Live Free or Die Hard* has issues that can't be overlooked. In an effort to increase the scope, Wiseman's action covers nearly the entirety of the Eastern seaboard (a complaint I continue to have against *Die Hard with a Vengeance*). "In a sense, America itself becomes the building McClane is trapped in," Bomback said about their plotting, but that approach eliminates the claustrophobic intensity of the first two *Die Hard* movies.[3] There's also the lingering and toxic thread regarding McClane's family, and the fact that they now hate his guts. It's a narrative choice that rubs me the wrong way. Lucy wants nothing to do with her father in their first awkward scene together. She refuses to take his phone calls. She's using her mother's maiden name of Gennaro. And she may have fibbed to her boyfriend about her dad's . . . life status.

"You told this jerkoff I was dead?" McClane exclaims as he breaks up Lucy's make-out session on the college girl's campus.

"I may have exaggerated a little bit," she barks back.

Ultimately, Willis's ability to recapture McClane's disdain for authority and fondness for being the fly in the ointment, the monkey in the wrench, and the pain in the ass for the terrorist of the moment puts *Live Free* on the same level as *Die Hard* and *Die Harder*, in my opinion. As I observed in the review I wrote for FilmCritic.com at the time of release, "The action in *Live Free* gets increasingly bombastic, and only the final confrontation involving a semi truck and an F-35 fighter jet pushes the envelope beyond the realm of credibility. There's nothing quite as good as McClane jumping off a roof with a fire hose wrapped around his waist, and there's nothing quite as laughable as the character surfing on top of a dump truck as an aqueduct fills with rushing water. *Live Free* works best because it gives us two additional hours with a character we thought Hollywood had retired. Willis slips comfortably back into McClane's shoes for another rescue mission, and we happily go along for the ride."[4]

Of course, Willis has since retired—just, not in time to prevent the atrocious *A Good Day to Die Hard* from being made.

Roger Ebert famously wrote about Rob Reiner's fantasy comedy *North* (coincidentally costarring Willis), "I hated this movie. Hated, hated, hated, hated, hated this movie. Hated it. Hated every simpering, stupid, vacant, audience-insulting moment of it. Hated the sensibility that thought anyone would like it. Hated the implied insult to the audience by its belief that anyone would be entertained by it."[5]

That's how I feel about John Moore's loathsome *A Good Day to Die Hard*, a joyless catastrophe that sends McClane to Russia for a nonsensical mission alongside his grown son, Jack (Jai Courtney). It's embarrassing to consider this an official entry into the *Die Hard* canon, as it bears no resemblance to its predecessors, and makes a mockery of the ingredients that made the initial film special.

In my original review published on *CinemaBlend*, I called *Good Day* "silly, incoherent and cartoonish to a fault," while also observing, "[d]ying no longer is hard for Bruce Willis's besieged New York cop . . . it's downright impossible. The resilient hero who once swallowed his fears to prevent random acts of terrorism is gone, replaced by a walking, talking superego whose bloodlust compels him to 'kill all the scumbags,' as he succinctly puts it. Justice, his own survival, and the lives of innocents around him are side effects this cyborg savior rarely considers."[6]

It's not just that Moore has zero ability to stage an articulate action sequence, though believe me, that's a serious issue. *Good Day* offers little more than a mind-numbing barrage of stale quips, crunching metal, and exploding body parts. "If a traditional action scene utilizes 250 edits, Moore shoehorns nearly 1,000 cuts into each headache-inducing stunt sequence," I wrote, "panning and zooming with reckless abandon as the superhuman McClane steamrolls over Russian bystanders, leaps from radioactive buildings, and swings from the tail of a helicopter like a kite string caught in a hurricane."

The central and inexcusable issue I have with *A Good Day to Die Hard* is that Moore and his credited screenwriters—and Willis, who's guilty by association—interpret John McClane in a way that contradicts the heroic fiber that previous helmers John McTiernan, Renny Harlin, and Wiseman worked hard to establish. The team on *Good Day* possesses no understanding of why audiences rooted for the underdog McClane for decades. They turn the once vulnerable, human, and sympathetic do-gooder into a sadistic, selfish fiend who murders hundreds of faceless bad guys, not out of any sense of duty or honor, but because they're in his way. They misunderstand McClane at the root level.

This exchange angers me. When choreographing potential action set pieces for *Good Day*, Moore and his team scouted Moscow, ending up in gridlock traffic while driving along the city's circular Garden Ring roadway. Moore concluded that this would be an ideal location for an extended chase scene they had been contemplating.

"It made perfect sense," Moore said. "If John McClane was gridlocked, John McClane would drive over traffic."[7]

And so, McClane does. In the final *Good Day* cut, John steals a Mercedes-Benz G-Class SUV so he can pursue Jack, who is also chasing the film's primary adversary, Alik (Radivoje Bukvic), away from a courthouse. Before hijacking the vehicle, McClane punches out an innocent Russian driver, screaming, "Do you think I understand a word you say?" And finally, in a disgusting display of wanton carnage, McClane drives the SUV on top of a traffic jam, demolishing mostly empty vehicles but undoubtedly crushing helpless drivers in the process. Moore even includes audio of a woman's scream as McClane crushes her car, shouting "Sorry, ma'am," before racing away.

Compare this *A Good Day to Die Hard* scene to a similar chase in McTiernan's superior *Die Hard with a Vengeance* to see how far Moore (and Willis) allowed McClane to fall. The sequence begins with our hero and Zeus (Samuel L. Jackson) on a payphone with Simon. They're told there is "a significant amount of explosive in the trash receptacle next to you." If they try to run, Simon claims he'll ignite it.

"Yeah, nobody's going to run, but I got a hundred people out here," McClane pleads. He's thinking about possible innocent victims, not himself. When Simon misleads McClane by telling him he and Zeus solved the St. Ives riddle too slowly, our hero again doesn't run. He shouts warnings at nearby pedestrians and dives on as many of them as he possibly can, trying to serve and protect in what he thinks are his final moments.

That's the selfless heroism I associate with McClane. And it only continues from there. Told by Simon that they need to travel ninety blocks in New York traffic to reach the Wall Street subway station in thirty minutes, McClane and Zeus commandeer a taxi cab (without physically assaulting the driver) and head directly through Central Park. Because, as we learn, "the best way south is not Ninth Avenue. It's through the Park." And as they race across the occupied greenways, McClane lays on the car horn, stays off the bike paths, and does everything in his power not to aim for the people—except maybe the mime.

It's one comparison. But analyzing these conflicting approaches to Willis's signature action hero in *Die Hard with a Vengeance* versus *A Good Day to Die Hard* illustrates the line separating John McClane from being a commendable, compassionate, and upstanding cinematic role model from being the reckless, callous renegade who ends up being no better than the villains he's trying to subdue. I don't recognize John McClane in this fifth and final *Die Hard* movie. Moreso, I reject this personification.

"You're not going to open up to me right before we die. No, that's not your thing," Jack yells at his father. "Killing bad guys. That's your thing!"

If that's what you believe McClane's "thing" is, then you watched the *Die Hard* movies incorrectly and left with the wrong lessons.

"Need a hug?" John sarcastically asks Jack at one point.

"We're not really a hugging family," Jack replies, and John agrees.

Except once upon a time, you were. The closing moments of both *Die Hard* and *Die Hard 2: Die Harder* found John lovingly embracing Holly, having laid his body on the line to ensure her safety. *Live Free* ends with Lucy wrapping her arms around her father and proclaiming, "I knew you would come for me." Where did that guy go? Why did Willis allow his legacy character to stop being the sensitive, emotional hero confessing to his wife through tears that he feared he'd never see her again?

And how is it possible that the nauseating *A Good Day to Die Hard* still isn't the Die Hard frachise's lowest point?

—4—

Willis drove the final nail into the *Die Hard* coffin on October 18, 2020. That evening, during a primetime NFL contest between the Green Bay Packers and the Tampa Bay Buccaneers, Willis reprised his legendary character John McClane one last time—not for a movie, despite years of persistent rumors swirling around a possible *Die Hard 6*; not even for a prestige television program made with the support of a pedigreed streaming platform.

No, Willis's final performance as his signature cop, John McClane, appears in a two-minute advertisement produced by Advance Auto Parts to help sell DieHard car batteries. The hero we first met on an airplane landing at LAX ends up driving off into the night, with his one-time limo driver Argyle (De'voreaux White) at the wheel. He jumps through a plate glass window. He crawls through an air vent. He recognizes Theo (Clarence Gilyard), an original member of Hans Gruber's team, despite the fact the two characters never once crossed paths in *Die Hard*. And when Argyle attempts to deliver McClane's catchphrase, "Yippee-ki-yay," John cuts him off and jokes, "Hey, that's my line."

It was. It is. It always will be. Almost every male movie star at the time passed on *Die Hard* before the role fell to Willis. It was the part he was born to play. Willis recognized John McClane as one of the working-class guys he knew from back home in New Jersey.

"'*Die Hard* is probably the closest I've come to showing what is in my heart on screen," Willis said in a 1988 interview. "In *Die Hard*, even though I'm acting, a lot of what is in me came through. I really wanted to play a vulnerable guy. I didn't want to be a superhero who's a larger than life guy that nobody really knows. I don't know any superheroes. I know guys who are afraid and have anxiety. And I think you know people like that, too. That's what I wanted to play. I really wanted to be honest about the moment you go through when you think your life is about to end. I wanted to play somebody who was afraid to die."[8]

And by doing so, he created a character who will live forever.

CONCLUSION

BRUCE WILLIS'S MOUNT RUSHMORE

Official movie poster for Terry Gilliam's *12 Monkeys*, starring Bruce Willis. *Author's Collection*

The phrase "give me your Mount Rushmore" operates as a measuring stick for almost any topic. The exercise asks someone to list off the four items that they personally think best represents the category in question. You can go broad with it. "Give me your Mount Rushmore of NBA basketball players." My own list would be Michael Jordan, LeBron James, Bill Russell, and Larry Bird. You can also get very specific with it. "Give me your Mount Rushmore of Van Halen songs with David Lee Roth singing lead vocals." For me, that's "Ain't Talkin' 'Bout Love" from their debut album, "Dance the Night Away" off *Van Halen 2*, "Unchained" off *Fair Warning*, and 1984's seminal radio hit, "Jump."

You know what's coming next. What's your Mount Rushmore for Bruce Willis movies? Note, I specified movies, which means *Moonlighting* is off the table, and automatically moved to an Honorable Mention category. The show's impact is unquestionable. We might not get Willis without *Moonlighting*, and David Addison is an iconic character, so you could easily carve his features into the Willis Mount Rushmore. But we're focusing on films for this exercise. Those are the rules.

John McTiernan's *Die Hard* has to be on there. It's a perfect action movie, a flawlessly paced Christmas thriller about an undercover cop disrupting European criminals from escaping Nakatomi Plaza with millions in stolen bearer bonds. The Hollywood sensation created its own genre as it made Willis an overnight global superstar. But blue-collar hero John McClane also became the blueprint for numerous underdog law enforcement agents Willis went on to play for the remainder of his career. He never managed to fill McClane's shoes—or lack of shoes—but he delivered a number of entertaining movies in his effort to replicate *Die Hard*'s success.

Quentin Tarantino's *Pulp Fiction* gets my second spot on Willis's Mount Rushmore. It's arguably the best movie, start to finish, that Willis has been involved with. And Tarantino asks Willis to shuffle through a staggering amount of difficult emotions over the course of his character's short story, "The Gold Watch," including pride, self-doubt, elation, love, fear, and bone-chilling terror. *Pulp Fiction* also begins Willis's experimentation with his own quiet, commanding screen presence, which would bolster the remarkable features *The Sixth Sense*, *Unbreakable*, *Sin City*, *12 Monkeys*, and *Looper*.

Speaking of which, I'm going with M. Night Shyamalan's *Unbreakable* for my third spot. I already hear you complaining that I'm leaving Willis's first collaboration with Shyamalan off the Mount. But *The Sixth Sense* walked so that *Unbreakable* could run. It's the better of the two movies, and probably Shyamalan's best film, overall. The mellow, deliberately paced superhero-origin story helped kick off the comic-book craze that swept through the industry, but it sidesteps special effects in favor of a spectacular Willis performance as David Dunne, a strong man who's slow to accept his possible invulnerability. Like *Sixth Sense*, *Unbreakable* surprised audiences with a twist ending, though this time, the twist wasn't the entire point. As Roger Ebert wrote, "If this movie were about nothing else, it would be a full portrait of a man in crisis, at work and at home." Credit Willis for embodying that human conflict in the most compelling way possible.

Finally, my Mount Rushmore concludes with what I believe is Willis's best performance, and that's as possible time traveler James Cole in Terry Gilliam's mesmerizing *12 Monkeys*. Willis so effectively conveys Cole's uncertainty about his reality that we're never completely sure if he's truly from the future, or just a present-day, incapacitated asylum patient. Brad Pitt got all the attention, and the accolades, for chewing scenery through *12 Monkeys*. But it's Willis's brilliant central performance, quietly reacting to Pitt's lunacy, that stands the test of time in this movie's wake.

Your choices may be different, and none of them would be wrong. Willis left his fans with an incredible body of work to appreciate, one that spanned decades. The New Jersey kid climbed to Hollywood's highest heights. Even harder, he figured out how to stay there for the duration of his A-list career. He survived trends and sustained his viability by choosing challenging creative partners, lucrative franchise screenplays, intriguing indie projects, and a bevy of fledgling filmmakers who needed his support to get a foot in the door.

Willis's charmed life came up during a particularly insightful conversation with PBS interviewer Charlie Rose in 2002. The actor typically derided the press, an attitude provoked by his experiences with invasive tabloid journalists over the years. But when asked about the self-satisfaction Willis had to be feeling about all that he had accomplished in his chosen field, the star got refreshingly candid.

"I've been really fortunate," he said. "I consider myself to be really blessed by God. I don't know how it happened, or why. I know actors that are ten times better actors than I am who don't get work, or don't get offered films. I don't know why it happens, and I do. I really don't. I mean, the films that I've done, some of them have made some money. Some substantial money. So the studios would like to see more of that substantial money come in. That's the easy part to understand."[1]

He's not wrong. The box-office tracker the Numbers reports that Willis's movies have earned more than $5.2 billion in worldwide aggregate box office. But Willis, in his own words, would tell you it's not about the money and never has been.

"I want to try and live my life as a good man. And be able to look back when it's done and say I did that, for the most part," Willis once told an interviewer. "I want to be a good father to my children. I want to cultivate the friendships that I have, and keep those things working. It's important to me. Family is important to me. And giving back. I mean, I've been given a lot of things. Things that I'd never expected, and things that exceed anything that I ever could have possibly imagined. So it's not that difficult to give back."[2]

And while his final stages appear to be marked by an unexpected battle with a complicated language disorder, it's that fighting spirit that Willis has shown throughout the course of his professional career that we will remember. No matter how successful, he managed to maintain an underdog status that kept audiences around the globe rooting for him, cheering him on, and celebrating his triumphs. That resilience, that fortitude, and that grit colored Willis's final words to the crowd that had gathered for his Comedy Central Roast in 2018.

"Nothing can keep me down," Willis growled at the audience, that permanent shit-eating grin replaced with a scowl. "I've been attacked by terrorists, asteroids, film critics, music critics, restaurant critics, divorce lawyers, male-pattern baldness, and none of it—none of it—stopped me.

"Because I am still Bruce fucking Willis."[3]

Yippee ki-yay.

Portions of this book were written between March 2022 and August 2023 in New York City; Los Angeles, San Francisco, and San Diego; London; Charlotte, North Carolina; and Key Largo, Florida. Wherever I went, Bruce followed. The ride was spectacular. I hope I did him justice.

APPENDIX

CAPSULE REVIEWS OF EVERY BRUCE WILLIS FILM

The First Deadly Sin (1980): Bruce Willis's feature film debut, a blink-and-you-missed it appearance in a morose Frank Sinatra potboiler about a New York City police detective connecting the dots on a potential serial killer. Look for Willis wearing a hat as he passes Sinatra on his way into a restaurant. Every actor has to start somewhere. The delicious irony of Willis kicking off in a Sinatra feature is that *Die Hard*'s literary source material—Roderick Thorp's *Nothing Lasts Forever*—was a sequel to the author's *The Detective*, which Sinatra adapted in 1968. As a result, Sinatra had to pass on the option to play detective Joe Leland in *Die Hard* before the part could be recast. He did (Ol' Blue Eyes would have been seventy-two years old around the time of filming). Joe Leland became John McClane. And Hollywood history was made. (★★☆☆)

The Verdict (1982): Paul Newman mesmerizes in Sidney Lumet's brooding and melancholic courtroom drama about an alcoholic ambulance chaser trying to redeem his soul by winning a tangled case. *The Verdict* earned Newman his sixth Oscar nomination in the Best Actor category, and belongs on the short list of roles you'd show to anyone questioning how gripping the performer could be on screen. It's mentioned here because of Willis's brief stint as a courtroom attendee, spotted over Newman's shoulders in select scenes. (★★★★)

Blind Date (1987): Like many who came before him, Willis used broad comedy as his bridge from television success to movie stardom, playing a hapless office worker in need of a date for an important work function. Willis mainly sets up, then reacts to, the outlandish physical comedy executed by *Night Court*'s John Larroquette and a recklessly drunk Kim Basinger. But that sly smile he flashes in the closing moments of the film—as his character stands over a pool, ready to dive in—finally shows the charismatic leading man Willis was destined to become. (★★⯪☆)

Sunset (1988): Wyatt Earp (James Garner) agrees to mentor a red-hot cinematic Western star (Willis), then both find themselves mixed up in a muddled murder mystery. Garner is remarkably suave as the confident lawman, and Willis already fits the part of a brash movie star enjoying his view from Hollywood's summit. But the drawn-out and dull *Sunset* says nothing interesting about celebrity, lacks the savage observations of Blake Edwards's comedic features, and wrings zero suspense out of its criminal subplot. And that's the truth . . . give or take a lie or two. (★⯪☆☆)

Die Hard (1988): The quintessential underdog action flick. John McTiernan's white-knuckle roller-coaster ride reinvented a genre as it made blue-collar, Regular Joe heroes credible. Willis's sarcastic wit counters Alan Rickman's icy arrogance at every turn, and the pacing remains tight and composed between each of the film's spectacular set pieces. The rare occasion where every element works, producing a perfect high-octane thriller and one of Hollywood history's most enjoyable rides. (★★★★)

In Country (1989): A well-intentioned but mawkish antiwar two-hander about an inquisitive teenage girl (Emily Lloyd) tending to her Vietnam veteran uncle (Willis) while also hoping to learn more about her killed-in-action father and the atrocities both men faced overseas. Willis gives an extraordinary performance, mixing his radiant movie-star confidence with the nonchalant demeanor of a Kentucky ranch hand. *In Country* feels like a deliberate pushback against his overnight *Die Hard* success, a necessary reminder to the industry—and probably himself—that he could be effective in an against-the-grain character-actor role. But while Willis operates with a scalpel, director Norman Jewison (*Moonstruck*, *In the Heat of the Night*) and the remaining cast bludgeon the material with an emotional sledgehammer, pulverizing even the most sincere anti-war messages found in the script. (★★☆☆)

Look Who's Talking (1989): Single mom Molly (Kirstie Alley) and her handsome babysitter James (John Travolta) fall in and out of a romantic entanglement as they bond over a shared love for Molly's son, Mikey (voiced by Willis). It's a cute gimmick, and Willis's one liners—delivered with enthusiasm and ample amounts of charm—are the highlight of the whole endeavor. Too bad writer-director Amy Heckerling has no plot beyond her amusing premise, so Travolta and Alley mostly flounder through sequences that are so contrived, any audience member over the age of two can see where they're going. (★★☆☆)

Die Hard 2 (1990): Director Renny Harlin recycles beats from John McTiernan's masterpiece—terrorists raise hell during the Christmas holiday, and only John McClane (Willis) stands in their way—but can't quite make lightning strike the same spot twice. While not as taut as its predecessor, *Die Hard 2* does benefit from a still-eager Willis punishing his body thanks to McClane's signature won't-quit attitude, and the ensemble of character actors in supporting parts (William Sadler, Franco Nero, John Amos, Dennis Franz) keep the dialogue sharp, colorful, and loaded with attitude. (★★★⯪)

Look Who's Talking Too (1990): Heckerling gets the band back together for a cash-grab sequel that's crude, childish, racist, and sexist. To his credit, Willis continues to mine decent laughs by voicing the inner thoughts of a toddler, this time dealing with the frustrations of potty training—I'm permanently scarred by the sight of Mel Brooks voicing the monstrous Mr. Toilet Man—and the arrival of a little sister (voiced by Roseanne Barr). (★⯪☆☆)

The Bonfire of the Vanities (1990): A miscalculation on almost every level. Brian De Palma was the wrong choice to adapt Tom Wolfe's satirical novel about race and class warfare into a sensationalist version of New York City. Too-nice Tom Hanks doesn't understand how to play Sherman McCoy, a Wall Street baron and self-professed "Master of the Universe" whose life unravels when he's part of a highly publicized hit-and-run accident. Additional casting mistakes and a misunderstanding of tone doom the rest of *Bonfire*, though I thoroughly enjoyed Willis as Peter Fallow, a failing journalist who rides

McCoy's coattails to literary success, and becomes a media-created monster in the process. Willis understood the assignment, so his nimble performance remains the only salvageable aspect of this otherwise disappointing misfire. (★☆☆☆)

Mortal Thoughts (1991): Willis told talk-show host Charlie Rose that he considered this to be "one of my top two or three films" during a 2002 interview. It's easy to understand why. Alan Rudolph's sordid psychological thriller centered around spousal abuse allows the actor to test his range—and challenge his fan base—by playing a despicable, abusive alcoholic. Too bad Rudolph doesn't comprehend subtlety, and the film's explorations of guilt are woefully melodramatic. The draw, at the time, was seeing celebrity couple Willis and Demi Moore sharing scenes together. But Willis's convincing portrayal of a manipulative scumbag is the sole reason *Mortal Thoughts* should be remembered today. (★★☆☆)

Hudson Hawk (1991): An ambitious and enjoyable mess of a movie that takes such enormous swings—Willis and Danny Aiello play singing cat burglars who are blackmailed into stealing pieces of a machine invented by Leonardo da Vinci—it almost earns a pass for its absurd plotting and surrealistic buffoonery. Loosely inspired by an original Willis idea (the actor receives his first and only "story by" credits), the madcap *Hudson Hawk* resembles a live-action Looney Tunes cartoon, packed with assassins named after candy bars, a network of papal spies protecting the Vatican, and an inspired ambulance chase across the Brooklyn Bridge. The whole thing is overly complicated and relentlessly silly, but you have to admire its originality, born out of an unwillingness to play by traditional filmmaking rules. (★★★☆)

Billy Bathgate (1991): In the opening scene of Robert Benton's period mobster picture, Willis sinks his teeth into some tantalizing Tom Stoppard dialogue while verbally sparring with a menacing Dustin Hoffman, a terrified Nicole Kidman, and a subdued Steve Buscemi. It's the film's high point. Willis shuffles through a full assortment of emotions—defiance, contrition, sorrow, and anger—during ten impactful minutes, mainly because he's playing a man who's tied to a chair with his feet buried in cement after angering the wrong criminals. The first half of *Billy Bathgate* fills in their gaps, with Hoffman's Dutch Schultz mentoring an Irish kid from the neighborhood (Loren Dean), and getting double-crossed by Bo Weinberg (Willis), his top lieutenant. Rarely has Willis been more cocky, dapper, and magnetic as he woos Kidman and backstabs Hoffman. He dominates his handful of scenes, which are all the more ominous because we know his character's watery fate. It also means he's absent from the film's bland and uneven second half, which shifts into a homespun small-town fable and a flavorless forbidden-romance story that feels totally detached from the movie we started watching. (★★☆☆)

The Last Boy Scout (1991): *Lethal Weapon* scribe Shane Black penned this ballsy buddy-cop thriller about a disgraced private detective (Willis) and a washed-up NFL quarterback (Damon Wayans) teaming up to prevent the assassination of the senator who's opposed to legalized gambling in Los Angeles. A weathered and beaten Willis excels as a streetwise, chain-smoking investigator. Joe Hallenbeck is Willis's coolest action character not named John McClane. If only the heavily rewritten third act didn't spin so out of control—with Wayans riding a horse through a professional football game and stopping a sniper's bullet with a well-thrown spiral—this would be revered as a 1990s action classic instead of just a competent entertainer. (★★★☆)

The Player (1992): Paranoia and guilt engulf a Hollywood studio executive (Tim Robbins) after death threats scrawled on postcards start arriving at his office. Director Robert Altman's fly-on-the-wall approach to dialogue captures innocuous film-industry banter, though the mildly scathing Hollywood jabs eventually take a back seat to a flavorless murder mystery. Willis's lone scene, where he rescues Julia Roberts at the conclusion of a fake film, acts as a cynical punchline about artistic integrity, which gets compromised on a daily basis in the soulless studio system. (★★★☆)

Death Becomes Her (1992): A spectacular oddity from Robert Zemeckis that flies in the face of everything audiences had come to expect from Willis— and that's a wonderful thing. Willis's henpecked character largely supports two swing-for-the-fences performances from Meryl Streep and Goldie Hawn, playing lifelong rivals fighting over a youth-inducing potion. He displays incredible control while playing a man spinning out of control as the macabre and murderous mayhem spirals around him. Sadly, this is one of the last broad comedic performances to which Willis would completely surrender himself. (★★★☆)

Loaded Weapon 1 (1993): Samuel L. Jackson and Emilio Estevez earn legitimate laughs in this cameo-laden send up of *Basic Instinct*, *Silence of the Lambs*, *Wayne's World*, and (of course) the Joel Silver-produced *Lethal Weapon* franchise. Relentlessly silly, but also frequently laugh-out-loud funny, the film slips Willis into one amusing scene that lampoons both *Die Hard* and Mel Gibson's explosive beach scene where heavily armed goons shoot up the wrong mobile home. (★★★☆)

Striking Distance (1993): Right before *Pulp Fiction* refocused his career, Willis detoured into this peculiar serial-killer thriller set in the Pittsburgh River Rescue community. That, alone, helps *Striking Distance* stand apart from competing stories in the action genre, and Willis keeps the whole thing watchable with an admirable version of his beleaguered-cop routine. (The face he makes while firing a flare gun at an escaping vehicle is a Willis signature, and makes me chuckle every time I see it.) By the end, though, too many half-explored storylines, a wave of amateurishly executed police cliches, and a miscast Sarah Jessica Parker combine to sink this almost-passable yet too predictable story. (★☆☆☆)

Pulp Fiction (1994): Quentin Tarantino's sleazy criminal masterpiece weaves riveting, interlocking vignettes about hit men, gangster wives, $5 milkshakes, a lost gold watch, a briefcase, and a too-proud boxer (Willis) unwilling to throw a marquee bout—earning him the type of trouble he never could have imagined. Everyone in the ensemble is excellent, though Willis's incredibly controlled performance as Butch held the audience in the palm of his tightly clenched fist as he walked a tightrope between life, death, and sexual violations, just to reacquire a prized keepsake from his past. (★★★★)

North (1994): An obnoxious fable about an overachieving, attention-craving young boy (Elijah Wood) who travels the globe in search of replacement parents because his own are too self-absorbed. The film's message? Families everywhere are awful. An endearing Willis is the only cast member who understands how to play the foolishness in Alan Zweibel's script. Everything else, from the costuming and the performances to the overall storytelling, is hyper-exaggerated to the point of farce, which would be acceptable if it was the slightest bit funny. Director Rob Reiner aimed for whimsical but missed, badly. (★★☆☆)

Color of Night (1994): This one is remembered for Willis's decision to do full-frontal nudity on screen, unheard of for a male A-lister of his stature. The rest of *Color of Night* is forgettable, a sleazy B-movie melodrama that would get relegated to late-night cable television if not for the presence of a bankable, marquee-worthy star in its leading role. Willis plays a colorblind psychoanalyst escaping to Los Angeles after one of his patients commits suicide, only to get caught up in an equally sticky murder mystery involving one of his head-shrinking colleagues (Scott Bakula). Willis takes the material seriously and plays it relatively straight. It's an unusual choice, though, because everyone else involved overacts with gusto, accepting the fact that they're stuck in a campy, shlocky, erotic thriller that can't be salvaged. (★★☆☆)

Nobody's Fool (1994): A harmless Paul Newman vehicle that's too gentle for its own good but features a welcome turn by Willis as an arrogant, philandering businessman playing foil to Newman at every turn. *Nobody's Fool* came out during the height of Willis's popularity, but he gladly accepted a supporting role just to share scenes with an icon, and his loose and confident performance suggests Willis enjoyed every moment of it. (★★★☆)

Die Hard with a Vengeance (1995): McTiernan returns to the franchise he launched and delivers a terrific buddy-action film—Willis and costar Samuel L. Jackson are an incendiary pairing—that also bends the rules of what made *Die Hard* special. Gone are the challenging confines of an office building or a crowded airport, so John McClane pinballs around New York

City and Canada trying to take down another terrorist (Jeremy Irons) with a unique grudge. (★★★☆)

Four Rooms (1995): Four directors tell four salacious tales, all set in an L.A. hotel on New Year's Eve. This terrible anthology garnered attention because indie film darlings Quentin Tarantino and Robert Rodriguez helmed two of the four shorts, casting famous friends such as Antonio Banderas, Salma Hayek, Madonna, Marisa Tomei, and Willis in supporting roles. Unfortunately, childish humor, tedious execution, and Tim Roth's embarrassingly cartoonish performance as Ted the Bellhop make *Four Rooms* unwatchable, even as a quirky storytelling experiment. (★☆☆☆)

12 Monkeys (1995): Arguably Willis's greatest performance, here playing a possible time traveler sent back from a disease-riddled future to obtain information on the virus that wiped out humanity. Willis shows off his complete range of emotions as a man who's unsure which reality he can trust—director Terry Gilliam wants audiences to debate whether or not the dystopian future from which Willis travels actually exists or is all in his head. And while costar Brad Pitt received an Academy Award nomination for the showier role of a paranoid patient in a mental-health facility, it's Willis who mesmerizes with his stoic silence, his expressive facial reactions, and his powerful reflection on our inability to change fate. Remarkable work by Willis in an infinitely rewarding sci-fi thriller. (★★★★)

Last Man Standing (1996): Walter Hill (*48 Hours*, HBO's *Deadwood*) remakes Akira Kurosawa's samurai drama *Yojimbo* into a tougher-than-leather bordertown gangster picture that fits Willis like a glove. The story doesn't reinvent the wheel. A stoic stranger rolls into a ghost town, encounters warring criminal groups (and a crooked sheriff), and decides to earn money cleaning up the scorched and blood-soaked streets. But the formidable Willis proves that his rugged demeanor, ice-cold confidence, and resilient heroism enhance the genre's run-of-the-mill elements, making me wonder why he didn't try to do more westerns or period gangster movies over the course of his career. (★★★☆)

Beavis and Butt-Head Do America (1996): For a while, Mike Judge's sexually frustrated, impulsive, metal-head morons held American pop culture in one hand, and their television remote in the other. Their first feature film begins when Beavis and Butt-Head's TV gets stolen, sending them on a nationwide search for a replacement. I have no idea why Willis agreed to voice Muddy Grimes, a drunk who mistakenly hires the lead idiots to whack his wife (voiced by Demi Moore). "You said whack . . ." But the famous couple both commit to the crude humor and get laughs without pulling focus off Judge's silly, illiterate antiheroes. (★★★☆)

The Fifth Element (1997): Luc Besson's goofy, sexy space opera finds a former Special Forces major turned taxi driver (Willis) protecting the lone valuable weapon (Milla Jovovich) that can destroy an impending Great Evil. Willis largely adheres to his confident action-hero blueprint, allowing the rest of Besson's bonkers futuristic universe to unfurl with reckless abandon around him. But the actor's stoicism and rugged presence provides Besson with the ideal balance to the picture's amplified sci-fi ingenuity. (★★★☆)

The Jackal (1997): A monotonous manhunt drama about an IRA terrorist (Richard Gere) hoping to shave time off of his prison sentence by helping the FBI capture "The Jackal" (Willis), a KGB contract killer operating miles off of the grid. While not a comedy, *The Jackal* is unintentionally hilarious, and would be completely disposable if not for the unforgettable array of comical wigs and accents Willis employs to disguise himself from his government pursuers. (★★☆☆)

Mercury Rising (1998): In the steady parade of law-enforcement officers played by Willis over the years, FBI agent Art Jeffries from *Mercury Rising* stands out for his passionate paternal streak, forged by a hostage crisis massacre in the film's opening minutes that leads to teenagers dying on his watch. Genuine compassion penetrates Willis's rugged exterior once he's assigned to protect Simon (Miko Hughes), a nine-year-old savant targeted for assassination by our own government after he cracks a $2 billion weapons code hidden in a book of puzzles. Neither Alec Baldwin's performance as an NSA heavy, nor

Harold Becker's direction, could be described as "subtle." But the protective urgency Willis brings to Jeffries varies up his usual action shtick and gives us real reason to root for this hero. (★★☆☆)

Armageddon (1998): Slick, brainless Hollywood blockbuster fare at its finest. Willis leads a loveable team of unsophisticated oil-rig drillers into outer space so they can bury a nuclear bomb in the heart of a meteor that's barreling toward Earth. Everything that can go wrong does, but Willis holds the entire endeavor together with the right amount of leadership, heart, and humor, making Michael Bay's bombastic thriller the better of the two "asteroid" thrillers released in theaters that year. (★★★☆)

The Siege (1998): Real-world fears of potential domestic terrorism infuse tension throughout Ed Zwick's paranoid but unfocused political thriller. Denzel Washington and Annette Bening credibly represent the human agents on the front lines of our country's escalating war on international threats, but it's a stoic Willis who personifies government overreach by playing a loyal US Army general willing to compromise his own beliefs and accept the order of martial law on US soil if it means preventing more attacks. (★★☆☆)

Breakfast of Champions (1999): Willis reunites with *Mortal Thoughts* director Alan Rudolph for an adaptation to Kurt Vonnegut's popular bestselling novel of the same name. This satirical black comedy is difficult to find. No streaming service carries it. Imported, non-US DVD copies can be purchased on Amazon for around $40. It's almost as if Willis found and destroyed all the negatives, hoping no one would ever see his performance as suicidal Midwestern car salesman Dwayne Hoover. I searched far and wide for a viewable version of *Champions*, but unfortunately . . . (No Rating)

The Sixth Sense (1999): Still one of the most effective twist endings in Hollywood history. But M. Night Shyamalan's wounded and tragic ghost story has repeat-viewing value because of Willis's tender chemistry with a spectacular Haley Joel Osment (who earned a well-deserved Oscar nomination), and the enormous control the film's leading man maintains on the screenplay's various secrets. This crowd-pleaser is Willis's highest-grossing movie for a reason. (★★★★)

The Story of Us (1999): Casting Willis and Michelle Pfeiffer in a sad dissection of a fifteen-year marriage that's now on the rocks sounds exhilarating. And the duo forge bona fide emotional bonds as they narrate Ben and Katie Jordan's crumbling relationship, which started off playful and romantic but gradually fizzled as career, kids, and life interfered. Unfortunately, Rob Reiner's lackluster direction pummels *The Story of Us* into two beautiful movie stars screaming their frustrations, and stock rom-com supporting players (including Rita Wilson and Paul Reiser) rattling off sitcom-worthy observations about the opposite sex. Strong performances in service of a grating script, lazily executed. (★½☆☆)

The Whole Nine Yards (2000): *Friends* costar Matthew Perry exerts an obscene amount of spastic energy to wring laughs from an otherwise harebrained screenplay about a hapless dentist wedged into a gangster conflict after an infamous contract killer (Willis) moves in next door. Willis counters Perry's hyper-anxiety with a silky-smooth demeanor. It allows him to charm the pants off an amusing Amanda Peet, and mesh seamlessly with the giant teddy bear, Michael Clarke Duncan. Too bad the story doesn't ask Willis to do much beyond act calm, cool, and collected—something the performer can, and does, do in his sleep. (★★☆☆)

The Kid (2000): A welcome departure for Willis into the realm of gentle family comedy. As a straight-talking (i.e., rude) image consultant, Willis allows himself to be something we don't always see on screen: unlikable. But as this better-than-average version of a familiar story—a corporate jerk reconnects with his inner child—plays out, Willis skillfully balances hilarious antics with heart, and the pitter-patter precision to his line deliveries reminds us how capable Bruce is at making a good script dance. (★★★☆)

Unbreakable (2000): After unassuming security guard David Dunn (Willis) survives a devastating train derailment and shows no injuries, his son (Spencer

Treat Clark)—as well as an overzealous comic book enthusiast (Samuel L. Jackson)—struggle to convince Dunn that he has superpowers. The somber and complex *Unbreakable* arrived at a time when superhero features were little more than superficial eye candy (*Spawn*, *Steel*, and *Batman and Robin* preceded it), so its stoicism and character-driven mythology lent gravitas to a genre many dismissed as adolescent. It helps that Willis and Jackson are equal parts fantastic as opposing sides of a superhero coin, fleshing out Shyamalan's slow-burn until it becomes an unforgettable origin story for a brand-new hero and villain. (★★★★)

Bandits (2001): *Armageddon* costars Willis and Billy Bob Thornton continue to mine their quirky comedic chemistry as the titular bandits—best friends and bank robbers who embark on an impromptu crime spree to fund their retirement. The charmingly neurotic Thornton milks a hypochondriac routine for consistent laughs, while Willis bounces playfully off of both him and a luminescent Cate Blanchett, generating sparks as a bored housewife swept up in the duo's caper. The meandering script isn't as sharp as the film's three leads, but their performances make this ride more than enjoyable. (★★★☆)

Hart's War (2002): A thinking-man's military story (plenty of conversations, very little combat), *Hart's War* explores the expected dramatic tensions between the US soldiers in a German POW camp and their Nazi captors, but also some unexpected hostilities—driven by racial divides—between the American men packed tight into their cramped quarters. The main plot morphs into a courtroom drama with a dedicated lieutenant (a young and hungry Colin Farrell) defending a Black pilot (Terrence Howard) against a murder he didn't commit. An excellent Willis uses his natural gravitas to play a US Army colonel who inspires, leads, but eventually intimidates the weary American POWs under his charge. It's a solid, important feature, though one can't help but wonder how much better *Hart's War* might have been if original director Alfonso Cuaron (*Roma*, *Gravity*) didn't abandon it to film *Y Tu Mama, Tambien* instead. (★★★☆)

Grand Champion (2002): A single mom (Joey Lauren Adams) and her children—one of them played by Emma Roberts—bond while raising a calf named Hokey for a steer competition in Texas. "Hokey" also describes this tissue-soft, sweet-natured, but corny family story, which somehow lured country music legend George Strait to appear as himself in the film (performing "Hokey Pokey"), and Dixie Chicks lead singer Natalie Maines as a rodeo announcer. Also look for a pregnant Julia Roberts playing a country fair ticket taker (she gets a charming scene with her niece, Emma), while Willis brings mild tension as a wealthy tycoon hoping to buy Hokey at auction. That's serious star power. Shame that none of it gives *Grand Champion* an ounce of spark. (★★☆☆)

Tears of the Sun (2003): A tense, morally conflicted, but mature military exercise that puts human faces on the sins and atrocities of war. Director Antoine Fuqua plunges audiences behind enemy lines with a no-nonsense, highly trained navy lieutenant (Willis) ordered to extract an American doctor (Monica Bellucci) from combat-riddled Nigeria before rebel guerilla forces invade their camp, even though it means leaving indigenous people behind to be slaughtered. War is hell in Fuqua's punishing jungles, and allegiances are challenged when situations become grim. But the courage, heroism, and compassion we frequently see in Willis eventually pierces through his character's squinty-eyed fortitude, leading to an inspirational finale. (★★★☆)

Rugrats Go Wild (2003): Nickelodeon crossed two of their popular animated series together—*Rugrats* and *The Wild Thornberrys*—for an imaginative adventure involving a disastrous family vacation at sea. And yes, Willis lends his voice (and a blast of scruffy energy) to the character of the family dog, Scout, who babysits the Rugrats kids while they are stranded on a deserted island. "Why is Willis in this?" you might ask. Consider that his and Demi Moore's daughters were born in 1988, 1991, and 1994, so Nickelodeon no doubt played consistently in the Willis household, and he wanted to be part of a movie his children could enjoy. (★★★☆)

Charlie's Angels: Full Throttle (2003): Willis shows up briefly as a Department of Justice official—perhaps as a favor to Demi Moore, the movie's seductive villain—in this spectacularly disappointing sequel that can't recapture any of the go-for-broke glee that made McG's original *Charlie's Angels* so much fun. (★☆☆☆)

The Whole Ten Yards (2004): Flop sweat pours off this very busy, but woefully unfunny, sequel to the surprise 2000 hit. Willis, who was so cool in the original, throws a steady stream of ridiculous choices against the wall hoping anything will stick—wigs, bunny slippers, mood swings, and a fascination with cleaning that was absent in the original movie. But farting grandmothers, erectile dysfunction gags, homophobic punchlines, and a hyperactive Kevin Pollack constantly slapping his gangster cronies are an antidote to actual comedy. It is loud, boorish, and just plain bad. (★☆☆☆)

Ocean's Twelve (2004): Before "meta" became the buzzword for every comedy under the sun, Willis participated in an enormously clever and oddball comedic bit buried inside of Steven Soderbergh's European *Ocean's* jaunt. To help pull off a heist, Julia Roberts's character Tess attempts to impersonate the real-life *Pretty Woman* star, and Willis plays himself recognizing Julia in a posh Rome hotel. Everyone involved dials into the lunacy of the situation, and Willis's understanding of his own celebrity grounds what could have been too facetious. Instead, it's just zany enough to work. (★★★☆)

Hostage (2005): Another Willis hero haunted by the death of a child under his watch. This time, hostage negotiator Jeff Talley (Willis) confronts unsettled demons while trying to rescue a deceitful family being held at gunpoint by three inexperienced and unpredictable thieves. What starts as an unplanned home invasion escalates into a full-blown situation, efficiently staged by director Florent-Emilio Siri. Willis mostly acts into a phone or walkie talkie, giving sleazy Ben Foster and volatile Jonathan Tucker ample room to chew scenery. *Hostage* also entertains with an unexpected *Die Hard* nod, a larger threat involving top-secret information stored on a DVD and a touching scene between Willis and his actual daughter Rumer. (★★★☆)

Sin City (2005): A thick layer of moral sludge coats Robert Rodriguez and Frank Miller's adaptation of the latter's acclaimed graphic novel. The unchecked depravity makes it difficult to embrace the unquestionable visual artistry that went into recreating the stark, bleak, neo-noir ingredients of Miller's gruesome crime stories. Willis gets the best story in this anthology, playing a beat cop with a bum ticker who goes to extremes to protect a young girl from the rapist who has targeted her. But the whole of *Sin City* suffers from overkill (as well as too much killing), and the longer this exercise drags on, the more it resembles a bloated corpse you might find floating in the city's putrid sewers. (★★☆☆)

Alpha Dog (2006): Nick Cassavetes coaxes incredible performances from his crew of talented young actors (Emile Hirsch, Ben Foster, Anton Yelchin, Justin Timberlake, and Amanda Seyfried) as they tell the true-life story of Jesse James Hollywood, an affluent suburban drug dealer obsessed with L.A. gangster culture who kidnapped a kid and set off a tragic chain of events. The deeply sad *Alpha Dog* takes a seedy street-level approach to an amateur, misogynistic criminal community—you better believe that Hirsch's gang-leader character has a *Scarface* movie poster on his bedroom wall—and is frequently disturbing in its realistic depictions of teenage violence. Willis defers to the up-and-comers, appearing in a few scenes as Hirsch's father, supplier, and negative influence. (★★★☆)

Lucky Number Slevin (2006): Willis fits comfortably into the pocket created by the snap-crackle-and-pop dialogue of director Paul McGuigan's elevated-noir crime thriller. Revealing too much about his character's motives would be a sin. So let's just say a sleek and shadowy Willis helps to facilitate a sophisticated scheme involving mistaken identity, decades-old revenge, and the ongoing feud between two cartoon-caricature crime lords, "The Boss" (Morgan Freeman) and "The Rabbi" (Ben Kingsley). A spectacular cast of character actors finds the rhythm in Jason Smilovic's hip script, leaving McGuigan to go a little overboard with camera tricks and set design, ensuring that *Slevin* has style to spare. (★★★☆)

16 Blocks (2006): Willis's lone collaboration with versatile director Richard Donner (*Superman, Lethal Weapon*) is a riveting race-the-clock cop thriller that riffs on the actor's penchant for being the wrong guy, in the wrong place, at the wrong time. Detective Jack Mosley (Willis) almost clocks out after an overnight shift but is forced by his superior to escort a chatterbox witness (Mos Def) from a jail cell to a courthouse to testify against dirty cops. Many shootouts follow. But Donner allows Willis time to linger in Mosley's deep character flaws, generating pathos for a complicated hero who has been ground down by life. His wounded performance, and terrific chemistry with Def, gives us plenty to chew on in between the film's suspenseful action sequences. (★★★☆)

Over the Hedge (2006): When a starving raccoon (Willis) tries to steal a hibernating bear's food stash, he's forced to recruit an assortment of woodland creatures to help him replace all of the rations before winter ends in a week. *Over the Hedge* proves that the smooth-talking Willis should have done more voiceover work during his career. (At least, films that don't include Beavis and Butthead.) The freedom and safety of the recording booth allowed him to unleash a boundless comedic energy that fueled both this and the two *Look Who's Talking* movies. The spirited *Hedge* has an inspired vocal cast, and Willis's peppy delivery helps him be every bit as funny as Garry Shandling, Steve Carell, Catherine O'Hara, and Eugene Levy. (★★★☆)

Fast Food Nation (2006): Humorless, defanged satire that tries in vain to marry intelligent commentary on the abusive immigrant experience in the American Southwest with the plodding, pointless story of a fast-food marketing executive (Greg Kinnear) investigating the amount of cow manure that's ending up in his company's hamburger patties. Willis is eerily convincing as a savvy corporate boss explaining away the health hazards of his industry as "the cost of doing business." But this, overall, is a rare swing and a miss for naturalistic filmmaker Richard Linklater, who's much better off helming his original, emotional screenplays like *Boyhood, Dazed and Confused*, and the exquisite *Before* trilogy. (★☆☆☆)

The Astronaut Farmer (2006): Willis joins Billy Bob Thornton for another story about outer space, though *The Astronaut Farmer* is sentimental and inspiring in all the places that *Armageddon* was bombastic and dumb. Thornton brings tenderness and real passion to the story of a Texas genius and former astronaut who's obsessed with fulfilling his dream of building his own working rocket. And Willis helps put Thornton's mission into perspective, playing a supportive NASA colleague who pitches in to make the ambitious goal attainable. Willis and Thornton's collaborations over the years were quite enjoyable, and pleasant movies like *Farmer* make me wish they worked together more. (★★★☆)

Planet Terror (2007): Quentin Tarantino and Robert Rodriguez revive the exploitation films of their youth, courtesy of a sleazy double feature that's accompanied by bogus trailers for fake flicks like *Machete* and *Werewolf Women of the SS*. Willis appears in Rodriguez's contribution, a zombie gore-fest set in and around a filthy, roadside Texas town. *Planet Terror* entertains by perfecting the look and feel of grainy film stock that's been scratched and worn by too many screenings. Meanwhile, the entire cast commits to the stomach-churning joke, from Rose McGowan's go-go dancer replacing her severed leg with a machine gun, to Willis morphing into a toxic, bulbous monster thanks to poison gas. There's nothing good or clean about *Planet Terror*, but it's a hell of a lot of fun. (★★★☆)

Perfect Stranger (2007): Investigative journalist Rowena Price (Halle Berry), disgusted by the male-driven corruption that keeps burying her stories, goes deep undercover to expose powerful advertising exec Harrison Hill (Willis) as a murderer. Late-night Cinemax movies boast better scripts than the cliche-ridden fan-fiction powering this aimless erotic mystery. You'd think Berry and Willis could salvage this, except they have the sexual spark of soaking-wet charcoal nuggets, and spend most of the movie chatting in Instant Message. (★☆☆☆)

Live Free or Die Hard (2007): More than a decade after *Die Hard with a Vengeance*, Willis cooked up a plausible reason to return to his signature role of John McClane, this time pitting the Energizer Bunny of action heroes against a cyberterrorist (Timothy Olyphant) seeking to freeze our nation's infrastructure over the July 4th weekend. McClane had become more Superman than Everyman by this stage of the franchise, but the actor's inherent cockiness—and the inclusion of some memorable set pieces—makes *Live Free* the last respectable *Die Hard* movie. (★★★☆)

Nancy Drew (2007): Adorably sweet adaptation of the timeless literary series, with Emma Roberts bringing wit, warmth, and a touch or neurosis to the title character as she works an unsolved mystery in modern-day Hollywood. Willis entertains in a brief cameo by playing himself, who is playing a vintage 1950s gumshoe in a glossy studio production. Roberts charms the actor when she interrupts him on set to clarify the history of Miranda Rights. He then offers the teenager the chance to direct the film—something I wish actually happened in real life, just so Willis could have played a 1950s detective in a feature. (★★★☆)

The Assassination of a High School President (2008): Willis brings a short-tempered frustration to his role of a high school principal with military PTSD who wants to get to the bottom of the theft of some SAT booklets. Director Brett Simon thinks he's reinventing the hardboiled, Dashiell Hammett–inspired private detective story *Chinatown*, but for high school's social hierarchy. Unfortunately, lead actor Reece Thompson is too milquetoast to play a teenaged Sam Spade, and *Looper* director Rian Johnson talked this exact same talk, only much better, in 2005's *Brick*, so watch that instead. (★★☆☆)

What Just Happened? (2008): Movie producer Art Linson's inside-baseball autobiography becomes a caustic, cameo-laden Hollywood satire in the hands of *Rain Man* and *Wag the Dog* director Barry Levinson. Willis is both credible and entertaining as a tantrum-throwing diva Hollywood star—reportedly modeled after Alec Baldwin—who refuses to shave his scraggly beard prior to a pivotal role, torturing the movie's shallow producer (Robert De Niro). Here's a backhanded compliment: Willis pulls the part of an egotistical superstar off with ease. (★★★☆)

Surrogates (2009): In the future, humans live dangerous lives without fear of repercussion by connecting their neural pathways to cybernetic replicas, or surrogates, and sending them out into the world. After someone invents a weapon that short-circuits surrogates in order to kill their human hosts, a former cop (Willis) abandons his bleach-blond android (also Willis) and enters the real world to diffuse the deadly device. *Surrogates* flirts with interesting debates about the morality of artificial intelligence, the possibility of becoming addicted to virtual reality, and the fearful way society might react to a surrogate's invention. But the film soon abandons those intelligent conversations to become a slick, muscular, but rote sci-fi action thriller. (★★☆☆)

Cop Out (2010): The title says it all. Willis coasts lazily through this uninspired buddy-cop comedy, failing to establish any chemistry with costar Tracy Morgan (they play partners on the police force but act like they met each other that morning) or to generate any interest in the simplistic plot. The jokes flop, the action is tepid, and everyone involved seems embarrassed to be there. (★☆☆☆)

The Expendables (2010): Sylvester Stallone's macho homage to 1980s action-movie excess is gruesome, violent, explosive, but predictable to a fault. The first film's only memorable moment is the amusing Planet Hollywood reunion, where Willis and Arnold Schwarzenegger join Stallone for a too-brief scene that sets up larger roles for both icons in the 2012 sequel. (★★☆☆)

Red (2010): Similar to *The Expendables*, *Red* relies on seasoned (OK, old) actors proving they still have what it takes to carry an explosive action-comedy. Once the novelty of seeing Helen Mirren in combat boots and a ball gown firing machine guns wears off, however, the overlong *Red* doesn't offer much that you haven't seen on screen before. Willis acts as the glue that holds this oddball ensemble of retired CIA operatives together, though a bemused Mary-Louise Parker earns Most Valuable Player status as a romance novel–reading call-center operator lured into the unfolding espionage. (★★☆☆)

Setup (2011): After Sonny (50 Cent) gets betrayed by his cronies during a diamond heist, he embarks on a vengeance mission through some depraved corners of his non-distinct city, forcing him to collaborate with colorful characters like "The Mob Boss" (Willis), "The Card Shark" (Antonio Esfandiari) and "The Butcher." Fitty carries this needlessly gruesome trudge through the criminal underbelly, which lacks tension or compelling stakes. And while Willis injects dark humor into his predictable gangster role, your movie will have a low ceiling when your second lead is the flavorless, emotionally stunted Ryan Phillippe. (★★☆☆)

Catch .44 (2011): Everything about writer-director Aaron Harvey's *Catch .44* screams "Tarantino knockoff," from the gratuitous violence and use of jangly surf rock to the wordier-than-necessary monologues delivered by seedy, sexy criminals. Even the narrative structure apes *Pulp Fiction*, starting off with a shootout at a roadside diner but systematically rewinding the plot to show different characters—including Willis's drug kingpin, Mel—arriving at the spot. Willis makes the most of his lone conversation with Forest Whitaker, playing a fellow crook. The rest is derivative, though I did chuckle when three ladies pop a cassette of Willis's *The Return of Bruno* into their car's tape deck and crank "Respect Yourself" until one of them demands that they "throw this shit out the window." (★★☆☆)

Lay the Favorite (2012): Director Stephen Frears (*High Fidelity, The Queen*) spotlights a colorful corner of Las Vegas that's rarely shown on screen, where a professional sports gambler (Willis) forges a profitable relationship with a wannabe cocktail waitress (Rebecca Hall), much to the chagrin of his volatile and jealous wife, Tulip (Catherine Zeta-Jones). Willis is endearingly quirky as the ringmaster of this off-the-strip circus, decked out in tourist-worthy T-shirts and Bermuda shorts with his tube socks pulled up to his knees. He shuffles shallow plot points like cards in a deck, alternating between the wide-eyed enthusiasm of winning and the violent outbursts that usually follow losing. But the trials and tribulations of these comedic degenerates don't ever amount to very much beyond ninety minutes of amusing, trailer-park eye candy. (★★⯨☆)

The Cold Light of Day (2012): A fine line separates relentlessly exhilarating from painfully excruciating. *Cold Light of Day* ends up on the wrong side of that division. A miscast (and distractingly bad) Henry Cavill sweats, screams, and flails about as an uptight yuppie immersed in illogical spy games after his family is kidnapped during a European vacation. Willis initially appears as Cavill's condescending father, whose CIA history triggers his son's impromptu rescue mission. But you can stop watching *Cold Light of Day* once the calm and calculated Willis exits the story around the thirty-minute mark. The movie doesn't get any better in his absence, though you do see Sigourney Weaver firing semi-automatic machine guns in a pointless parking-garage shootout. (★⯪☆☆)

Moonrise Kingdom (2012): Wes Anderson's warmest movie, which wrings tender emotions out of a first-love teenage romance without sacrificing any of the eccentricities the director's fans appreciate and expect. There's remarkable rhythm and precision to Anderson's dialogue and staging, and he continuously invites recurring cast members (Bill Murray, Jason Schwartzman) because they know how to dance to his beats. But it's most thrilling when Anderson invites a newcomer—like Willis, as Captain Sharp of the island of New Penzance—and they sing in harmony with the material. It's a real shame Willis didn't do another Anderson film before retiring. (★★★⯪)

The Expendables 2 (2012): Stallone's big, dumb action franchise grows bigger and dumber, but also receives a slick polish from studio-friendly action director Simon West (*Con Air, Lara Croft: Tomb Raider*). Watching Willis, Schwarzenegger, Stallone, and Chuck Norris engage Jean-Claude Van Damme in a firefight provides a nostalgic kick for audiences of a certain age. But *Expendables 2* proves that the franchise, at its peak, offers very little beyond the short-lived adrenaline rush that comes with seeing action icons reciting each other's catch phrases as they mow down faceless adversaries. (★★★☆)

Looper (2012): Intelligent science fiction continues to bring out the best in Willis, who is both intimidating and sympathetic as a futuristic hit man forced to confront his younger self (Joseph Gordon-Levitt) and possibly prevent an innocent child from growing into a tyrannical dictator. One of the last films where Willis willingly gave himself over to a filmmaker with a strong vision and challenging screenplay, resulting in a spectacular, white-knuckle thriller that should stand the test of time. (★★★☆)

Fire with Fire (2012): Adequate vengeance pic follows a firefighter (Josh Duhamel) into protective custody after he witnesses a convenience store robbery and murder conducted by an eclectic mobster (Vincent D'Onofrio) with a lengthy rap sheet. Willis is feisty, focused, and defiant as a police lieutenant working all angles to bring the crime lord to justice. His lone scene with D'Onofrio—a standoff where the latter affects a Cajun accent and waxes poetic about the Seven Deadly Sins—is worth the price of admission. (★★☆☆)

A Good Day to Die Hard (2013): A travesty. Willis's John McClane has gone from formidable everyman to an indestructible killing machine, this time sent on a rampage through Moscow as he aims to assist his CIA agent son (Jai Courtney). Poorly shot, terribly scripted, and nonsensical. It's greatest sin, however, is in making the once-beloved McClane into a bitter, unlikeable jerk as it pounds the final nail into the *Die Hard* franchise's coffin. (★☆☆☆)

G.I. Joe: Retaliation (2013): Paramount hires Dwayne "The Rock" Johnson, Channing Tatum, and Bruce Willis to resuscitate its flat, Hasbro toy–inspired franchise. It works. They help deliver a slick, exciting, and genuinely entertaining piece of blockbuster escapism. Jon M. Chu (*Step Up 3D, Crazy Rich Asians*) cooks up inspired action set pieces—the ninja fight on the side of a mountain is unforgettable—and the battle-ready cast brings the proper balance of humor and arrogance to a sequel that works well because it knows exactly how ridiculous it's allowed to be without going off the rails. (★★★☆)

Red 2 (2013): Funny and fast-moving, *Red 2* improves on its predecessor by hiring proven comedic director Dean Parisot (*Galaxy Quest, Curb Your Enthusiasm*) and fully embracing the exaggerated lunacy of the central premise.

Willis appears to be having more fun than usual bouncing off of his original costars. He and Mary-Louise Parker's substantial chemistry keep us invested through the requisite action-sequel bombast. And Sir Anthony Hopkins plugs seamlessly into the story's goofiness as an unstable scientist who possesses valuable information about a top-secret weapons project. Finally, kudos to Parisot for cooking up an automobile stunt on the streets of Paris that rivals Willis's slow-motion cop-car moment from the first film. (★★★☆)

Sin City: A Dame to Kill For (2014): Robert Rodriguez returns to the sordid, sleazy streets of Frank Miller's *Sin City* for four more stylish, but now repetitive, neo-noir crime stories. Newcomers Joseph Gordon-Levitt, Julia Garner, Ray Liotta, Juno Temple, Eva Green, and Josh Brolin assimilate nicely, though Willis's contributions are severely limited, given his death by suicide in the original *Sin City*. Look for him playing Hartigan's ghost throughout, sulking and glaring and wishing he could do more to protect Nancy (Jessica Alba), the love of his life. (★★☆☆)

The Prince (2014): When a retired assassin (Jason Patric) suspects his college-aged daughter has been kidnapped, his investigation plunges him into New Orleans's sordid drug underworld, and puts him on a collision course with his one-time rival (Willis). *The Prince* is Patric's show (the title is the nickname Willis's character gave him), and he commendably carries it with intense paternal concern and the convincing ability to break bones when needed. Willis, meanwhile, mostly pulls strings from the safety of his kingpin headquarters, but still cuts a menacing profile and exceeds Patric's ferocity during their inevitable confrontation. (★★★☆)

Vice (2015): Male clients at the futuristic facility Vice pay top dollar to the CEO (Willis) to act out their most depraved fantasies on life-like female androids, dubbed Artificials. The emaciated plot sputters into gear once one Artificial (Ambyr Childers) becomes self-aware and escapes, jeopardizing the entire Vice operation. There's potential in this premise. Unfortunately, clumsy action sequences and a ham-fisted approach to the story's complicated morality debates turn *Vice* into a grotesque, misogynistic snuff film—and a boring one, at that. At least Willis perks up in the few scenes he shares with a gnarly Thomas Jane, who chews scenery as a frustrated cop trying to dismantle the hedonistic temple. (★★☆☆)

Rock the Kasbah (2015): Bill Murray can't salvage this unfunny, rambling slog about a washed-up talent manager wandering around Afghanistan after a USO tour falls apart. If director Barry Levinson has a point to make here, it never becomes clear. Admittedly, *Rock the Kasbah* perks up every time Willis appears as a heavily armed, tattooed mercenary blackmailing Murray's character into letting him provide security. They have comedic sparks, and their out-of-the-blue riff on bestselling author Danielle Steel is the movie's most amusing bit. The rest is obnoxious. (★★☆☆)

Extraction (2015): Fledgling CIA operative Harry Turner (Kellan Lutz) launches a lone-wolf mission when his father, agency legend Leonard Turner (Willis), gets captured by terrorists. Generic to a fault, *Extraction* mostly keeps Willis off screen, hoping the anemic screen presence of both Lutz and costar Gina Carano can overcome the moronic script and uninspired, *Bourne*-style fight choreography. They can't. (★☆☆☆)

Precious Cargo (2016): Former *Saved by the Bell* heartthrob Mark-Paul Gosselaar brings something that is desperately missing from too many of these generic Willis shoot-'em-up dramas: a sense of humor. His cocky swagger, and chemistry with costar Claire Forlani, elevates a spirited action flick about experienced thieves teaming up to steal a cache of precious gems so they can pay back a ruthless crime boss (Willis). Director Max Adams makes clever use of his coastal Mississippi setting, staging jet ski chases and speedboat fights for Gosselaar. And Willis responds to the snappy screenplay by slathering extra relish on his cliched villainous monologues. Fast-moving and fun. (★★★☆)

Marauders (2016): Christopher Meloni excels as a hard-nosed FBI agent hunting down a precise team of Good Samaritan bank robbers. Willis plays a bank president with shocking ties to the unpredictable and absorbing plot. Also, director Steven C. Miller injects a modern noir style and a confident energy that helps keep this movie's motor humming. (★★★☆)

Split (2016): M. Night Shyamalan's chiller about an unpredictable kidnapper with dissociative identity disorder (a tour de force for James McAvoy) becomes a backdoor *Unbreakable* sequel the moment Willis reprises his role of David Dunn in a mid-credits scene. His one line of dialogue, "Mr. Glass," sets up 2019's trilogy capper, *Glass*. (★★★☆)

Once Upon a Time in Venice (2017): The movie that allows you to see a bucknaked Willis (and a strategically utilized stunt double) skateboard around Southern California, hide a gun between his butt cheeks, and wear a bright red wig and lipstick while hunting down his stolen dog. The movie's so shaggy and stupid, it's impossible to recommend, despite funny cameos and two goofily amusing performances by Willis and John Goodman, who share a pleasant beach-bum vibe that deserves a stronger story. (★★☆☆)

First Kill (2017): A corporate executive (Hayden Christensen) takes his family from the city to the country for a deer hunt, hoping the male bonding will toughen up his bullied child. What starts as a well-acted and thoughtful father-son story about a generational rite of passage, however, derails into predictable territories once the duo witness a murder in the woods. And while Christensen relishes his scenes as a doting dad, his transformation from Wall Street broker to proficient action hero is less convincing. *First Kill* does kickstart Willis's consistent run of "local chief of police" performances, teaming him with Christensen but mainly saddling him with wearisome exposition dumps that flesh out a dull kidnapping plot. (★★☆☆)

Acts of Violence (2018): A disturbingly sadistic crime thriller about three distraught brothers, two with serious military experience, who wage war on a sex-trafficking operation after goons kidnap their sister. Willis is spry, invested, and convincingly sympathetic as a local police detective racing to retrieve the girl before her brothers burn his entire jurisdiction to the ground. His subplot takes a backseat to the brothers on their mission, but his occasional scenes at least represent the legitimacy of law enforcement, which often gets overlooked in single-minded vengeance stories such as this. (★★☆☆)

Death Wish (2018): Playing a grieving husband and father, Willis adds a slight pulse to this otherwise cold-hearted vengeance story, a modernized (and more sadistic) retelling of the Charles Bronson–led thriller of the same name. Having Willis's amateur vigilante also be a trauma surgeon is an inspired plot development. But the story's brazen stance on gun violence is tone deaf for its time, making this remake feel like more of a relic than its 1974 predecessor. (★★☆☆)

Reprisal (2018): There's nothing original to be found in this tedious and clumsily constructed bank-robber thriller starring Frank Grillo as a traumatized branch manager, and a glum, disinterested Willis as a retired cop drawn into investigating the crime. Willis doesn't pretend to be engaged with the banal story, and given the material, it's hard to blame him. (★☆☆☆)

Air Strike (2018): Men, women, children, and pigs (yes, even pigs) are in constant danger of being bombed from the skies in Xiao Feng's mawkish combat melodrama. *Air Strike* tells individual stories of heroism centered around China's military defending itself against Imperial Japanese forces during World War II. And Willis appears sporadically, as if dropped in from a different story altogether, playing a US military advisor to the Chinese Air Force. The aerial sequences are exciting; but this film's original title, *The Bombing*, makes a lot more sense, as Zeng can't go longer than five minutes without unleashing a barrage of computer-generated explosions caused by waves of bombs dropped from soaring planes. (★☆☆☆)

Glass (2019): M. Night Shyamalan concludes his *Eastrail 177* trilogy with a heady dissertation on heroism, villainy, and the legitimacy of comic-book lore. Shyamalan sets *Glass* in a psychiatric ward, where Dr. Ellie Staple (Sarah Paulson) psychoanalyzes our main character's delusions of grandeur to see if they're a substitute for perceived superpowers. Ambiguous storytelling has us questioning the reality Shyamalan created back in *Unbreakable*— right up until two final twists (one ludicrous, one satisfying) bring the unconventional comic-book origin story to an acceptable conclusion. (★★★☆)

The Lego Movie 2: The Second Part (2019): Such a disappointment. This inevitable but unnecessary sequel to the Oscar-nominated *The Lego Movie* suffers from a weak story as it sends Emmet Brickowski (Chris Pratt) on a second adventure through the Lego landscape. New characters Rex Dangervest (also Pratt) and Queen Watevra Wa'Nabi (Tiffany Haddish) are more obnoxious than funny, though Will Arnett's delusional Batman continues to steal the show. Willis voices himself as a Lego, poking fun at his bald scalp and John McClane's penchant for crawling around in air ducts. (★★☆☆)

Motherless Brooklyn (2019): A fascinating disaster, the kind of cinematic car crash you can't turn away from because each new creative decision dilutes the impact of the finished film. Saddle Edward Norton with all the blame. He writes, directs, produces, and stars as a 1950s private investigator obsessed with figuring out who murdered his mentor (Willis). Only, the film's too polished to pass as a noir experiment, the characters are broadly drawn caricatures, and Norton relies heavily on a mawkish narration to fill in his gaping narrative holes. Worst of all, Norton's PI suffers from Tourette's, and his verbal outbursts are laughably distracting instead of sympathetic. Willis gets shot and killed in the first fifteen minutes. You can turn *Brooklyn* off then, and not miss much. (★☆☆☆)

Between Two Ferns: The Movie (2019): Zach Galifianakis takes his extremely funny online skit about a public access talk show and stretches it into a sporadically amusing behind-the-scenes mockumentary. The comedian's interplay with fellow actors gets big laughs. But the interstitial fodder about Galifianakis hitting the road to save his failing show falls flat. Willis only appears as himself for two seconds in archival footage, so don't feel guilty about skipping this movie to watch his full appearance on *Between Two Ferns*, instead. (★★☆☆)

10 Minutes Gone (2019): Michael Chiklis starred in FX's magnificent *The Shield*. He deserves far better than witless garbage like *10 Minutes Gone*, where he plays a career criminal trying to piece together what went wrong following a botched bank robbery. The intense actor does what he can, but the laughable script twists itself into a pretzel with double and triple crosses the screenwriter mistakenly believes are shocking. Using a recurring gimmick found in these late-stage Willis crime thrillers, *10 Minutes Gone* stations the actor in one location, then shows him interacting with his costars via cellphone while they scurry around shooting separate, more intense scenes. The trick allows Willis to film his minimal scenes in just a few days, limiting his required time on set. But it also means he rarely feels like he's part of the overall story. In the case of *10 Minutes Gone*, that's a blessing. (★☆☆☆)

Trauma Center (2019): A suitable standout of the late-stage Willis thrillers, during which the actor fully engages with the formularized story of an injured witness (Nicky Whelan) struggling to avoid two corrupt cops who fear that the bullet they left in her thigh is forensics evidence that can link them to a crime. Whelan's steely performance keeps us invested as this overwhelmed victim unlocks the resources that will keep her alive. Meanwhile, director Matt Eskandari makes good use of the titular location and embraces a simplistic directorial approach that sustains the tension of his film's premise. Hardly groundbreaking, but it delivers what it promises. (★★★☆)

Survive the Night (2020): Criminal siblings making a run for the border hold a trauma surgeon (Chad Michael Murray) and his family hostage until he agrees to operate on one of the wounded brothers. Willis plays a retired sheriff (of course), and is convincingly tender as the father of Murray's doctor. But *Survive* suffers from the same sluggish pacing, improbable plotting, and wooden performances that populate almost every Willis movie from 2020 onward. (★☆☆☆)

Hard Kill (2020): A ridiculous plot involving a stolen artificial intelligence system and a kidnapping sets up an interminable firefight between teams of mercenaries in a dilapidated warehouse. Willis hardly registers, playing a distraught father who is bankrolling one of the combat units, so they'll retrieve his kidnapped daughter. Rumor has it *Trauma Center* and *Survive the Night* director Eskandari only had ten days to film this idiotic terrorist thriller. The lack of effort shows. (★☆☆☆)

Breach (2020): In the year 2242, a select few humans board a transport ship built to remove them from our decimated planet. While en route to their intergalactic destination, the survivors encounter a slug-like creature that systematically picks off crew members in vicious fashion. *Breach* never becomes anything more than a dumbed-down and incredibly bloody copy of Sir Ridley Scott's *Alien*. But Willis, for his part, is livelier than normal as the ship's hard-ass captain, making an otherwise predictable story palatable by beefing up his trademark tough-guy bravado. (★★☆☆)

Cosmic Sin (2021): First contact with an alien race in 2524 triggers a potential extraterrestrial zombie invasion, which a futuristic band of soldiers must now prevent. *Cosmic Sin* continues Willis's low-budget sci-fi run, and makes good use of its limited funds to create an admirable space environment, even if Willis—playing a seasoned military veteran—doesn't do nearly enough on-screen to live up to his nickname "The Blood General." *Cosmic Sin* starts and ends so abruptly, it plays like half of a movie. But the half we get is mildly entertaining. (★★☆☆)

Midnight in the Switchgrass (2021): After producing a steady stream of direct-to-video thrillers—many featuring Willis in miniscule roles—Randall Emmett tries his hand at directing, with uneven results. Emile Hirsch gives a passionate performance as a Florida cop tracking a truck-driving serial killer (a creepy Lukas Haas), while Megan Fox holds her own as an undercover FBI agent contributing to the investigation. But the cast can't overcome Emmett's shortcomings as a first-time director, and Willis only gets a handful of scenes—and absolutely zero narrative meat—as Fox's partner. (★☆☆☆)

Out of Death (2021): Grieving beauty Shannon (Jamie King), hiking up a rural trail to scatter her father's ashes, stumbles upon a band of corrupt sheriffs operating a heroin ring. Willis appears in a minor role as a vacationing cop trying to help keep Shannon alive. But the effects of his aphasia are evident in his speech, and reports claim he only spent one day on set. Not that Willis in his prime could resuscitate this movie's threadbare screenplay, stagnant pacing, strained character development, and rigid performances from the supporting players. Dreadful on every level. (★☆☆☆)

Survive the Game (2021): Two criminals doing an embarrassing Joker-and-Harley or Mickey-and-Mallory routine choose a random country house to hole up in. The trouble is, the house belongs to a suicidal military specialist (Chad Michael Murray), and a predictable hostage formula unfolds once the generic players are in place. *Survive the Game* looks like it was filmed in three days, on a fifteen-dollar budget. As for Willis, he plays a veteran police officer with thirty years on the job who gets shot by the criminal duo in the opening scene, somehow resurfaces later, and contributes nothing to the story. (★☆☆☆)

Apex (2021): A derivative premise, where the richest members of a futuristic society pay top dollar to hunt human prey as sport. Willis actually spices up the formula by playing an incredibly dangerous prisoner dropped onto Apex Island who ends up being smarter than his pursuers in the ghastly game. But the cast consists of dreadful nonactors, warm bodies who dispose of each other, gruesomely. And only Neal McDonough brings the heat as a skilled surgeon able to go the distance with Willis, both in the story and as a worthy costar. I'll give *Apex* an extra half star for the funny *Unbreakable* joke it slips into its script, and a weird bit where Willis riffs on Shakespeare after finding a skull in the wilderness. (★★☆☆)

Deadlock (2021): Best described as "*Die Hard* at a Hydroelectric Plant," with a lethargic Willis leading a group of terrorists hellbent on opening a dam and flooding an entire community for vengeful reasons tied to a drug bust gone bad. Patrick Muldoon is convincing as Army Ranger Mack Carr, this movie's version of John McClane. But Willis misses a golden opportunity to muster enough energy to match him as his Hans Gruber. (★★☆☆)

Fortress (2021): An ex-CIA operative (Willis) with a pitch-black past sequesters himself inside a heavily-guarded retirement facility while a team of mercenaries try to infiltrate the fortress and take him out. Willis affects a grizzled vocal delivery that comes off as slurred speech, which diminishes the impact of the scenes where he tries to reconnect with his estranged son (Jesse Metcalfe). Not that it matters much, as their interesting familial wrinkle gets buried beneath a spray of bullets and bloodshed in the film's predictable second half. Credit Chad Michael Murray for trying to salvage this rubbish with a scenery-devouring turn as the movie's main villain. (★★☆☆)

American Siege (2021): A marginally interesting (but still poorly constructed) entry in the "Willis films for a few days in rural Georgia" canon. What starts out as a predictable hostage situation takes some dark, weird turns before reaching its inevitable, bloody shootout. *Siege* gets bonus points for being unpredictable, though the central plot—involving corrupt law enforcement agents and illegal pharmaceutical labs—grows too perplexing for its own good. Willis holds up his end as the county sheriff, managing the escalating tensions and rediscovering some of his fading heroism when it's time to stand up and do the right thing. (★★☆☆)

Gasoline Alley (2022): I'm running out of fresh ways to describe yet another surly Willis turn as a burned-out detective assisting on a murder case. At the same time, Willis had run out of fresh ways to play the role. Luke Wilson receives far more screen time as Willis's wild card of a partner, but the true standout is street-tough Devon Sawa, playing a murder suspect with a checkered past whose personal investigation blows the lid off of a sleazy sex-trafficking operation. Compelling story, dull execution. (★★☆☆)

A Day to Die (2022): Choppy and unsurprising crime thriller about an ex-military operative (Kevin Dillon) and his highly trained team attempting a series of complicated heists in order to save his kidnapped wife and pay back $2 million they owe to a sadistic local gangster (Leon) and a corrupt police chief (Willis). Leon is smooth as silk, but the only thing dying on the day you choose to watch this will be your attention span. (★☆☆☆)

Fortress: Sniper's Eye (2022): A listless and sloppily staged sequel to 2021's *Fortress* that sends Willis's ex-CIA agent on a mission to rescue Sasha (Natali Yura), the Russian wife of his cunning adversary, Frederick (Chad Michael Murray). Only, Sasha is part of a larger, more devious scheme, and her husband isn't as deceased as we were led to believe after *Fortress. Sniper's Eye* flounders as it tries to expand its story with a wave of new but boring characters. As for Willis, he spends half of the movie recuperating in a hospital bed, and the other half tied to a chair. Far from riveting. (★☆☆☆)

Vendetta (2022): This by-the-numbers vengeance story has a shockingly vulgar and cruel script, which follows a bloodthirsty father (Clive Standen) systematically hunting down the gang members who murdered his teenage daughter as part of a random initiation task. Having once played the grieving dad in Eli Roth's *Death Wish*, Willis flips the script to play the crime boss awaiting Standen at the end of his quest. Only Thomas Jane livens up the proceedings when he sporadically joins scenes as Dante, a smooth-talking arms dealer. But his bit part isn't long enough to make this mediocre, predictable, and poorly acted feature memorable. (★☆☆☆)

Corrective Measures (2022): A highly original and entertaining premise fuels this tough-guy action comedy, where radiation poisoning leads to drastic mutations in the human race, creating armies of super-powered villains. As a response, the Overseer (Michael Rooker) creates San Tiburon, a prison designed to contain and neutralize the most deranged criminals. Willis relishes his part as legendary psychopath "The Lobe," the facility's kingpin who eventually lights the fuse that ignites this powder keg. In fact, all of *Measures* is way more amusing than expected, thanks to Willis, Rooker, Tom Cavanagh, and Dan Payne—playing a Punisher-type vigilante named Payback—recognizing the material's camp value and bringing levity to the chaos. (★★⯨☆)

Wrong Place (2022): This schizophrenic rural thriller casts Willis as Frank, a security guard dealing with the recent loss of his wife, a cancer diagnosis for his daughter (*Twilight*'s Ashley Greene), and a band of meth dealers vowing revenge for the leader Frank shot in the leg. Director Mike Burns (*Out of Death*) continues to display no understanding of basic filmmaking concepts such as acting, editing, music cues, or coherent narrative. Willis, meanwhile, lumbers along in his now-familiar, Midwest mode of autopilot. Even by the reduced standards of the actor's late-career surge, this is horrible. (★☆☆☆)

Wire Room (2022): Shane Mueller (Willis) heads up the sophisticated surveillance center of the title, an intelligence hub that collects unlimited evidence against global criminals. On his first night on the job, "rookie" agent Justin Rosa (Kevin Dillon) must protect a "Walmart Jason Statham" he's monitoring from dirty cops and vengeful members of the Baja cartel. *Wire Room* lacks any urgency as it plods through its illogical motions. This is Dillon's show, but I got a kick out of Willis's character basically being stationed at a dive bar for the bulk of the movie, only occasionally stepping outside to take phone calls and move the plot along. (★★☆☆)

Paradise City (2022): Credit to *Paradise City* for this: it's the only movie I'm aware of that involves Hawaiian bail bondsmen scouring the islands in hopes of bagging a notorious cop killer. Their mission detours into the beachfront mixed-martial arts community, and a strip club where the dancers are ex-Marines. But even though Willis appears fully engaged in the narrative, the movie's flashes of originality can't transcend the derivative action and asinine script. Plus, the juicy promise of a *Pulp Fiction* reunion between Willis and Travolta gets filmed in a way that you can tell they never shared a set, or properly interacted once. Shame on me for expecting more. (★★☆☆)

Detective Knight: Rogue (2022): The "Knight" in the title refers to the chess piece, which can move around the board in unpredictable ways. And this movie, the first in a trilogy focused on Detective James Edward Knight (Willis), avoids being too predictable itself as it pits a renegade cop against a washed-up former NFL quarterback Casey Rhodes (Beau Mirchoff), who now makes ends meet leading a band of thieves. *Rogue* actually spends time on character development, giving Rhodes a sympathetic backstory and shading Knight's professional résumé so he's closer to crooked than he is to clean. Here's what's heartbreaking: anyone paying the slightest bit of attention can spot the places director Edward John Drake blatantly cheats by using body doubles in place of his leading man, going so far as to put a werewolf mask on Knight for the Halloween-set finale so Willis can let a stuntman do all the work. (★★☆☆)

Detective Knight: Redemption (2022): The Halloween-set *Detective Knight: Rogue* transitions to the Christmas-set *Redemption*, with Knight (Willis) being sprung from prison so he can round up the bloodthirsty, Santa suit–wearing disciples of a sadistic, bank-robbing preacher (Paul Johansson, melodramatic instead of menacing). Willis appears in the bare minimum number of scenes that still allow the producers to feature him prominently on the poster and not get sued for false advertising. The remainder of the film falls on Beau Mirchoff's Casey Rhodes character, though the emotional hook of his estranged family (from *Rogue*) gets sidelined for Johansson's violent outbursts. I did chuckle when a teenager played "Ode to Joy" on the cello in a throwaway scene, no doubt a nod to *Die Hard*, Willis's more famous Christmastime movie. (★★☆☆)

Detective Knight: Independence (2023): Awful, even by the declining standards of the *Detective Knight* series. The disjointed main plot moves like molasses as it sics Willis's sketchy cop on a homicidal EMT (Jack Kilmer) posing as a cop to wreak havoc over the July 4th holiday. The trilogy's last, and worst, chapter suffers from slapdash editing, incompetent performances by the supporting cast, low-budget production values, and laughable dialogue strung through an unfocused, paper-thin script. (★☆☆☆)

White Elephant (2023): One of the more heartbreaking installments in the concluding stage of Willis's career. Not because of the film's lack of quality—and believe me, *White Elephant* offers an embarrassing script and rotten performances by actors (Michale Rooker, John Malkovich) who should be above this. But more because Willis's scenes are genuinely depressing, as director Jesse V. Johnson has to edit around the actor and insert shoddy dialogue patches to cover the clear affect aphasia was having on his ability to perform. *White Elephant* is inept. But it'll mainly be remembered as the movie so drastically affected by Willis's declining health that Johnson declined further opportunities to work with the superstar out of sympathy, telling the *Los Angeles Times*, "We are all Bruce Willis fans, and the arrangement felt wrong and ultimately a rather sad end to an incredible career, one that none of us felt comfortable with." (★☆☆☆)

Assassin (2023): In the not-so-distant future, humans invent technology that allows them to digitally insert their consciousness into another being, then pilot them like drones for covert military missions. The inventive premise is executed with more skill than the rest of these run-of-the-mill thrillers, and the twist waiting at the end is satisfying. Willis plays Valmora, the head of the task force that uses this tech. He mostly takes a backseat, however, to the potent Nomzamo Mbatha, playing the wife of a deceased soldier who is forced to complete her husband's assignment. The mediocre but watchable *Assassins* takes on added weight by being Willis's last official movie. Given his track record over his final five years of acting, it was unlikely Willis was going to end his career on a high note. But I take solace in knowing that, in terms of a final film for this Hollywood legend, things could have been much worse. (★★☆☆)

NOTES

Author's Note

1. Bruce Willis quoted in Paul Fischer, "A Change of Image for Macho Willis," *Girl.com*, March 2016, https://www.girl.com.au/bruce-willis-16 -blocks-interview.htm.

Introduction

1. Demi Moore's Instagram post, March 30, 2022, https://www.insta gram.com/p/Cbu-CyELWio.

2. Haley Joel Osment's Instagram post, March 31, 2022, https://www .instagram.com/p/CbxmD9GFwGk/.

3. John Travolta's Instagram post, March 31, 2022, https://www.insta gram.com/p/CbxmnHJLbl1.

4. Author interview with Emily Blunt, July 7, 2023.

5. Arnold Schwarzenegger, "Arnold Schwarzenegger Weighs in on Bruce Willis' Retirement, Gives Us the Best Response," *CinemaBlend*, May 27, 2023.

6. John Goodman, *Face to Face with Connie Chung*, December 1990, video, https://www.youtube.com/watch?v=e8xlLlpLhxI.

7. Bruce Willis box-office stats, The Numbers, https://www.the-numbers .com/box-office-star-records/worldwide/lifetime-acting/top-grossing-stars.

8. "Rewind: Bruce Willis on Movie Choices, Career Moves and *Pulp Fiction*," Bruce Willis interview with Mark Greczmiel, 1994, video, https:// www.youtube.com/watch?v=Pjfb_ziARS0.

9. Rian Johnson on ReelBlend, November 23, 2022, video, https://www .youtube.com/watch?v=AidrB-BFQLE.

10. Bruce Willis, *Inside the Actor's Studio* (interview with James Lipton), *The Stranger Fiction*, September 10, 2001, video, https://thestrangerfiction .com/inside-the-actors-studio-bruce-willis/.

11. Richard Hack, "*'Moonlighting'* First Episode: THR's 1985 Review," *Hollywood Reporter*, March 3, 1985, https://www.hollywoodreporter.com/tv/ tv-news/moonlighting-first-episode-1985-review-819796/.

12. John J. O'Connor, "*TV View: 'Moonlighting' Delivers Wit and Style*," *New York Times*, December 1, 1985, https://www.nytimes.com/1985/12/01/ arts/tv-view-moonlighting-delivers-wit-and-style.html.

13. Willis, *Inside the Actor's Studio*.

14. Matthew Perry, *Friends, Lovers, and the Big Terrible Thing* (New York: Flatiron Books, 2022).

15. "Bob Dole vs. Hollywood," *Washington Post*, June 6, 1995, https:// www.washingtonpost.com/archive/politics/1995/06/06/dole-v-hollywood/ 5ab73a2a-0259-4162-909e-ddf31111da13/.

16. Ed Gross, "*Die Hard* Is 30—Meet the 1988 Bruce Willis in a Recovered Interview, *Closer Weekly*, June 6, 2018, https://www.closerweekly.com/ posts/bruce-willis-die-hard-161288/.

17. "Buce Willis, Just a Guy, Just a Very Fortunate Guy," *Rolling Stone*, December 8, 2000, https://www.rollingstone.com/tv-movies/tv-movie-news/ bruce-willis-171842/.

18. Demi Moore, *Inside Out* (New York: Harper Perennial, 2020).

19. Meg James and Amy Kaufman, "Concerns about Willis' Declining Cognitive State Swirled Around Sets in Recent Years, *L.A. Times*, March 30, 2022, https://www.latimes.com/entertainment-arts/movies/story/2022-03-30/ bruce-willis-aphasia-memory-loss-cognitive-disorder.

20. Sharon Stone, "Sharon Stone Reveals All," *Harper's Bazaar*, August 14, 2015, https://www.harpersbazaar.com/culture/features/a11741/sharon -stone-nude-0915/.

21. Emilia Clarke, "A Battle for My Life," *New Yorker*, March 21, 2019, https://www.newyorker.com/culture/personal-history/emilia-clarke-a-battle -for-my-life-brain-aneurysm-surgery-game-of-thrones.

22. "A Statement from the Willis Family, Association for Frontotemporal Degeneration, February 16, 2023, https://www.theaftd.org/mnlstatement 23/.

23. "Bruce Willis *Die Hard*—Bobbie Wygant Archive," 1988, video, https://www.youtube.com/watch?v=cqfn2IiTJ8U.

24. Sylvester Stallone to Terry Wogan in "Sylvester Stallone, Arnold Schwarzenegger, Bruce Willis—interview, Wogan, October 23, 1991, video, https://www.youtube.com/watch?v=nprv44xdiUA.

Section One Introduction

1. "Bruce Willis Speaks to Charlie Rose," *The Charlie Rose Show*, 2002, video, https://www.youtube.com/watch?v=6P-VgMhWNlM.

Chapter One

1. "Bruce Willis Talks about Comedy Style and Working with Blake Edwards," March 27, 1987, video, https://www.gettyimages.com/detail/video/willis-interview-news-footage/1270535580.

2. Roger Ebert, "*Blind Date*," *Chicago Sun-Times*, March 27, 1987, https://www.rogerebert.com/reviews/blind-date-1987.

3. Willis, *Inside the Actor's Studio*.

Chapter Two

1. "Rewind: Bruce Willis on predicting movie success: *Die Hard, Look Who's Talking, Hudson Hawk* & More," Bruce Willis interview with Mark Greczmiel, 1994, video, https://www.youtube.com/watch?v=t6RsYteeC9Q.

2. Willis, *Inside the Actor's Studio*.

3. Gene Siskel, "*The Bonfire of the Vanities*," *Chicago Tribune*, December 21, 1990, https://www.chicagotribune.com/news/ct-xpm-1990-12-21-900 4150626-story.html.

4. Bruce Willis and Robert Kraft Reminisce on *Hudson Hawk*, February 5, 2008, video, https://www.youtube.com/watch?v=N6odkKcJcBo.

5. "Siskel and Ebert review (1991): *Soapdish*, *What About Bob?*, *Hudson Hawk* and *Only the Lonely*," *Siskel & Ebert*, 1991, video, https://www.youtube.com/watch?v=3koR821rK4w.

6. "Bruce Willis *Hudson Hawk*—Bobbie Wygant Archive," 1991, video, https://www.youtube.com/watch?v=8Y4eWHh_728.

7. Willis and Kraft Reminisce.

8. Matt Zoller Seitz, "The Making of Silent Bruce," *Vulture*, August 2022, https://www.vulture.com/2022/08/silent-bruce-willis.html.

9. Michael Lehmann on the *Hudson Hawk* DVD commentary.

10. Author interview with Fred Topel.

11. Author interview with Douglas Davidson.

12. Willis and Kraft Reminisce.

13. "Rewind: Bruce Willis on predicting movie success."

14. *Hudson Hawk* Blu-ray review, The Film Junkies, September 26, 2022, https://thefilmjunkies.com/hudson-hawk-special-edition-blu-ray-review/.

Chapter Three

1. Adam Nayman, "Bruce Willis: Minimalist Star Power," *New Yorker*, April 6, 2022, https://www.newyorker.com/culture/cultural-comment/bruce-williss-minimalist-star-power.

2. Wynter Mitchell Rohrbaugh, *Screen Drafts* podcast, Planet Hollywood episode, August 23, 2021.

3. Steve Starkey, *Death Becomes Her* DVD "Making Of" featurette.

4. David Koepp, *Death Becomes Her* DVD "Making Of" featurette.

5. Rick Carter, *Death Becomes Her* DVD "Making Of" featurette.

6. Robert Zemeckis, *Death Becomes Her* DVD "Making Of" featurette.

7. Goldie Hawn, *Death Becomes Her* Interview, CNN, 1992, video, https://www.youtube.com/watch?v=db52HKw05uI.

8. Jordan Crucchiola, *Screen Drafts* podcast.

9. Rohrbaugh, *Screen Drafts* podcast.

10. Drew McWeeny, *Screen Drafts* podcast.

11. Joshua Grannell, *"Death Becomes Her* at 30,"The AV Club, https://www.avclub.com/death-becomes-her-anniversary-peaches-christ-queer-cult-1849350520.

Chapter Four

1. Kelly Lawler, *"Friends*: As It Prepares to Leave Netflix, Why We Won't Shut Up about It," *USA Today*, September 16, 2019, https://www.usatoday.com/story/entertainment/tv/2019/09/16/friends-25th-anniversary-why-we-cant-let-them-go/2154983001/.
2. Perry, *Friends, Lovers.*
3. Perry, *Friends, Lovers.*
4. Perry, *Friends, Lovers.*
5. Roger Ebert, *"The Whole Nine Yards* Review," *Chicago Sun-Times*, February 18, 2000, https://www.rogerebert.com/reviews/the-whole-nine-yards-2000.
6. Perry, *Friends, Lovers.*

Chapter Five

1. Robert Altman, *The Player* DVD commentary.
2. Steven Soderbergh, *Ocean's Twelve* DVD commentary.
3. Soderbergh, DVD commentary.
4. Stephanie Zacharek, *"Ocean's Twelve,"* Salon, December 10, 2004, https://www.salon.com/2004/12/10/oceans_12/.
5. George Nolfi, *Ocean's Twelve* DVD commentary.
6. Soderbergh, DVD commentary.
7. George Clooney, *"Ocean's Thirteen*: The Interview," *Time*, May 30, 2007, https://content.time.com/time/subscriber/article/0,33009,1627003,00.html.
8. Soderbergh, DVD commentary.
9. Soderbergh, DVD commentary.

Section Two Introduction

1. Willis, *Inside the Actor's Studio*.
2. Terry J. Leonard, *Die Hard with a Vengeance* DVD, "Making Of" featurette.
3. "Bruce Willis Speaks to Charlie Rose."
4. Bruce Willis, *Die Hard with a Vengeance* DVD, "Making Of" featurette.

Chapter Six

1. Joel Silver, quoted in Joe Berkowitz, "Producer Joel Silver on Crafting and Complicating the Buddy Action Movie Formula," Fast Company, May 20, 2016, https://www.fastcompany.com/3059941/producer-joel-silver-on-cultivating-and-complicating-the-buddy-action-movie-for.
2. Roger Ebert, "*Rush Hour* review," *Chicago Sun-Times*, September 18, 1998, https://www.rogerebert.com/reviews/rush-hour-1998.
3. Willis, *Inside the Actor's Studio*.
4. Desson Thomson, "*The Last Boy Scout*," *Washington Post*. December 13, 1991, https://www.washingtonpost.com/wp-srv/style/longterm/movies/videos/thelastboyscoutrhowe_a0ae8c.htm.
5. Bill Cosford, "Bad Script Dooms *The Last Boy Scout*," *Miami Herald*, December 14, 1991, https://www.newspapers.com/clip/83625117/the-last-boy-scout/.

Chapter Seven

1. Stephanie Zacharek, "16 Blocks," *Salon*, March 2, 2006, https://www.salon.com/2006/03/03/16_blocks/.
2. Roger Ebert, "*16 Blocks* Review," *Chicago Sun-Times*, March 2, 2006, https://www.rogerebert.com/reviews/16-blocks-2006.
3. "Bruce Willis interview for *16 Blocks*," Addicted to TV, 2006, video, https://www.youtube.com/watch?v=fRALvcU99Xo.

Chapter Eight

1. "Harrison Ford: 'I Know Who the F*** I Am,'" *Hollywood Reporter*, February 8, 2023, https://www.hollywoodreporter.com/tv/tv-features/harrison -ford-interview-shrinking-indy-5-1923-1235318736/.

2. "Helen Mirren Interview—*Red*," Collider, January 29, 2012, video, https://www.youtube.com/watch?v=fYeFOXeshEs.

3. "Bruce Willis: Funny Press Conference in Berlin!" (for *Red*), TIK online, video, https://www.youtube.com/watch?v=RiGhn0FllHU.

4. "Bruce Willis: Funny Press Conference."

5. Bruce Willis: *Red* interview with Clevver Movies, https://www.you tube.com/watch?v=Oa4pxbQC7iQ.

6. "Bruce Willis: Funny Press Conference."

7. "Bruce Willis: Funny Press Conference."

8. "Harrison Ford: 'I Know."

9. Ben Derico and James Clayton, Bruce Willis Denies Selling Rights to His Face," BBC, October 2, 2022, https://www.bbc.com/news/technology -63106024.

Chapter Nine

1. Maria LaScala, "Wow," *Ethelmae's Blog*, https://ethelmae.wordpress .com/2009/10/25/wow/.

2. Sylvester Stallone quoted in Mike Scott, "Sylvester Stallone and *The Expendables*: There's Nothing Small about It," NOLA.com, *New Orleans Times Picayune*, July 6, 2009, https://www.nola.com/entertainment_life/ movies_tv/article_f2d00c5f-d1cb-52f5-8a84-e835a7f30cb3.html.

3. Simon West quoted in B. Allen Grange, "Director Simon West Talks *Expendables 2*," MovieWeb, August 14, 2012, https://movieweb.com/ exclusive-director-simon-west-talks-the-expendables-2/.

4. West quoted in "Director Simon West."

Chapter Ten

1. Todd Gilchrist, "*G.I. Joe 2* Director Jon M. Chu on Courting Bruce Willis and Creating a Sequel 'For People Who Don't Know Anything about G.I. Joe,'" *Hollywood Reporter*, April 23, 2012, https://www.hollywood reporter.com/movies/movie-news/gi-joe-2-retaliation-jon-chu-bruce-willis-d wayne-rock-johnson-justin-bieber-never-say-never-315065/.

2. Ben Child, "Bruce Willis Bored with Making Action Movies," *Guardian*, August 13, 2013, https://www.theguardian.com/film/2013/aug/13/bruce -willis-bored-action-movies-interviews.

3. Willis, quoted in Rebecca Ford, "Bruce Willis Wins a Beard Bet, Dwayne Johnson Rocks as Roadblock," *Hollywood Reporter*, March 29, 2013, https://www.hollywoodreporter.com/movies/movie-news/gi-joe-retaliation -premiere-bruce-431754/.

4. Bruce Willis, *G.I. Joe*, DVD "Making Of" featurette, https://www .youtube.com/watch?v=GlsWG5_OQ0E.

Section Three Introduction

1. "Interview with Bruce Willis about *The Fifth Element*," studio interview at the Cannes Film Festival, 1997, video, https://www.youtube.com/ watch?v=gvjZ9zxHO7c.

Chapter Eleven

1. Patrice Ledoux quoted in Alex Ritman, "*The Fifth Element*: How Luc Besson's Space Opera Conquered Cannes 25 Years Ago," *Hollywood Reporter*, May 17, 2022, https://www.hollywoodreporter.com/movies/movie-news/the -fifth-element-cannes-1997-luc-besson-1235146998/.

2. "*5th Element* Cannes Opening Night Party 2/4," video, https://www .youtube.com/watch?v=wp_MHv2Wmvo.

3. "Bruce Willis Talks to Joe Leydon about *The Fifth Element*," 1997, video, https://www.youtube.com/watch?v=GkdlGn958M8.

4. Marc Savlov, "*The Fifth Element* review," *Austin Chronicle*, May 9, 1997, https://www.austinchronicle.com/events/film/1997-05-09/the-fifth-element/.

5. "Bruce Willis Talks to Joe Leydon."

6. Gene Siskel, "*Element* Entertains and Thrills," *Chicago Tribune*, May 9, 1997, https://www.chicagotribune.com/news/ct-xpm-1997-05-09-9705090146-story.html.

7. "*The Fifth Element* Opens the 50th Cannes Film Festival," Screen-Ocean, Reuters, April 19, 1997, video, https://reuters.screenocean.com/record/386997.

8. "Bruce Willis Talks to Joe Leydon."

Chapter Twelve

1. Kevin Polowy, "M. Night Shyamalan on the 'Power' of Bruce Willis, the Movie He Bet His House on, and His One Film People Watch on Their Deathbeds," Yahoo Entertainment, February 2, 2023, https://www.yahoo.com/entertainment/m-night-shyamalan-best-movies-the-sixth-sense-unbreakable-the-village-bruce-willis-215254721.html.

2. Terry Gilliam interview in "The Hamster Factor (And Other Tales of *12 Monkeys*)," video, https://www.youtube.com/watch?v=ufyWxk5__YI.

3. Roger Ebert, "*12 Monkeys*," RogerEbert.com, January 5, 1996, https://www.rogerebert.com/reviews/12-monkeys-1996.

4. "Bruce Willis *Twelve Monkeys*—Bobbie Wygant Archive," 1995, video, https://www.youtube.com/watch?v=t6JYpCfY8-0.

Chapter Thirteen

1. Author interview with Emily Blunt, July 7, 2023.

2. Joseph Gordon-Levitt on Working with Bruce Willis, *Looper* DVD commentary, December 12, 2012, https://www.youtube.com/watch?v=5mqOSSm7aIs.

3. Rian Johnson on the *Looper* DVD commentary.

4. Rian Johnson, Quoted in Kyle Buchanan, "The Toughest Scene I Wrote: Writer/Director Rian Johnson on *Looper*," *Vulture*, December 21, 2012, https://www.vulture.com/2012/12/toughest-scene-i-wrote-rian -johnson-on-looper.html.

5. Gordon-Levitt, on Working with Bruce Willis.

6. Bruce Willis, quoted in Tom Chiarella, "The Collected Wisdom of Bruce Willis, 1:32–3:45 P.M., Thursday," *Esquire*, May 21, 2012, https:// www.esquire.com/news-politics/a14060/bruce-willis-interview-0612/.

Chapter Fourteen

1. "Asteroid 2013 TV135 Could Hit Earth in 2032, but NASA Says Not to Worry," ABC News, October 19, 2013, https://abcnews.go.com/ Technology/asteroid-2013-tv135-collision-earth/story?id=20622551.

2. "Asteroid 2013 TV135 Could Hit Earth in 2032."

3. "Bayhem," Urban Dictionary, https://www.urbandictionary.com/ define.php?term=Bayhem.

4. Ben Affleck on the *Armageddon* DVD commentary.

5. Roger Ebert, "*Armageddon* review," *Chicago Sun-Times*, July 1, 1998, https://www.rogerebert.com/reviews/armageddon-1998.

Section Four Introduction

1. Author interview with Matt Damon, July 7, 2023.

Chapter Fifteen

1. "Quentin Tarantino and Sally Menke on Editing," Cinema Garm- onbozia, August 17, 2017, video, https://www.youtube.com/watch?v=vqh PWfOxMwA.

2. Sally Menke, "'Quentin Tarantino and I Clicked,'" *Guardian*, Decem- ber 5, 2009, https://www.theguardian.com/film/2009/dec/06/sally-menke -quentin-tarantino-editing.

3. Quentin Tarantino, *ReelBlend* podcast, July 19, 2022.

4. Tarantino, *ReelBlend*.

5. Jill Gerston, "Finally, Bruce Willis Gets Invited to the Ball," *New York Times*, October 2, 1994, https://www.nytimes.com/1994/10/02/movies/film-finally-bruce-willis-gets-invited-to-the-ball.html.

6. "Bruce Willis, *Pulp Fiction*—Bobbie Wygant Archive," September 27, 1994, video, https://www.youtube.com/watch?v=jwKarojdjGA.

7. Willis to Wygant.

8. Tarantino on "How Bruce Willis Got Cast for Pulp Fiction," *2 Bears, 1 Cave* podcast, November 22, 2022, https://www.youtube.com/watch?v=jBitGA1GrKw.

9. Mark Seal, "Cinema Tarantino: The Making of *Pulp Fiction*," *Vanity Fair*, February 13, 2013, https://www.vanityfair.com/hollywood/2013/03/making-of-pulp-fiction-oral-history.

Chapter Sixteen

1. Shyamalan on "*The Sixth Sense*: Reflections from the Set," Filmingmentary, May 12, 2020, video, https://www.youtube.com/watch?v=SPSS9a8r7TI.

2. Willis, Reflections.

3. Roger Ebert, "Disney's *The Kid* review," *Chicago Sun Times*, July 7, 2000, https://www.rogerebert.com/reviews/disneys-the-kid-2000.

4. "M. Night Shyamalan: I Owe Bruce Willis My Career," Tass, January 2019, https://tass.com/society/1040680.

Chapter Seventeen

1. "Bruce Willis on *Bonfire of the Vanities*," Conversation in the Arts and Humanities with John C. Tibbetts, 1990, video, https://www.youtube.com/watch?v=PsDPkjbP5qA.

2. David Sheff, "Bruce Willis," *Playboy*, February 1996, https://www.davidsheff.com/bruce-willis-1996.

3. "Bruce Willis *Bonfire of the Vanities*—Bobbie Wygant Archive,"1990, video, https://www.youtube.com/watch?v=uqGZmYL2FOM.

4. Alejandro Gonzalez Inarritu, "73 of the Best Quotes about Filmmaking," Filmcrux, https://www.filmcrux.com/blog/best-filmmaking-quotes.

5. Sheff, "Bruce Willis."

6. "Bruce Willis on *Bonfire*," Tibbetts.

7. Sheff, "Bruce Willis."

8. "Bruce Willis on *Bonfire*," Tibbetts.

9. Salamon, Interview in "The Plot Thickens," Turner Classic Movies, Episode 3, https://www.youtube.com/watch?v=Ih2h-4vJc3o.

10. De Palma, Interview in "The Plot Thickens," Turner Classic Movies, Episode 1, https://www.youtube.com/watch?v=4ucm8Wv4-b0.

11. "Bruce Willis on *Bonfire*," Tibbetts.

Chapter Eighteen

1. Benton quoted in Robert W. Welkos, "Yes, Virginia, That's Bruce Willis," *Greensboro News & Record*, February 9, 2015, https://greensboro.com/yes-virginia-thats-bruce-willis/article_89567826-c3fd-553f-ad19-c189386b4ef5.html.

2. Wes Anderson quoted in "The Circle of Wes Expands," *Slate*, May 17, 2012, https://www.slate.com/articles/video/conversations_with_slate/2012/05/wes_anderson_on_directing_bruce_willis_edward_norton_for_the_first_time_video_.html.

3. Wes Anderson quoted in Lindsey Bahr, "*Moonrise Kingdom* director Wes Anderson would care about awards if . . . ," *Entertainment Weekly*, January 9, 2013, https://ew.com/article/2013/01/09/moonrise-kingdom-director-wes-anderson-talks-awards/.

4. Frank Miller interview, Kubert School Media, 2016, video, https://www.youtube.com/watch?v=Xo7frKC0N2E&t=2431s.

5. Rodriguez interviewed on *Sin City* (2005)—"How It Went Down: Convincing Frank Miller to Make the Film," DVD featurette, Archives of Kino, video, https://www.youtube.com/watch?v=D-R5Vls-Y1U.

6. Tarantino interview, *Sin City* (2005)—"Special Guest Director Quentin Tarantino," DVD featurette, The Archives of Kino, video, https://www.youtube.com/watch?v=J03y7K0JAD0.

7. Bruce Willis in "Director's Commentary: *Sin City*, Quentin Tarantino Robert Rodriguez, Frank Miller, with Bruce Willis, video, https://www.youtube.com/watch?v=8coTokXZf8E.

8. Willis, "Director's Commentary."

9. Bruce Willis interview for *The Story of Us*, "Rewind: Bruce Willis on Going Bald and Early Gig as Movie Extra Opposite Paul Newman," 1999, video, https://www.youtube.com/watch?v=Fp9XCwxKPtQ.

10. Kenneth Turan, "*Nobody's Fool*," *Los Angeles Times*, December 23, 1994, http://articles.latimes.com/1994-12-23/entertainment/ca-12101_1 _paul-newman.

11. Caryn James, "*Nobody's Fool*," *New York Times*, December 23, 1994, https://www.nytimes.com/1994/12/23/movies/film-review-paul-newman -in-blue-collar-gear.html.

Section Five Introduction

1. "Kevin Smith Panel @ Comic-Con 2012: Bashes Bruce Willis of *Die Hard*," video, https://www.youtube.com/watch?v=kPiVlU9PXgQ.

2. Willis, quoted in Chris Nashawaty, "Bruce Willis: 'If I Hadn't Done *Die Hard*,' I'd Rip It Off,'" *Entertainment Weekly*, June 14, 2007, https://ew .com/article/2007/06/14/bruce-willis-if-i-hadnt-done-die-hard-id-rip-it/.

Chapter Nineteen

1. Jeb Stuart quoted in Karen Butler, "Writer Jeb Stuart Settles Debate: *Die Hard* Is a Christmas Movie," UPI, December 10, 2022, https://www.upi .com/Entertainment_News/Movies/2022/12/10/die-hard-christmas-movie/ 3541670677910/.

2. John McTiernan, on *Empire Film Podcast*, August 5, 2022, https:// open.spotify.com/show/5WtA4Y7DFbQzkj42B2zxfb.

3. "John McTiernan on Why Die Hard Is a Christmas Movie," American Film Institute, video, https://www.youtube.com/watch?v=PR-XHOTv8nU.

4. McTiernan, AFI.

5. McTiernan, AFI.

6. Jeb Stuart, quoted in James Mottram and David S. Cohen, *Die Hard: The Ultimate Visual History* (New York: Insight Editions, 2018).

7. McTiernan, AFI.

8. Willis, quoted in Mottram and Cohen, *Ultimate Visual History*.

9. "Bruce Willis *Die Hard*—Bobbie Wygant Archive," 1988, video, https://www.youtube.com/watch?v=cqfn2IiTJ8U.

10. Jason Bailey, "How *Die Hard* Changed the Action Genre," *Vulture*, July 10, 2018, https://www.vulture.com/2018/07/how-die-hard-changed -the-action-game.html.

11. A. Martines, "*The Last Action Heroes* by Nick de Semlyn Focuses on 8 Action Stars," *Morning Edition*, NPR, June 6, 2023, https://www.npr .org/2023/06/06/1180361017/the-last-action-heroes-by-nick-de-semlyen -focuses-on-8-action-stars.

12. Bruce Willis quoted in Mottram and Cohen, *Ultimate Visual History*.

Chapter Twenty

1. Renny Harlin, quoted in Mottram and Cohen, *Ultimate Visual History*.

2. Doug Richardson, quoted in Mottram and Cohen, *Ultimate Visual History*.

3. William Wisher, quoted in Mottram and Cohen, *Ultimate Visual History*.

4. McQuarrie quoted in, Brian Davids, "*Mission: Impossible* Director Christopher McQuarrie on the Dark Plotline Cut from *Fallout*," *Hollywood Reporter*, July 30, 2018, https://www.hollywoodreporter.com/movies/movie -news/mission-impossible-tom-cruise-pushed-a-dark-plot-was-cut-1130744 /.

5. Jonathan Hensleigh, *Die Hard With a Vengeance* alternate ending commentary track, https://www.youtube.com/watch?v=ORUuDiIB5Wk.

6. Bruce Willis, *Die Hard with a Vengeance*, DVD featurette, video, https://www.youtube.com/watch?v=QnR_tKhRZWw.

7. Willis, quoted in Mottram and Cohen, *Ultimate Visual History*.

Chapter Twenty-One

1. Willis, quoted in Mottram and Cohen, *Ultimate Visual History*.
2. Willis, quoted in Mottram and Cohen, *Ultimate Visual History*.
3. Bomback, quoted in Mottram and Cohen, *Ultimate Visual History*.
4. Author's *Live Free or Die Hard* review, FilmCritic.com, June 27, 2007, https://web.archive.org/web/20070629115343/http://www.filmcritic.com/misc/emporium.nsf/reviews/Live-Free-or-Die-Hard.
5. Roger Ebert, *North* review, *Chicago Sun-Times*, July 22, 1994, https://www.rogerebert.com/reviews/north-1994.
6. Author's *A Good Day to Die Hard* review, *CinemaBlend*, February 13, 2013, https://www.cinemablend.com/reviews/Good-Day-Die-Hard-6304.html.
7. Moore, quoted in Mottram and Cohen, *Ultimate Visual History*.
8. Willis, quoted in Ed Gross, "Bruce Willis Talks *Die Hard*," *Closer Weekly*, June 6, 2018, https://www.closerweekly.com/posts/bruce-willis-die-hard-161288/.

Conclusion

1. "Bruce Willis Speaks to Charlie Rose."
2. "Bruce Willis Shares What He Really Wants in This Raw Uncut Interview," Reba Merrill, 2000, video, http://www.youtube.com/watch?v=PN1LSF0X5c0.
3. Willis, in "Comedy Central Roast of Bruce Willis," July 29, 2018, https://www.cc.com/episodes/r8a57d/roast-of-bruce-willis-roast-of-bruce-willis-ep-1.

INDEX